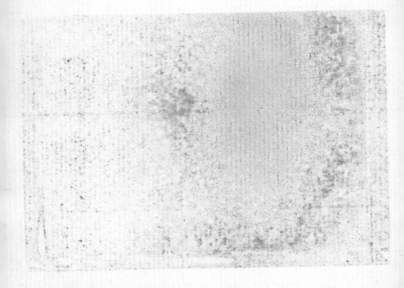

ENGLISH RECUSANT LITERATURE
1558–1640

Selected and Edited by
D. M. ROGERS

Volume 327

ROBERT POINTZ
Testimonies for the Real Presence
1566

ROBERT POINTZ

Testimonies for the Real Presence

1566

The Scolar Press

1977

ISBN o 85967 343 x

*Published and printed in Great Britain by
The Scolar Press Limited, 59-61 East Parade,
Ilkley, Yorkshire and
39 Great Russell Street,
London WC1*

NOTE

Reproduced (original size) from a copy in the Fellows' Library at Winchester College, by permission of the Warden and Fellows. The last page is slightly damaged, the affected words being '*Petri Louanij*'.

References: Allison and Rogers 656; STC 20082.

soester

TESTIMONIES

FOR THE REAL PRESENCE

of Chriſtes body and blood in the bleſſed
Sacramēt of the aultar ſet foorth at large,
& faithfully tranſlated, out of ſix auncient
fathers which lyued far within the firſt ſix
hundred yeres , together with certain
notes, declaring the force of thoſe teſtimonies, and detecting ſometimes the Sacramentaries falſe dealing , as
more plainly appeareth in
the other ſyde of this
leaf.

*By Robert Pointz ſtudent in
Diuinitie.*

Athanaſ. ad Epict. contra Hæret.
Si vultis filij patrum eſſe, non debetis ſen-
tire diuerſa ab ijs, quę patres ipſi coſcri-
pſerunt.
If ye will be children of the Fathers, you muſt
not diſſent from thoſe thinges which the Fathers them ſelues haue writ.

LOVANII,

Apud Ioannem Foulerum.
M. D. LXVI.

The summes of the Chapters.

To the Reader.

Least thou shouldest wonder (gentle Reader) vpon what occasiõ I write oftentimes in my notes hereafter folowing, as vnto one particular person, hauing now sette them foorth to be common to other, I thought good to let thee vnderstand, that as well the testimonies of the doctors as those notes of mine were gathered of me specially for one frindes sake, who desiered to be satisfied at my hand in this matter of the blessed Sacrament. whose reasonable request as I could not with honestye repel, in consideratiõ both of my duety vnto God & my good will towards him, especially wher as God hath willed euery man to haue care of his neighbor, and to vse whatsoeuer small talent to his honor, when occasion is offered : so deuisinge with my selfe how I might best accomplish the same, I resolued at length to translate part of that which the auncient fathers haue writen herein. which way seemed for one of my state and condition most meete, both for because by that meanes I my selfe should least of all medle in the matter, and also because the same should best of all through the auncient fathers graue auctority persuade the trueth.

Wherevpon consideringe further what meanes I might best vse , to make it throughly perceaued , how plainly those graue & learned doctors doe confirme the Catholike faith, I thought there could be no way either more indifferent, or more conuenient, then so to translate them, that the whole discourse of eche Doctor might fully appeare. persuadinge my self that as by common practise it is proued, that ye eye iudgeth much better of ye thinge which is sett fully before it, then if it see but a glims thereof only: so my sayd frind should iudge more vprightly & more sincerely of ye auncient doctors verdict in this matter by seinge them so fully & amply alleaged.

And that some of their wordes and sentences which doe most plainly confirme ye Catholike faith and destroy the contrary might be somewhat better marked : I thought good to adioyne therevnto those notes of my owne , wherby ye only might be somtyme set forth a litle plainer & with a few moe wordes which the doctors them selues teach briefly. I thought it not amisse also in those notes to discourse now & then somewhat largely vppon other matters, accordinge as either ye doctors themselues, or the aduersaries of ye reall presence haue by reason of their misusinge of the holy doctors, geuen me iust occasion.

Now if it be demaunded how I durst

venture to publishe that vnto other, which
at the beginning I ment vnto one priuate
frind only: truly I cã not better aunswer,
then with that most common & most true
saying: Man proposeth, but god disposeth.
For as he disposeth al things most swete=
ly , and turneth often times wicked in=
tentes vnto good endes : so I haue great
cause to hope, that this change of my good
purpose into a better, came by his good di
sposition also: especially whereas it is his
property to further alwayes & not to hin=
der good purposes, as which procede al=
together from him: and seing on the other
syde ÿ special cõmendation of a good pur=
pose is, to cõmunicat ÿ vnto many, which
may be good and profitable for them. For
therby, I hauing ÿ same intêt to doe good
vnto many according to my power which
I had to profite one, was easely persuaded
to change my sayd purpose : considering
withall that ÿ same reason proueth it may
profite many , by which I was at the be=
ginning persuaded it might doe good to
one. For this I considered with my selfe.
whatsoeuer sort he be of, that shal happen
hereupon, it may alwaies be profitable
for him, to see the consent of the auncient
fathers of the Church in this chief matter
of religion at large set foorth ,which may
direct his whole beliefe in these most
        A iij   perilous

perilous dayes full of sectes & diuisions.

If he be already sounde and Catholike, it may comfort and confirme him much to see those holy Fathers, which are now doutles blessed Saintes in heauē, to haue so amply by their writinge witnessed that which is now impugned by the Sacramē taries and of al Catholikes defended: and thereby he may assure himselfe to be in the right way, and to mantayne the true religion. If he be one of them which are wa ueringe, being vncertaine which syde to sticke vnto by reason of the number of bo kes which he seeth write, and the number both of scriptures & doctors on eche syde alleaged: then if he himselfe will, he may take speciall commoditie by readinge of these testimonies. For hereby he shal finde iust occasion to cleaue wholy vnto the Ca tholike faith, whē as by the doctors whole discourses, he himselfe shall perceaue throughly, how they haue preached and taught the same. Moreouer he shalbe able to iudge, both how truely the Catholike writers allege in their workes ý sayinges of the fathers, & also how deceytfully and falsely the Protestantes oftentimes deale with men in that behalfe. And therby he may take iust occasion to discredit their whole doctrine, which as it is in dede no thinge but a fardell of lyes, so it can not other=

otherwise be mainteined and nourished, then by matter lyke vnto it selfe, that is to say by lying and falsifyinge.

Now that third sort of men, which hartely embraceth the cōtrary religion I take to be deuided into two sortes. And as for the one which consisteth of those false dealers thē selues, which haue so maliciously conspired against the Catholike Church, that in al their doinges they protest neuer to returne thervnto againe, be their vaine bragges neuer so much discouered, and the auncient fathers neuer so plainly proued to make against them, as there is smal hope that this or any other meane will do them good: so I trust few of that sort are amonge the vnlearned, for whose instruction this is chiefly set foorth. I trust they are of that sorte only which are the teachers & ringleaders, who being puffed vp with the pryde of a litle knowledge, easely become malitiouse & desperate. Neither is it marueile if there be small hope that any thinge will doe such any good, seinge the holy scripture it selfe hath so longe before by the example of others like vnto them both in name and conditions, admonished vs so expressely of their extreme malice and stubbornesse. For we reade in the storie of the Byble that certaine of the

A iiij   rulers

rulers of Juda after the death of the good high priest Joiada, obteined by flattery & faire wordes of Joas the Kyng to forsake the Church of the Lord God of their forefathers, & to set vp Idols after their own fansi in woddes & groues. wherevpon it foloweth in the text, that God was highly displeased with them, mittebátque eis Prophetas vt reuerterétur ad dominum, quos Protestantes illi audire nolebant: and he sent vnto the Prophetes that they should returne againe vnto him, but they Protestantes, that is to say, they makinge their solemne protestations would not heare them. In which few wordes the malice of ye chief Protestantes of these our dayes is manifestly prophesied of, and plainly described: of those J say, which wil not harken to the auncient Fathers so many and sundry waies callinge and crpinge vnto them to returne vnto God their Father, & to the holy Catholike Church their mother, both which they haue at one time forsaken. But as J sayd before, J trust there be not many of that sort, J trust they are only as the scripture saieth, Protestantes illi, which we may englishe, those protestantes, or that kind of malitiouse Protestants.

2. Parali. cap. 24.

   For there is an other sort of very earnest Prote-

Protestantes, which are not seduced by malice, but of a certaine zeale and simplicitie, being after a sort exceding zealous of the truth. And therefore there is good hope that God will deale mercifully with them, as he did with S. Paul and others. Neither doe I dispaire, but vnto such the reading of these auncient Fathers thus fully alleged may doe much good: specially if they them selues will not close their eyes, whē the truth shal shyne clerely before them. Yea and although many of them be gone so far in this blind zeale (as I my selfe do know certaine) that they make this one of the most surest groundes and principles of their religion, to say their conscience beareth them witnesse of the truth, and that the spirite instructeth them: yet I haue good hope and trust in God, that these testimonies thus amply set foorth, by which their misinformed consciences may finde far better witnesses of the truth, shall do them no small good.

For if they wilbe content syncerely to folow the counsell of holy Scripture, as they pretende specially to doe in that point (being in dede much deceaued, for that they lacke those singular reuelations and speciall graces, by whiche Sainct Paule and others might

A v   boldly

boldly so speake) they must first of all trye
that spirite which they say instructeth and
guydeth them , whether it be of God or
no . For so S. Ihon counseyleth saying.

1.Ioã. 4. Nolite omni spiritui credere, sed probate
spiritus si ex Deo sint. Beleue not euery
spirite but trye ỹ spirites whether they be
of God. And what better waye can they
haue to make such a tryall , then by comparing that which their spirite teacheth,
with the doctrine of S. Chrysostome , S.
Cyprian, S. Augustine, and the rest hereafter folowinge , who were by all mens
iudgemẽt truly inspired of the holy Ghost
and must nedes by these mens owne confession if they haue any reason or shame-
fastnes ,be much more worthy credit then
they them selues are? If then they shall
(as they must nedes) find by reading these testimonies,that holy spirit which inspired those auncient Fathers, to haue
taught cleane contrarie to that wherrof
their fond conscience beareth them witnesse , they will I hope beginne by litle
and litle to mistrust that priuate spirte of
their owne fancy, and submit them selues
to that truth which is here by the auncient
Fathers generally approued and alowed.
And this must they nedes doe onlesse they
turne their simplicitie into presumption,
and their vnskilfull zeale into wilfull malice.

lite. which if they doe, then others may
yet take good by their example, and vn=
derstanding what spꝛite beareth rule in
them, beware how they fall into that kind
of foolish zeale, which by S. Paules iudge
ment is voyde of all knowlege and dis=
cretion.

And thus thou vnderstandest (gentill
Reader) how vppon hope to doe good
vnto many, I was moued to make this
commō vnto thee and other, which at the
first I had appointed to be pꝛiuate vnto
one frind only. Neither could other mens
much moꝛe learned bookes set foorth al=
ready of this selfe same matter staye this
my purpose, when I considered withall
how one disease in diuerse men is not com
monly cured by one medicine: but that
sundꝛie complections demaunde diuerse
compositions, oꝛ at the least one kinde of
medicine diuersely tempered. wherefoꝛe
sith this is done of me vppon respect only
to doe good, in such soꝛt as my simple abi=
litie serueth, do thou also construe all
things to the best, and be not offended
though my purpose being changed I haue
not yet altered in my notes that maner of
wꝛiting which I vsed at the first. And if
my simple notes mislike thee, either be=
cause to the Catholike I shall iustly seeme
to haue omitted many things and passed
                                    ouer

To the Reader.

ouer many stronge argumentes slightly, or because to other I may perchance seme sometyme to speake roughly, thē yet take in good part my other small labor, and what so euer thou art, take some good by the auncient Fathers testimonies, which do so euidently by them selues note vnto thee the Catholike faith. wherevnto if thou take hereby any occasion to returne, or therein to continue more stedfast, so I shall litle esteme whatsoeuer blame may otherwise be layed to my charge, and also shal thinke my great good will and small payne sufficiently recompensed.

Robert Pointz.

Faultes escaped in printing.

lefe.	fide.	line.	fault.	Correction.
2	1	4	man	may
5	2	24	from pinacle	from the pinacle
6	1	31	fpecially	fpecially
21	2	28	rife	rife
22	1	26	nerce	nere
21	2	6	appeareft	appeare♉
24	2	30	whereof	were of
32	2	3	ont	out
Jbid.		8	alfo	alfo
39	1	15	a	all
42	1	9	the	that
48	1	14	endure	endue
55	1	1	fake	Afke
83	1	5	brought paffe	brought to paffe
Jb. in ý margēt 81.i Ɱat.				De ꝓdit. Iud.
Jbid.2		31	lifter	after
103	2	19	fubftance	fuftenance
121	2	4	which	Jn which
123	1	29	withneffe	whitneffe
140	2	12	afhmed	afhamed
146	1	1	fenfe	fentence
147	1	3	appofeth	oppofeth
156	2	9	out all	out of all
158	1	15	enturally	naturally
159	1	20	liueth	liuely
160	1	13	wrote out	he wrote out
Jbid.2		4	aduerfus	aduerfus.
162	1	19	which	with
168	2	13	thim	him
178	1	15	it not	is not
184	1	19	perfpicuitie	perfpicuitie
192	1	22	naturally	naturall
199	1	8	counfell	Counfellers

Magnus Basilius in Homil.
contra Sabel. & Arr.

Te pacatum reddat traditio: Dominus
ita docuit: Apostoli prędicauerunt : Patres
custodiuerunt : confirmarunt martyres:
sufficiat dicere sic edoctus sum.

Let tradition content thee : Our Lord
hath so taught: The Apostles haue so prea
ched: The Fathers haue so obſerued: The
Martyrs haue cõfirmed it:let it be inough
to ſay, thus haue I bene taught.

Idem Basilius in sua ad Antiochenam
Ecclesiam Epist.

Fidem nos neque ab alijs scriptam uobis
recentiorem suscipimus, neque ipsi mentis
nostræ germina tradere audemus: ne humana figmenta existimentur esse verba religionis, sed quæ a sanctis patribus edocti
sumus , ea interrogantibus nos annun-
tiamus.

we neither receaue a later faith written
for vs of others , nor dare we deliuer de=
uiſes that ſpring out of our owne head,
leaſt matters of religiõ ſhould be thought
to be mens feyned inuentions : but what
things we haue bene taught of ẙ holy Fathers, thoſe we declare vnto ſuch as aſke
vs.

Augustin. lib. 2. contra Iulian. Pelag.

Nunquid Cyprianus, Hilarius, Ambrosius & Ioannes (Chrysostomus) de plebeia fece Sellulariorum? &c.

Nunquid milites? nunquid Scholastici auditoriales? nunquid Nautæ, Tabernarij, Cetarij, Coquilani? nunquid adolescentes ex monachis dissoluti? & paulo post:

Isti episcopi sunt, docti, graues, sancti, veritatis acerrimi defensores aduersus garrulas vanitates.

what say you to these men, Cyprian, Hilarie, Ambrose, and Ihon Chrysostom, are they of the rascall sort of sitting Craftesmen? &c. Are they Souldiars? Are they Scholers that for the fashion only haunt lessons? Are they Mariners, Tapsters or Prentises, Fishetonters, Scoullians? Are they ponkers such as of Monkes become dissolute Renegats? (& a litle after.)

Nay, these are Bishops, learned, graue, holy, most ernest defendours of the truth against babling vanities.

Regiæ Maieſtatis priuilegio conceſſum eſt
Roberto Poyntz Anglo, vti per aliquem
Typographorum admiſſorum impune
ei liceat imprimi curare, & per omnes
Burgundicæ ditionis regiones diſtra-
here, librum inſcriptum: Teſtimonies
for the reall preſence, &c. & omnibus alijs
inhibitum, ne eundem abſque eiuſdem
Roberti conſenſu imprimant, vel alibi
impreſſum diſtrahant. Datum Bru-
xellæ 20. Auguſti. Anno 1565.

Subſig.
Facutwez.

❡ The places of the new Testament which principally belong to the blessed Sacramēt, together with a short introduction to the testimonies of the Fathers.

There is no one saying more truely verified of Christ our sauiour, then that which is spoken by the Prophet Esay, where he saith: Quid est quod vltra facere debui vineæ meę, & non feci ei? what is it ꝑ I ought to doe more vnto my vineyard, and I haue not done to it? for certainly his bountifull goodnesse hath bene alwayes such toward mākind, that he hath omitted nothing that might serue to bring vs to that heauenly heritage, which he hath most derely purchased for vs.

And therefore emōg many other things this one semeth vnto me worthily noted of many learned men and good writers, as a speciall token of the great desire which he hath of our saluation: that he hath prouided the greatest mysteries of our redemption so often to be repeted and witnessed in the new Testament: to th'end no man should haue any iust occasion to doubt of them, or any lawfull excuse of his incredulity and misbeliefe. which thing is principally obserued in the chief and highest mysteries, to witnesse not only ꝑ certenty, but also the dignity and maiesty of them.

And therfore notwīstādig thei were al fore
B   signified

The first Chapiter.

Esai. 5.

The chief mysteries of our Religion are oftē repeted in scripture.

signified and prophecied in the olde testament, as well by the figures and ceremonies of the lawe, as by the wordes & dedes of Patriarches and Prophetes: yet Christ him self to make the same more playne, and that they should be the better regarded, allwayes warned his disciples before hand of those great mysteries which were to come, and they fayled not according to his ensample to commend the same to the faithful after his ascension, by theyr dayly practise and preaching.

In suche sorte that as the tyme is commenly deuided in to thrice partes, the tyme past, present, and the time come: so we find those great mysteries for the most part three seueral tymes witnesshed and rehershed vnto vs in holy scripture. for we read howe Christe firste solenly promised them, how he afterward fulfilled his promise, and last of al how y̍ Apostles by theyr preaching and writing confirmed them. But that this may appeare more euident by some playne example, what greater mysterly is there of our redemption then the death and passion of the sonne of God by which we are redemed? of whiche thing Christe very often warned his disciples long before it came to passe, neither signified only that he should be killed and put to death, but also after what manner and sorte, saying, Like as Moy=

r.
Ioan.3.

Moyses lyfted vp the serpent in the wil=
dernesse : euen so must the sonne of man be
lifted vp, that euery one which beleueth in
him man not perishe. And in an other place
he hath these wordes. And if I be lifted vp
frō ȳ earth, I shall draw all thinges to my
selfe. which the Euangelist him selfe expoū=
deth immediatly saying. He spake this signifying what death he should dye, Now it
can not be doubted but this promisse was
perfitely performed (accordingly as all the
foure Euangelists do witnesse) at the tyme
of his passion. And last of all, nothing is
more commenly preached and taught in the
Actes of the Apostles, and Epistles of S.
Paule and others, then the same death and
Crosse of Christe. The like may easely be
shewed in those other high mysteries of his
resurrection, ascension, and the comming of
the holy Ghost, &c.

Also the holy Sacramēt of baptisme taking his vertue and strength of Christ his
passion & being the only dore whereby we
entre to saluatiō, is with no lesse diligence
commended vnto vs by Christ and his A-
postles. For Christ first in that swete talke
he had with Nicodemus teacheth before
hande, that onlesse a man be borne again
of water and the holy Ghost he can not
enter into the kingdome of heauen. And
anon after his resurrection we read that he

B ij   in dede

"
"
"
"
"
Ioan. 12.
"
"
2.

3.

1.
Ioan. 3.

2.

in dede instituted that holy Sacrament, ₢ gaue his disciples auctority to minister the same, saying : All power is geuen me in heauen ₢ in earth , goe ye therefore ₢ teach all nations , baptising them in the name of the Father , and of the Sonne, and of the holy Ghost. And finally we find the same confirmed by the practise of the Apostles. As whē after S. Peters sermon there were baptised three thousand persons. likewise diuerse in Samaria by S . Philippe , and in other places by S. Paul and the rest.

Now to come vnto my principall purpose. The blessed Sacrament of the altar being no small mystery, but in dede ý very chiefe treasor of all Christen religion, ₢ the perfection of all other Sacramēts: it was most requisite ý the same should likewise be at diuerse tymes, and in diuerse places of holy scripture, highly cōmēded vnto vs. wherefore Christ tendering so hartely our health, and knowing so assuredly what a great comfort the same should be vnto all good folke : as by the strength and vertue whereof, they might passe quietly through this vale of misery, and safely arriue vnto the hill of God, where they should enioy ₢ see him face to face to their endlesse confort: he foreseing also al that mischief, which the Deuill and his wicked membres the miscreans ₢ heretiks should practise to ouer= throwe

Matt.28.

,,

,,

3. ,,

Acto.2.
&8.

The verity of the blessed Sacrament at three special times witnessed in holy scripture.

throwe the same, prouided that the veritie
thereof should be at three seuerall tymes
most plainly & manifestly witnessed, accor=
dingly as it may be perceaued in the other
mysteries before mentioned. For we haue
first the promise of this holy Sacrament
most solemly made by Christ in the sixt of
S. Johns Ghospel, together with a plaine
declaration of the substance, and contentes
thereof, which he saith shalbe his flesh and
blood. Also he there teacheth, how necessary
the receauing of this foode shalbe , to all
y couet after euerlasting saluation. Seco=
darily we haue y fulfilling of that promise
at his last supper, where he instituted this
blessed Sacrament and gaue his Apostles
authority to doe the same by those wordes:
Hoc facite in meam commemorationem,
Do or make this for y remembrance of me.
all which is most perfitely described by the
other thre Euangelistes. Last of al S. Paul
witnesseth the practise thereof in y Church
of the Corinthians: to whom he writeth,
that he deliuered the the same thing which
he receaued of Christ his Lord and master.
Now as the holy Ghost hath prouided all
these testimonies most plainly to agree in
setting foorth one truth: so y same hath inspired also the holy Doctors of the Church
merueilously to consent as wel in their expositions made vppon those special places,

B 3   as where

as where soeuer els they happen to intreat
of this matter. But because all that they
write hereof is commonly grounded vpon
some texte in one of those places, to thend
you may better vnderstand the expositions
of the holy doctours (which I entend by
God his helpe moste amply and fully to
transflat)and lesse troble your self in seeking
for the textes of holy scripture which they
shall allege,as also that you may first of all
begin with the sure foundation, and considre how plainly Christ him selfe speaketh
herein : I haue thought good first of all to
set before your eyes those speciall places
of holy scripture according to that ordre of
tyme which(as I noted vntoyou before)is
obserued in them. First therefore the words
write in the sixt of S. Johns Gospel which
Christ spake at Capharnaum wher he promised the institution of this diuine Sacramēt,iust ȳ Easter twelue moneth before he
instituted the same at his laste supper in
Hierusalem, are these.   I am the lyuely
Ioan.6. bread which came downe from heauen, if
  „   any man eate of this bread he shall liue for
  „   euer,and the bread which I shal geue is my
  „   flesh, which I shall geue for the lyfe of the
  „   world. Then the Iewes fell at variance
  „   emongst them selues saying. How can this
  „   man geue vs his flesh to eate?Then Iesus
  „   said vnto them:verely, verely,I say vnto
                                    you,

you, but if ye eate the flesh of the sonne of
man, and drinke his blood, ye shall no haue
lyfe in you. He that eateth my fleshe and
drinketh my blood, hath euerlasting lyfe,
and I shall reyse him vp at the later day.
For my flesh is verely meat, and my blood
is verely drinke, he that eateth my fleshe
and drinketh my blood dwelleth in me, and
I in him. As the liuing Father sente me,
and I lyue for my Father, so he that eateth
me shall lyue also for me. This is the bread
which is come downe from heauen. not as
your fathers did eate Manna and aredead,
he that eateth this bread shall line for euer.

This communication oure Lorde had
with the Iewes teaching in the Synagog
at Capharnaum. And many therefore of
his Disciples hearing these thinges saied,
this is an hard talke, who can heare him?
But our saniour knowing in him self that
his disciples murmured hereat, saied vnto
thē. Doth this offend you? what then if you
shal see ȳ sonne of man ascend vp whereas
he was before? The spirit is ȳ which quic
kneth, ȳ flesh auaileth nothing. The words
which I haue spoken to you be spirit & life.
And this much of those words which Christ
thē vttered at what time he promised (as ȳ
wordes them selues doe plainly declare) to
geue his fleshe to be eaten in the blessed
sacramēt. Now you shall heare those which

B iiŋ   he

he pronounced twelue monethes after, at his laſt ſupper when he inſtituted the ſame bleſſed Sacrament, and accompliſhed that his foreſayed promiſe.

Matt.26. *As they were at ſupper Ieſus toke bread,
Marc. 14 gaue thākes, & bleſſed, & brake & gaue to his
Luc.22. Diſciples ſaying: Take, and eate, this is
      ,, my body whiche is geuen for you. This
      ,, doe for the remēmbrance of me. Like=
      ,, wiſe taking the chalice after he had ſupped
      ,, he gaue thankes, and gaue it them ſaying:
      ,, Take, and diuide among you, and drinke
      ,, all of this. This is my blood of y̆ new Te=
      ,, ſtament. This is the chalice, the new Te=
      ,, ſtament in my blood, which for you and for
      ,, many ſhalbe ſhed for the remiſſion of ſyn=
      ,, nes. I ſay verily vnto you that I will not
      ,, drinke from hence foorth of this generatiō
      ,, of the vine, vntill that day when I ſhall
      ,, drinke it new with you in the Kingdome
      ,, of my Father. And they dranke all thereof.

These are in effect all the words which y̆ three Euangeliſtes witneſſe to haue bene ſpoken of Chriſt at the inſtitution of y̆ bleſ=ſed Sacrament. It remayneth that I geue you likewiſe S. Paul his words, by which it appeareth, how he deliuered the ſame to be practiſed emōgſt the Corinthians, which Chriſt before inſtituted. S. Paules words
1.Cor. 11 are theſe. For I receaued of our Lord that
      ,, which I deliuered vnto you: for our Lord
                                                 Ieſus

Iesus ý same night he was betrayed,toke »
bread, & geuing thanks, brake, and sayed: »
take, & eate,This is my body, which shall »
be deliuered for you, do this for ý remem= »
brance of me. Likewise the chalice also af= »
ter he had supped, saying: This chalice is »
the new Testament in my blood, doe this »
so often as ye shal drinke, for ý remëbrance »
of me. For so ofte as ye shal eat this bread, »
and drinke of this chalice, ye shall shew »
foorth our Lordes death vntill he come. »
wherefore whosoeuer shall eate the bread »
and drinke of the chalice of our Lord vn= »
worthely, shalbe gilty of the body & blood »
of our Lord. But let a man examine him »
self,and so let him eate of the bread & drink »
of the chalice: for he that eateth and drin= »
keth vnworthely, eateth and drinketh his »
own iudgemët, not discerning the body of »
our Lord. Thus you haue those worthy »
testimonies of ý new Testament, by which
the true doctrine of this hygh mysterie the
blessed Sacrament of the altar is substan=
tially & perfitely confirmed, twise by Christ
his own mouth (accordingly as the fower
Euangelistes do witnesse) and once by his
elect vessell S. Paule, making a rehersall
only of Christes institution.

Of ý words noman doupteth, but whatso=
euer opinió or sect he be of cócernïg ý mat=
ter it self, he pretëdeth to reuerëce thë with
B 5 al his

all hys hart & stedfastly to beleue that whic̄h Chrift ment by them. So that herein the Catholikes and Proteſtātes doe agree very wel. for both do confeſſe aſwell theſe to be the words of the new teſtament, as alſo that they haue a trew meaning which is

wherein conſiſteth the whole cōtrouer- ſie of our ſpuie.

neceſſarily to be beleued. But which is the true ſenſe and meaniug of them, thereupon ariſeth al the ſtrife, and therin conſiſteth the whole weyght of the matter . For words ſerue properly to this end, to geue the rea- der or hearer to vnderſtand what his mind and meaning is that vttereth the. So that vnles we haue this true meaning, it ſkyl- leth very litle what one thinke or beleue of the words. It is moſt certayne alſo that the words of holy ſcriptur haue ben all- wayes , alleged not only of all manner of heretiks , were theyr hereſies neuer ſo falſe and abominable : but euen of the Diuell hym ſelfe the great graunfather of al here-

Matt. 4.

ſies and lyes, as it is ſpecially noted in that place where he tempted Chriſt to caſt hym ſelfe downe from pinacle of the temple. For to perſwade him thereunto he alleged in a wronge ſenſe thys place of ſcripture:

Pſal. 90.

Angelis ſuis mandauit de te. & cæt. He hath geuen his angels chargeof the y̌ thou hurte not thy fote againſte the ſtone . For thoſe words are not ment of ſuch an external and corporal protection wherby any mā ſhould
be

be moued to tempt god, neither of Meſſias only as the Diuel falſely applied them, but of the ſpiritual & inward protection whiche angels haue cōmitted thē ouer good men.

But we are on the other ſide againe moſt aſſured that although neither heretike nor diuel lacketh wordes of ſcripture to alleage for theyr falſhodes, yet they can neuer alleage therefore any one word truly & rightly vnderſtode. For truth always agreeth only with truth. & therefore euery word of holy ſcripture beinge moſt infallibly true it is not poſſible ỹ ſame ſhould at any time be truly alleged to proue a falſhod. The cōtrouerſie thē which at this day troubletħ Chriſtendō ſo much cōſiſting only in ỹ true meaning of Chriſtes words & in effect all together about ỹ true ſens of thoſe foure, This is my body, we ought earneſtely to thinke which may be the moſt ſure & ſafeſt way to attaine thereunto: eſpecially whereas both ỹ truth of al other queſtiōs now in controuerſie, & the whole ſtate of our ſouls health depēdeth after a ſort vpō ỹ true knowlege & true belieſe thereof.   If we conſider the whole courſe of a Chriſtē māslife, there is no one vertue more cōmended either by ỹ manifold teſtimonies of holy ſcripture, or exāple of Chriſt him ſelfe & al holy fathers, than humility, which as it ſerueth beſt in al caſes of a mās life, ſo it helpeth ſpecally to ỹ

true

The meane to vnderſtand ſcripture truly.

true vnderstanding of Gods word, as con=
trariwise pride is the rote of all heresy and
mysbeleife. And if you will haue the same
proued out of scripture it self, harken vnto
those words of Ecclesiasticus, where it is

Eccl. 5.

sayd: Esto mansuetus ad audiendum verbū
Dei, vt intelligas, & cum sapientia proferas
responsum verum. Be lowly and meeke to
heare the word of God, that thou mayst vn
derstand, and with wisedome bring foorth
a true answer. This sure foundation being
then layed, that we may by this meanes be
assured of the true vnderstanding of Chri=
stes words: let vs yⁱ desire to attayne there=
vnto, sticke vnto this sure ground: let vs
put in practise this humility: let vs not
proudly take vppon our selues by confe=
rence of scripture only to find out so high a
mysterie, neither let vs trust our owne
braynes only. For as we may easely mis=
construe any one place: so may we no lesse
easely be deceaued in the interpretation of
many, which we endeuour to try and exa=

The iudge-
ment of
auncient fa
thers
ought to
be prefer-
red before
our own
sense.

mine by the same. we ought rather hum=
bly become scholers vnto such as long be=
fore our tyme haue not without the mani=
fest assistance of the holy Ghost most dili=
gently studied holy scriptures, & truly ex=
pounded them: we ought not wedde our
consent to y⁰ sense, which our selues or some
other of our age haue inuented, specially if
the

the same be found contrary to $\bar{y}$ sense of the auncient holy Fathers. For what token of humility appeareth in him, who preferreth his owne fansy before $\bar{y}$ iudgement of such learned Doctors? Or what greater pride can ther be, the for $\bar{y}$ new learning of a few sprõg vp within these thirty or forty yeres to condemne their learning which hath bene wel nigh thirten hundred yeres of al Christendome generally receaued & approued?

Holy scripture teacheth also $\bar{y}$ the lippes of Priestes do kepe the true knowledge of Gods law: & willeth vs to seke $\bar{y}$ vnderstanding thereof at their hãds. what more worthy Prelats wil you seke for, then those holy Bishops, S.Chrysostome, S.Cyrill, S.Cyprian, S.Ambrose, S.Augustine, & such like? who attayneth to $\bar{y}$ true meanig of Christes words, if they did not, which so happily succeded $\bar{y}$ Apostles them selues as wel in nerenesse of tyme, as godlynesse of life? what more indifferent iudges cã any man require then such, as without all partialty of either part $\bar{y}$ now striueth, haue writen truly & syncerely what them selues then taught, & what $\bar{y}$ whole Church then beleued so many hundred yeres before this cõtrouersie was either doubted or dreamed of? The Ecclesiasticall hystorie recording vnto vs $\bar{y}$ meanes which S.Basil $\bar{y}$ great & Gregory Nazianzen two perfite holy & great

Mala. 2◉

Lib.11. cap.9.

great learned diuines vsed for ẏ true vnder
standing of ẏ bokes of holy scripture repor
teth thus of thē. Eorũ intelligentiã & cæt.
They folowed ẏ vnderstādinge of those bo
kes not by theyr own presumtiõ, but accor
ding to ẏ wzitings & autozity of their foze=
fathers. who also thēselues receaued ẏ rule
by succescio frõ ẏ Apostles. Here we learne
not only ẏ these holy fathers by their good
ensāple haue cōfirmed ẏ vertue of humility
in pzeferring ẏ fozefathers iudgemēt befoze
their own, but also ẏ this rule of trying out
ẏ true meaning of holy scripture was by ẏ
Apostles thē selus cōmēded vnto vs. Now
if thes, two great clarks liuing not past 300
yeres after ẏ Apostles, reuerenced so much
theyr fozfathers which were of liklyhod ei=
ther about 200 yers ōli oz not so much elder
thē thēselues, how much moze oughtwe to
reuerēce & embzace their wzitinges which
ar thzise yea six tymes so many hūdzed yers
befoze vs? If they, whose perfitnesse of lyfe
was such who as ẏ same histozy witnesseth
sequestred thē selues ẏ space of thirtē yeres
frõ al other affayzes & secular studies to em
ploy this only, would not yet pzesume to
vnderstād scripture wout ẏ interpretation
of theyr ancesters: what pzesūption were it
foz any mā now a days in which al iniqui=
ty abundeth, & especially foz ẏ common sozt
which neuer study ẏ scripturs thirtene mo
nethes

nethes together, to trust their own phansy
sly & to refuse y̆ interpretatiõ which y̆ holy
doctors of y̆ chnrch & aunciẽt wꝛiters shall
ministre vnto thẽ? But as I haue alleged
this one exãple of two perfite good mẽ to
shew what we ought to do i this case:so I
could by a nũbꝛe of exãples most platly de=
ciphꝛe vnto you what kind of men they al=
wayes haue bene which do practise y̆ cõtra
ry. To auoid tediousnes I will rekon one
oꝛ to only. First therfoꝛe harke I pꝛay you
what is wꝛitẽ of those notoꝛious heretikes
the Arrians by a very reuerẽd & auncient
Catholike Bishop Alexander, as appe=
reth in y̆ Tripartite stoꝛy, in a letter of his
wherein he describeth perfetly the maners
of those olde heretikes. His woꝛdes are as
here foloweth.

It hathe
bene y̆ mã
ner of here
tikes al=
wayes to
refuse the
authoꝛitie
of aunciẽt
fathers.

Lib.1.ca.
14.

Hi enim qui contra deitatẽ filij Dei ca-
stra constituunt, neq́ue contra nos ingratas
calúnias exercere formidant: quoniã &cæ.
Foꝛ these Arrians (saiethe he) whiche doe
pitch their tentes and make battail against
the Deity of the sonne of god no meruel if
thei feare not spitefully to slannder vs
(Catholikes)seing they cannot abide that
any of the auncient fathers should be com=
pared tõ thẽ,neither can suffer to be cõsted
eqnal tõ such as haue bẽ our teachers & ma
sters frõ our youth,noꝛ admit any of those
whiche now ani where do beare like office,
　　　　　　　　　　　　to haue

>> to haue like measure of wisedome to them
>> selues, coūting them selues only to be wise
>> (being in dede poze wzetches and inuētozs
>> of strang opinions) ⁊ that vnto them only
>> those things haue bene reueled, which no
>> man vnder ⁊ son euer vnderstode before.

Also Eusebius declaringe howe one
Tatianus fell into sundzy abhominable
heresies hath emongest other these wozds,

Eccl. hiſ. which serue wel to this purpose : Elatione
li.4.c.29 nimia elatus tanquá qui se cęteris duceret
meliorem proprium maluit quám a veteri-
bus traditum docendi instituere stylum. He
being puffed vp with ouer much hautynes
as one that thought himselfe better then
all other, chose rather to folow his owne
peculiar maner of teaching, then that which
was deliuered of his ancesters. And a litle
after speakīg of ⁊ same heretike ⁊ his cōpa-
nions he describeth thē after this sort: Qui

Ibidem. vtútur quidé lege & Prophetis & Euágelijs,
sed propria quadá interpretatione scriptu-
rarū sensum peruertunt. which vse in dede
the law, the Prophetes ⁊ the Ghospel, but
doe peruert the sense of scriptures by expounding them after a certain peculiar and
pzinate fashion. Of Nestozius also ⁊ grand

Trip.hiſ. heretike this much is wzitten. Libris anti-
li.12.c.4. quorum interpretum dedignabatur incum-
bere, omnibusque se meliorem putabat esse.
He disdained to reade the bokes of ānciēt
interp

interpreters and preferred him self before al
other. Thus you see most euidently what
kind of men those haue bene allwayes,
which refused th'expositions of auncient
writers: you see both partes throughly pro
ued, aswell that humility, in embracing
the holy Fathers censure, is the way to
come by the true sense of the holy scripture,
as that pride on ẏ other side & presumption,
is the commen high way that leadeth vnto
all heresy and falshode.

wherefore I doubt not but as you hartely
detest these heretiks pride: so according to ẏ
good example of S. Basill & S. Gregory
Nazianze, you wil gladly with al humility
folowe that meaning of Christes wordes
concerning this hygh mystery of our redē-
tion conteined in the blessed Sacrament of
the altar, which the holy, learned, and auncient writers shal plainly declare vnto you.
whose sayinges I doe minde from thence
specially to translate, where they write most
fully and at larg of this matter, to thentent
you reading theyr whole discourse, not by
peace meale or in a few lynes, but many lea
ues together, may more perfitly be instructed in theyr doctrine, and haue no cause to
mistrust in me any false dealing: but rather
to perceaue many tymes the legerdemaine
of some Protestantes, whiche haue not blu-
shed to alleage halfe sentences for their syde
℃		when

when as the wordes going before or those which folow make clane against them. I will therefore translate vnto you first of all, that which S. Chrysostome the chiefe doctour amongste the Grecians hath written most largely vpon some parte of those places of scripture before rehersed.

℃ Testimonies out of S. Chrysostome vppon the sixth Chapiter of S. John.

The h.
Chapiter.

TO begin now with the sixth Chapiter of S. Jhon, that you may more plainly conceaue of what force that place is to proue the real presence of Christes flesh and blood in the blessed Sacrament, and also howe S. Chrysostoms wordes here doe come in: You shal first vnderstand, that the Jewes of Capharnaum (whiche thereof are commonly called Capharnites) after they had ben miraculously fede of Christ with fiue barly loues & two fishes being them selues in nomber about fyue thousand, retorned vnto Christ again, looking for some other like banket: and to prouoke him the more as they thought, began to bragge how their fathers dyd eate Manna in the desert, doing him to vnderstād thereby if he would get credite amōgst them, he should in like sort feed thē. whereuppon our sauiur tooke occasion to declare vnto them before hand, that miraculous & heauenly

Ioan. 6.

heauēly foode which he minded afterward
to ordein in his last supper & which should
not only aunswere their Manna: but so
far passe the same as a true body passeth a
shadow. And therefore he saied vnto them,
the bread which I shall geue is my flesh. &
that he ment by those wordes to leaue his
true flesh in dede to be eatē in stede of their
Māna: it appereth by that which soloweth
most euidently. For whereas the Caphar=
nite Iewes gruged strait way saying:how
cā this man geue vs his flesh to eat? imagi
ninge suche a grosse and homly eatynge of
Christes fleashe as of other common fleshe
which is bought in the shābles, he did not
take away that scruple as our Protestātes
do now a dayes with saying ỹ it should be
a bare figure ouly, or that they should eate
bread only and not fleshe, and feed on hym
only spiritually by fayth. He sayde none of
all these thinges but cleane contrary to con
found their gruging infidelity & to cōfirme
his former wordes added thervnto other of
more vehemēce saying:verely,verely,I say
vnto you,but if ye eate the flesh of the sōne
of man and drinke his bloode, ye shall not
haue lyfe in you, with many moe of lyke
perspicuity and playnesse. Nowe if Christ
had mente by these first wordes a figure
or tōkē only of his fleshe,how easely might
he haue satisfied the Iewes, who coulde so

An euidēt
argumēt
prouing
ỹ Christ
meant to
geue his
true flesh.

C ij   well

well away with figures beinge allwayes vsed therunto in Moyses Law. And what likelyhood is there, ẏ he being so merciful a Sauiour vnto al men, and bearing such a speciall affection to hys countrimen, that he neuer departed from them, but witnessed

Math. 15 that he was chiefly sent vnto the lost shepe of Israel, would not only not appease their grudging, but more increase ẏ same? In so muche that in the ende they quite forsoke him saying: this is an hard talke, who can heare him? whereas if he hadde ment a bare signe or figure, by telling the truth only, he might haue kept them continually in his company. Truely no man (I suppose) that thinketh wel of God, can imagine any such vnmercifulnes to haue bene in Christ. And therefore seing he made no such interpreta-tion, but contrariwise immediatly after their grudging, threatned thē, that onlesse they did eat his flesh and drinke his blood they should not haue life, & confirmed the same with his accustomed othe verily, verily: it seemeth vnto me a very strong argument, ẏ his meaning was to promise thē his true naturall flesh, & not a figure thereof only.

But to proue that he ment so in dede, hearken now what S. Chrysostom writeth vppon those stubborn wordes of the repi-ning Iewes: This is an hard talke, who can heare him? In the exposition whereof

afte r

after a few lines he hath as here foloweth.

⧆ It is ye part of a scholer not to enquire
curiously of ye which his master affirmeth,
but to heare & beleue , and attend a conue=
nient tyme for the resolution thereof. How
happened then here (say ye) the contrary?
& why went they backe? mary by reason of
theyr owne folly . For when this question
cometh in, quomodo aliquid fiat, how or by
what meanes any thing may be done , to=
gether therewith cometh incredulity and
lacke of faith. So Nicodemus beig trobled
with in him self sayd, how can a man entre
into his mothers womb again? and euen so
these men now are trobled saying, how can
this man geue vs his flesh to eate ?

But if thou askest this questiō: why didest
ye not say likewise at ye miracle of fiue loues:
How hath he increased them so much? Be=
cause they cared thē only for filling their bel
lies,& respected not the considering of ye
miracle. But the thing it self (you will say)
then taught them. Therefore they should
haue learned to beleue therby , that these
thinges also by him might easely be done.
For to that entent he wrought the former
miracle, that therby they should learne not
to discredite any more suche thinges as he
should tell them afterward. But they truely
were nothing better for those his sayings.
We are they which haue receaued the com=

Chryso.
Hom. 45
in Ioan.
"
"
"
"
"
"　1.
"
"
"
Ioan. 3.
"
"
"
"
"
"
"
"
"
"
"
"
"
"　2.
"
"
"
"
"

,, modity and benefit thereof. wherefore it is
,, necessarily to be learned how wonderfull
,, mysteries these are , why they were geuen,
,, and what profite aryseth by them . we are
,, one body & members of his flesh & bones.
,, And therefore suche as haue professed his

3. name ough to obey his precepts. Now that
,, we be not by loue only but in very dede tur
,, ned into his flesh , that is brought to passe
,, by the meate which he hath geuen vs . For
,, when he would declare his loue towardes

commi- vs , he mengled him selfe by meanes of his
scuit. body together with vs, and made him selfe
one with vs, that the body and the head,
,, should be vnited together . For this is the
,, manner of such as loue most intierly. This
,, Iob signified of those seruantes by whom
,, he was most beloued, which to expresse the

4. same loue sayd . who could graunt vs that
Iob. 31. we might be filled with his flesh? the which
,, thing Christe performed , to binde vs more
,, to loue him. And to witnesh his singular af
,, fectiō towardes vs he permitted him selfe
,, not to be seen only of such as are desirous,
,, but to be touched and eatē , and theyr teath
,, to be fasteued in his fleshe , and all men to
,, be filled and satisfied with the desire of him.
,, Let vs rise therefore from that table as it
,, were lions breathing out fyre, making the
,, diuell him selfe a feard, let vs haue in mind
,, our head , and thinke vppon the singular
loue

one whiche he hath shewed towardes vs.
Parentes oftentymes haue put foorth theyr
childrē to be nourished of other, but I (saith
Christ) do nourish you with my own flesh,
I geue my self vnto you, I fauour al men,
I geue all men good hope of the ioyes to
come. He that sheweth him selfe so louing
to vs in this life, will shew the same much
more in ỹ life to come. I vouchsafed (saith he
(to' be your brother I be came partaker for
your sakes of flesh and blood. And looke by
what thinges I was ioyned in one with
you, the same things I haue now exhibeted
and geuen again vnto you. This blood is
cause that the kingly image flourisheth in
vs, this blood suffereth not the beauty and
nobiliry of the soul which it watereth con=
tinually and nourisheth, at any ryme to de=
cay. Blood is not made by and by of the
meat that is eaten, onleste it be first chan=
ged into some other thing, but this blood
floweth to ỹ soule inmediatly without any
delay, and inueth it with a certaine great
strength. This mysticall blood driueth the
deuils far of from vs, and draweth the An
gels and Lord of Angels nerce vnto vs.
For the deuils when they see within vs ỹ
blood of our Lord, are put to flight, and ỹ
Angels make hast to assist vs. This blood
being shed, washed the whole world, of
which S. Paul to the Hebrewes speaketh

“
“
5.
“
“
“
“
“
“
“
“
6.
“
“
“
“
“
“
“
“
“
“
“
“

7.
The Sa
crament
putteth
Diuels to
flyght.

“

C 4　　very

,, very much. This blood purged the inward
,, places and the holy of holyes. If the figure
9.
Exod. 12 ,, thereof had such vtue in ꝑ Iewes Church,
,, being sprinkled on ꝑ postes of their dores
,, in the midst of Aegipt: much more ꝑ truth.
,, This blood signified ꝑ golden altar. with=
,, out this ꝑ hyghe Priest durst not entre into
,, ꝑ inward places. This blud made Priestes,
,, this blood in a figure purged synnes. In
,, which figure if it was of such force, if death
,, quaked at the shadow, how much more I
,, pray you will it feare ꝑ truth it self? This
,, is ꝑ health of our soules, by this our soule
,, is washed, hereby it is adorned & deked, he
,, reby it is inflamed. This maketh our mind
,, brighter thē fyre, & more shyning thē gold.

10. ,, The shedding of this blood caused hea=
,, uen to lye open vntovs. wonderful truly
,, are the mysteries of the Church, wonder=
,, ful is her closet or holy place. Out of Para=
,, dise springeth a fountain from which sensi=
,, ble riuers are deriued. From this table a
,, fountaine riseth which sendeth foorth spiri
,, tual fluddes. By this welspring bare wy=
,, lowes doe not grow, but trees ꝑ reach vp
,, to heauen it self, which always doe bring
,, foorth seasonable and sound fruits. If any
,, man be ouer hote or drye let him resort to
,, this fountayne and he shalbe refreshed. It
,, cleanseth al filth and vncleannesse, it aswa=
,, geth heates, not such as are caused by the
          sonne,

sonne, but such as fyery dartes doe print or "
fasten in vs. For it hath his spring from "
aboue and the water is from thence conti- "
nually renewed, from whence it hath his "
head. There are of this fountayn many ri- "
uers, which the holy Ghost sendeth abrode "
according to the wyl & arbitrement of God "
the sonne. Nether y way is made by mat- "
tocke & spade, but by opening our hartes & "
mynds. This is y fountayn of light which "
spreadeth abrode the beames of truth. The "
heauenly powers stand & behold y beauty "
of his flouigs. For they see y vertue & mer- "
neilous shyning brightnes of these things "
a great deale more plainly, then we can. "

And truly euē as if a man put a hand or "
tong in to gold y is melted, y same forthw "
is gylted ouer: so these things which are "
set before vs, do gylt our soules. This flud "
mounteth vp more vehemently then fyre, "
neither doth it burne, but dly washeth clean "
whatsoeuer it taketh. This blood was al- "
ways foresignified in y altars, & in y mur- "
der of iust men. This is the ornamēt of the "
world, this is y wherewith Christ redemed   11.
wherewith he decked y vniuersal Church. "
For euen as a man byeth & also decketh his "
bondmā with gold, so doth Christ vs w his "
blood. They which be partakers of this "
blood haue their abiding with the Angels, "
Archangels & celestiall powers. They are "

C 5   arayed

,, arrayed w̄ Christ his kyngly stole they are
,, garded & defended with spiritual weapons.
,, Twysh I haue sayd nothig, I shuld rather

12. ,, say they haue put on ȳ King him self. Now
,, as this is a great & wonderful thing, so if
,, ȳ be without spot whē thou doest approche
,, thereunto, then comest thou to thy health &
,, sauegard, but if with an euil cōscience, then
,, to thy paine & torment. For he that eateth &

1.Co. 11. ,, drinketh vnworthely ȳ blood of our Lorde
,, eateth & drinketh his own dānation. For if
,, they which defile ȳ kinges purple robe are
,, no lesse punished thē they which cut & mā-
,, gle ȳ same, what meruеil is it if they which
,, receaue the body of Christ with an vnclean
,, conscience, haue one punishment with thē

13. ,, ȳ with nayles fastened him to the crosse?
,, Consider what an horrible punishement

Deu. 17. S. Paul threatneth vnto such. who soeuer

Heb. 10. maketh voyde or breketh ȳ law of Moyses
,, (saith he) being conuinced thereof by two
,, or three witnesses is put to death without
,, any mercy. How much more then thinke
,, ye deserueth ȳ man to be more greuously
,, punished who shal tread the sonne of God
,, vnder his feate and shall esteme ȳ blood of
,, ȳ testament polluted or vile in which he is
,, sanctified? Let vs cōsidre therefore (welbe-
,, loued) what we haue to doe, seing we enioy
,, such benefites. when any filthy thought co-
,, meth into our mind, whē we perceaue our
                                        selues

selues caried away by ãger either in worde **"**
or dede,let vs thinke what we deserue,what **"**
spirit we haue receaued,& let vs kepe down **"**
our vnreasonable & brutish affections . let **"**
this be our cogitatiõ.how longe shal we be **"**
wholy geauẽ to thinges present & trãsitory? **"**
whẽ shal we be styrred vp to goodnes?how **"**
long wil it be before we thinke ernestly on **"**
our saluatiõ? Let vs cõsidre how many be= Faith on=
nefites Christ hath bestowed vpõ vs, & rẽ ly without
dre him thãkes therefore,let vs glorify him good wor
not by faith only,but by good workes also, kes suffi=
to th'ẽd we may obtein ẙ glory to come by ceth not.
ẙ grace & clemẽcy of our Lord Jesus Christ **"**
through whõ & to whõ be vnto the Father **"**
& the holy Ghoost glory for euer & euer. &c **"**

Now ẙ you may more euidẽtly perceaue
how this holy auncient Doctor impugneth
directly ẙ opiniõ cõcerning ẙ blessed Sacra
mẽt which is cõmẽly taught by ẙ Sacramẽ
tary Protestãts, I will brefly repete vnto
you some of those sẽtẽces,which in this his
discourse doe cheifly touch ẙ point:besechig
you to iudge indifferẽtly whether it may be
gathered by any of thẽ ẙ he taught ẙ figure
only of Christ his body to be in the Sacrament,& not rather the true, reall,& natural I,
body,which was borne of the virgin,& put
to death on the crosse for our synnes. And
first of al learn that good lesson of S . Chry
sostom,that we ought not be curiouse in
asking

asking how or by what meanes that which Christ affirmeth, is brought to passe.

This curiosity as it was the vndoing of the Capharnites, & sheweth that they lacked faith : so if you marke well, the same condemneth our Protestantes, & proueth manifestly, that whereas they bragge so much of their faith, saying by faith only they receaue Christ his body at their communion, in very dede they are altogether voyde of all true faith . To open which thing more plainly you shall note here, that as wel the incredulity of the Sacramentaries as of the Iewes procedeth of those curious interrogations which S . Chrysostome blameth: but after a diuerse manner, and by two diuerse extremities, of which the one is cleane contrary to the other. For whiles the Iewes imagined, when Christ talked of his flesh to be eaten, that they should eate the same, euen as they then saw it in the forme of flesh, neither lifted vp their mind to consiðre his Godhead & omnipotency, whereby he was as well able to geue his true flesh vnder an other forme, as to fede v. thousand men with v. loues:hauing, I say, their mind fixed vppon this extreme grosse imagination, they murmured within them selues saying in this sense:how can he geue vs his flesh to eate? how shall our stomake away with it? what a hard kind of talke is this?

this? is it not against nature that one man
should be nourished with an other mans
flesh? do not our mouthes & stomakes abhorre the same? And whereas Christ to
plucke their mind from that grosse ima- Ioan. 6.
gination sayd: The spirite is that which
quickneth the flesh auaileth nothing, meaning thereby, that their so fleshly & grosse
interpretation of his wordes was not to
be alowed, but that they should vnderstäd
them more spiritually: for so much as he
ment to geue his flesh vnder such a forme
and in such sort, together with his soule &
Godhead, that it should nothing anoye the
stomake, but greatly conforte both their
soule and body: they nothing attending to
Christes cöfortable words, but as mē alredy wedded to their grosse cöceiued opiniö,
went clean away, & vtterly forsoke him.

Now our Protestantes are in the other
extremitie, agreing neuerthelesse with the How the
Protestantes a-
gree & thē
Caphar-
naites and
wherein
they differ
Iewes in the mischief of incredulity, as it
happeneth in other like cases. for al extremes are wont to agree in ỹ which is ill, as
it is most manifest in ỹ example of a prodi-
gall man and a niggard: both which doe
agree in doing euil, and yet are they clean
contrary one to the other. but will you see
ỹ same plainly appeare betwixt ỹ Iewes &
the Protestants? As they were ouermuch
grosse & carnal, so our mē are ouer much figuratiue

tatiue and spiritual: They would not imagin how Christ was able to geue his fleshe
vnder any other forme , then that whiche
they saw. These men wil not conceiue how
possibly his true flesh may be côteined vnder the forme of bread as Christ appointed.
They toke ꝑ first parte of Christ his talke
only , and would not geue eare to the last
by whiche he condemned their grosse opinion. These men ground their heresy vppon the later wordes, taking chief hold of
them, and do not regard what he saied before concerning the truth of his fleshe. For
whereas Christ saied in his former words,
the bread whiche I shall geue is my fleshe:
They say cleane concrary, the bread which
Christe gaue is not his fleshe , but remaineth still bread, grounding their false opinion vppon those later wordes falsely
vnderstode , where Christe saied : the spirite geueth life, the flesh profiteth nothing.
For thereby he mêt not to deny that which
he had before promysed , but to controlle
the stubborn Iewes which vnderstode his
words so grossely.

Thus you see how the Iewes & Protestantes are in two diuerse extremites & after a sort one cleane côtrary to ꝑ other. But
in those interrogations which as S. Chrysostom wel noteth are arguments of incredulity & lack of faith they agree I warrant
you

you marueilous wel. For as y̆ Iewes vsed
many howes, so these men haue almost no
other thing in their mouthes, but how can
Christ his flesh, blood, and bones, be cõtei-
ned in so litle a rome? how can his body be
at one tyme in heauē and on the altar? how
can it be in a thousand places at once? how
can that be flesh, whiche our eyes, tast, fea-
ling, and other senses tell vs is bread? So
that as they begin like the Iewes, with
that interrogatiue particle of incredulity:
so the rest of their wordes tend alltogether
like the wordes of the Iewes, to the discre
diting of the omnipotent power of God.

For if they beleued that God were able
by his worde to bring all this to passe, seme
it neuer so muche against naturall reason:
they would neuer reason after such a sort,
but would only consider, whether Christe
spake any such words whereby it may appere he ment to worke suche a wondersull
miracle. For otherwise thei may by like interrogations discredite the whole Christen
faith & aske, how God made y̆ world of nothing? how his true Godhead came down
frõ heauē to be incarnat & yet remained stil,
in heauē? how he was cõceiued of y̆ blessed
womã his mother without sede of a man?
how he cam, flesh blood & bones out of his
mothers wombe she always continuing a
virgin? & so orderly go forward throuhout
the

the whole life of Chrift, to his paffion, re=
furrection, and afcenfion, which were alto=
gether full of miracles, fuch as our natural
reafon can neuer attaine vnto, and fuch as
we fhall quickly difcredite, if we vfe thofe
interrogatiues of ý Iewes & Proteftants.
Both which as they agree, by two fundry
extremes, in this infidelity of difcrediting
God his omnipotency: fo if you compare
both thofe extremities together, you fhall
find alfo that thefe mens extreme madneffe
deferueth much moꝛe blame, and far exce=
deth that of the Iewes.

The Pro
teftantes
incredu=
lity is
woꝛſe then
that of the
Iewes.

Foꝛ firft the Iewes beleued not yet that
Chꝛiſt was true God: neither yet that he
was able to perfoꝛme in dede whatfoeuer
he pꝛomiſed in woꝛd. which thing the Pro
teſtants muft nedes confeffe, if they will be
Chꝛiſtians. Secondarily they faw not vn=
der what foꝛme Chꝛiſt mynded to inftitute
his fleſh to be eaten, and therefoꝛe in that
refpect, are much moꝛe excuſable then our
Pꝛoteſtāts, which doe not only know that
he inftituted the fame at his laft fupper vn
der the foꝛme of bꝛead, but alfo haue ſeen
the pꝛactiſe of the Church, and general be=
lief of al Chꝛiſtendome continued fo many
hundꝛed yeres. Thirdly & laft, they vnder=
ſtode Chꝛiſtes woꝛds fo, ý they thought yet
he ment to geue them the true ſubſtance of
his fleſh, although they beleued not he
couId

could doe it conueniently, neither would abide to heare after how cōuenient a maner the same might be performed. But our protestantes thinke not at al that Christe ment to geue vs his true flesh, but cleane contrary both to Christes wordes and meaning, take away by theyr glosing the true substance of his flesh, and in stede thereof cōmend vnto vs bare bread & naked figures. For which three causes no dout the Iewish Capharnites shall at the day of iudgement ryse vp and cōdemne them, as those which of two extreme mischiefes and vntruthes haue chosen that which is most hereticall.

Now if you compare the true catholike faith with both these extremities, you shall find that it agreeth with neither of them, but kepeth the goldē meane betwixt both. For it vseth none of those incredulouse questions which S. Chrysostome condemneth, but simply beleueth that to be true which Christe affirmed. It cleaueth not to the first parte of Christes wordes only, as the Capharnites, who thought because he sayd his flesh was meat in dede thei should eate him visibly: nor yet to y latter part onlie with the protestants, who thinke because he saied: It is the spirite that geueth life, therefore his fleshe is to be eaten by faith only: but cōtrary to them both and in the right meane & true meaning betwene

both

The Catholike faith kepeth the meane.

both, adioyning al Chriftes wordes toge=
ther it concludeth, that vnder the forme of
bread Chriftes true flesh is really and sub=
ftantially receaued. By saying vnder the
forme of bread, it taketh away the Caphar=
nites grosse, and carnall imagination, by
saying true fleshe really and substantially
present, it condemneth the Proteftätes spri=
tish and faithlesse inuention.

I haue bene longer vpö this first sentēce
of S. Chrysoftom then I thought. but my
truft is, that the Proteftantes opiniö being
thus plainly set before you, together with y
Catholike beliefe, you shalbe able hereafter
much better to iudge which side is confir=
med by y ancient doctors. Now it remay=
neth that after you haue throughly cöside=
red how cömon that quomodo, which S.
Chrysoftom condēneth, is in y Proteftants
mouthes, & therefore concluded also with
him that they are in this behalfe incredu=
louse & without faith like the Capharnites,
you read forward & you shall find secondly
to be noted in S. Chrysoftom, y Chrift did
first work that great miracle of feadig fiue
thousand with fiue loaues & two fishes, to
thēd y Iewes should beleue that which he
minded to speake afterward cöcerning the
blessed Sacrament. whereby it appereth y
this should be as it is in dede a far greater
miracle then the other, But & if it be a bare
figure

2.

figure or signe only of Christ, then there is
not wrought so great a miracle in this, as
was by those fiue loues .yea rather thē ther
is here no miracle at all.For what maruell
is it, if one hauing a peece of bread put in
his mouth, and being warned besides tō
fede on Christ by faith, taketh occasiō there=
by to thinke on Christ? But that after the
words of consecration pronoūced by a law=
full Priest, the substance of bread should be
chāged into the substance of Christes body,
without any alteration of ye outward form,
this is an exceding greate miracle and far
passing mans reason. wherefore S. Chry=
sostom who therefore calleth these the wō=
derful mysteries confirmeth plainly hereby
the Catholike faith, and ouerthroweth that
false opinion of the Protestantes.

　　Thirdly you haue to note, that S. Chry=　　　3.
sostome saith we are by receauing this hea=
uenly foode not only spiritually or by loue
only, as the Protestantes teache, but really
also and truely made one with Christe and
turned into his flesh: so that our flesh (as
the other doctors hereafter do more plainly
declare) is by touching this holy fleshe of
Christe made to be after this life, glorionse
and immortal.And therefore to declare that
this effect commeth by the reall touching
and receauing of Christes fleshe into our
bodies, he vseth those effectuall wordes of
　　　　　　　　　　　D ij　　　　　　　our

flesh turned into his and of his fleshe mengled with ours . which kind of wordes are
very often tymes vsed of this doctor, and
are a most assured argumēt, that he beleued
as the Catholikes now do, that we receaue
Christes flesh really and truely.

4.   Your fourth note shalbe, to cōsider how
he applieth those wordes of Job, and with
all to marke the sensible words which him
selfe vseth to signifie a true eating and touching of Christes flesh in the Sacrament,
all which were vaine and foolishe if we receued into our mouth no flesh at al but bare
bread . For he signifieth plainly by most
plaine wordes , that we doe not only see
Christ our maker there presēt vnder ÿ form
of bread , but that we eate and touche and
fasten our teeth in his flesh , all whiche is
done no lesse really concerning the substāce
thereof, then if it were to be seen, tasted, and
touched in the propre and vsuall forme of
flesh.

5.   Fifthly note the comparison which is
made betwixt Christ and common parents
which doe put foorth their children to be
nourished of others, whereas Christ nourisheth vs with his owne flesh . Now if he
nourisheth vs not with his true flesh , but
with a figure thereof only, then how can
this comparison stand, or how nourisheth
he vs with his own flesh? Onlesse you will
say

say that the figure of a thing and the thing
it selfe, a painted man and a true man in
dede be all one, or that his owne flesh was
no true flesh, but figuratiue and phantasti-
cal, which was the heresie of Manicheus.

Note firtly, and note diligently, that he
saith Christ geueth vs the same things here
in the Sacrament, which he toke for our
sakes when he was made one wt vs. Now
when, I pray you, was God made one wt
mã, or toke any thing for our sake but whē
him selfe became man, and toke flesh of the
blessed virgin? And that flesh whiche he
toke in her blessed womb was it figuratiue
fantasticall and spirituall or was it not rather substantiall, reall and natural? which
if it be graunted, then must it nedes folow
by S. Chrysostoms wordes, that his reall,
substantiall and naturall flesh is also in the
blessed Sacrament. For he saieth, Christe
geueth vs the same thinges which he toke
of vs. If there be the same substance of
flesh and blood, then they are truly called
the same things, although they be vnder
other formes and inuisible, or not geuen
after the same manner. But if the same
substance of fleshe and blood be not present, then can they not at all truely be called the same. In the seuenth place note
that the blood of Christ displaceth diuells,
and that they hastely flie away frome

6.
The same
body and
blud is in the
blessed Sa-
crament ye
Christ
toke of the
virgin.

7.

D iij   the

the presence of this blessed sacramēt wherof because I my selfe can say somwhat of
myne own experience by reason of ẏ which
I haue sene practised in the Church, that
being ouer much to put in here, I will put
it by it selfe in the next chapter.

8.   Note furthermore in the eigth place, that
this is that blood which S. Paule speaketh
of in his epistle to the Hebrews. for there S.
Paule talketh chiefly of the true blood of
Christ, which was shedde once for al on the
crosse for our sinnes, willing the Iewes
therefore not to trust any lenger vppon
their old Sacrifices, wherein the blood of
goates and calues was offered, for asmuch
as that was a figure only of this truth,
& ẏ truth taking place the figure ought to
ceasse. If then those places where S. Paul
speketh of Christes true blood ẏ was shed
on the crosse, may be applied also vnto this
which is in ẏ blessed sacrament accordingly
as S. Chrysostom sayth: it must nedes folow that here is conteined the true blood
of Christ. Note also where he sayth, that the
bloode of the Paschal Lambe beinge sprinkled on the postes of the Iewes dores at
theyr departinge out of Egypte, was a
figure of this truth. For thereby it foloweth necessarily that in the Sacramēt ther
is Christes true blood, for so much as other
wise ẏ figure alone which was true blood
shoulđ

9.

should be a more lyuely representation of
Christes passió thē ỹ truth it self is. & so ac=
cording to ỹ Protestāts opinió, which doe
make this a bare figure of Christes blood ỹ
Iewes shalbe said rather to haue had the
truth, & we ỹ figure. For ỹ blood of gotes &
calues was a great deal more true figure of
Christes blood, thē bare bread & wine cā be.

But mark a litle after where S. Chryso=
stó saith most plainly: the shedding of this
blud caused heauē to lie opē vnto vs. what
blood hath he talked of al this while I prai
you, but of that whiche is conteined in the
blessed Sacrament? and what blood was
that, the shedding whereof opened heauen?
was it any other then the moste pretious
blood of Christe shed on the Crosse? Ioyne
then all together, and you shall finde that
this whiche is in the Sacrament, can be no
figuratiue or spirituall, but the most true
& natural bloud of Christe: onlesse you wil
say, that many kinds of bloud was shed for
vs on the crosse, which no christen man can
say: either ỹ Christes blood there shed was
figuratiue & phantasticall: which to say or
think is no lesse abhominable. S. Chrysostó
goeth forward w̄ the similitudes of foutai=
nes, riuers, fire, gold, & such like to set forth
ỹ beauty of this high Mystery: & repetig a=
gain ỹ same sēse, affirmeth this to be ỹ blud
wherew̄ Christ redeined ỹ whole Church.

10.

11.

D iij   And

And so concludeth that such as be worthely partakers hereof are not only appareled with the kinges garment, but haue
12. put on the king himselfe. Now iudge you
whether the king him selfe and a picture or
figure of the king be all one. I might vrge
also the great threatnings which he addeth
in the end comparing the vnworthy receauers of these highe mysteries vnto those
13. whiche fastened Christ to the Crosse which
could not take place if Christ in them were
not truely presente. But I haue bene alredi
ouer long with my notes and therefore I
wil reserue this matter vnto an other place
wishing you in the meane time to considre
throughly the whole dicourse of this holy
doctor, & besids other which your selfe may
find out, diligently to note these 13 places
which I haue specially marked out vnto
you, and in the very later end note that we
must glorifie God not by faith only but by
good works also: whereas the Protestates
doe teach that faith only sufficeth.

⸿A true report of many notable things but
specially concerning the blessed sacramēt,
which happened of late yeres in Rome &
in Padua at the casting out of deuilles.

The third
Chapiter.
NOw to speake at large of the great
vertue whiche this blessed Sacramēt hath against diuels, accordingly as I promised in the former chapiter:

piter: although $\tilde{y}$ stedfast faith of any Chri=
sten man may be able by the assistance of
God to ouercome them, yet that is well
worth the noting whiche S. Chrysostome
writeth of the presence of the blessed Sacra=
ment, signifying that thereby the same is
much rather brought to passe. For he saieth
in one place (whiche is aboute my fourth
note) $\tilde{y}$ by this table, we are made terrible
vnto $\tilde{y}$ diuel and able to make him afeard.
And in an other (wheruppon I haue made
my seuenth note) he saith again: This mysti
call blood driueth the diuell far of from vs.
And what marueyl? seing (as he ofte tymes
repeteth) our soule is marueilously streng=
thened thereby in faith, and with all maner
of spiritual weapons, that our enemy must
nedes be altogether discouraged specially
in presence of that worthy Capitain which
hath so valiatly triumphed ouer him. And
therefore (as it may appeare both in other
auncient hystories and be proued out of S.
Chrysostome in these places) the Churche
hath rightly vsed often tymes the presence
of this Sacrament to that speciall effect.
whereby the true presence of Christ whom
the diuel so feareth, is most sensibly confir=
med, to theyr great confusion, which will
haue it to be bare bread only.

    Many examples might be alleged out
of old writers for this purpose, but I will
D v   first

first put you in minde of that only which I my selfe being in Italy did see practised: that the glory of God in this blessed Sacrament, whiche through his mercifull goodnes hath so sensibly and manifestly appeareth euen in these our miserable daies, may not lie hydde: and also that you reading the same may credite S. Chrysostomes wordes more perfitly, & yeld al glory vnto y true presence of Christ in the blessed Sacrament, hauing a most euident argument thereof so faithfully confirmed by the eyes of him, whose report I trust you will not discredite in this behalfe. Neither yet shall you heare any great newes, but that truth repeted only in writing whiche I haue allredy told you by mouth, trusting that by this meanes it shalbe printed more depely in your memorie.

Two kindes of coniuration.

But first to auoyde many cauilles and obiections whiche are wonte to be made, against this casting out of diuells, I thinke it necessarie to let you vnderstād, that there are two kindes of coniuration. The one, whiche is comenlie called Sorcerie, Coniuringe, or witchecraft, is detestable in the sight of God: and therefore very much spoken against both in the old and new testament, and generally condemned, and punished through al Christendom, as well by y lawes ciuile as ecclesiastical. And the cause

Wherfore sorcery & witchecraft is vnlawful.

why

why this kinde deferueth fo much blame
is, for that they which vfe the fame, althouh
they pretend neuer fo much the name of
God, yet, they doe all thinges in deede by
the power of the diuell him felf and fo make
him theyr God. For the chiefe Diuel fore-
feing how he is like to gaine many foules
thereby obeyeth moft wiilingly in al thinges that fuch feruantes of his fhall com-
maunde him : and is content alfo to dif-
place at their requeft fomtymes the inferiour fprites, which haue poffeffed any bo
dy, or do troble and difquiet any houfe. for
he is affured that by fuche meanes he maketh bothe parties fynne greuoufly in the
fyght of God, and that onleffe they repēt he
fhal winne their foules for euer, which is a
thoufand times more acceptable to him thē
to trouble their bodies in this life. And fo
vppon this refpect he is ready to obey fuch
men or women, as will fo vfe hun at their
commaundement. And after this fort the Marc. 3.
Pharifies falfely obiected vnto Chrift, that
he did caft oute Diuells in the power of
Beelzebub the captayn diuell. whereby as
they blafphemoufly fignified, that he was
one of thofe Sorcerers whiche the lawe
fpeaketh againft, and that he wrought
not by the power of God; fo yet they declared therby truly this chiefe point wherein
the

the diuelishe & wicked coniuratiõ differeth
frõ ÿ which is godly & laudable, ÿ is to say,
in working by the power of Beelzebub the
chief diuell. Now although it is most euident that these wicked coniurers worke
altogether by the power of the diuel , and
how their doings are therefore in god his
sight most abhominable , for ÿ they call for
his helpe, who is in dede a most deadlie
enemie both vnto god and to themselues, &
doe in effect thereby make the diuell their
god: yet the diuel to allure men to serue
him in that kind , hath inuêted certain ar-
tes of Magik, & diuerse superstitious rules
wherby men shold be perswaded, that thei
worke rather by their own learning and
knowlege , then that they become subiect
therby vnto him. for by this meanes many
are entrapped in ÿ snare . which if they con
sidered depely, how far thei become therby
slaues and bond to the diuell, would neuer
I am sure studie those diuelishe practises,
nor vse in any matter the helpe of them.

And by this description of that naughtie
coniuration you may easely gather many
tokens to discerne when and of whom the
same is vsed. for first seing it is not lawful,
such as are experte therin will not practise
it opēli, but rather in secret, least thei shuld
be espied, and if thei do ani thing in an opē
place ÿ superstitious circles & strãge words

1.

2.

iii

in which thei put their cheife confidence, do commonly betray them, and which is most worthy to be noted, you shall seldom here that thei medle with deliuering ani person possessed, or doing ani deed that may seme good or vertuous: but rather do entangle theselues and are curious in seking out of things to come, & somtime doe seke to destroie & kil also, or at least wise if thei seme at any time to do anie good deed by their coniuring, thei are not wholi bent therevnto but at one time or other, bi medlinᵹ with other matters they bewraie them selues to worke bi the diuel, and not bi that lawfull meanes which god hath appointed.

Now y other kind of coniuration where of I haue to talke, is that lawfull autoritie which Christ gaue his Disciples and their successors in casting out of diuells, and deliuering men or women possessed from their tyrānie. neither do we read that thei called at ani time for the helpe of diuells, or vsed their aduise in sekinge out ani thingz that was losse or kept secret, but by the vertue of their office compelled them onlie to departe from thence where they did harme.

And this kind of coniuration hath bene continuallie mainteined in the Churche euer sence the Apostles time, and is commonlie called of the Greke name Exorcisme: as those whiche haue bene alwaies
specially

Of y lawfull coniuratiō vsed in y Church. Lucæ 9. & 10.

3.

specially appointed to that function are commenly called Exorcistes. which name although it be not now a daies so commen, because that office is seldome founde in any man seperately, but ioyned with the ordre of Priesthod, yet it signifieth stil a degre of holy ordres separat from the rest.

And in the primitiue Church when men toke more deliberation and tried thē selues more perfitely, before they ascended from one degree of holy ordres to an other, we read of diuerse which passed not this degre of an exorcist? And namely we read of one holy Martyr put to death vnder Diocletiā the Tyran which hereof to this day is called Petrus exorcista, in honour of whome and of Marcellinus his felowe Constantine the greate built a Church which standeth yet in Rome and is called of them Basilica Marcellini presbyteri & Petri Exorcistæ. The Church of Marcellin ÿ Priest & Peter the Exorcist. For as the history of their lifes most faithfully witnesseth this Peter was preuented by martyrdome, so that he could not take any higher degree, as to be Subdeacon or Deacon. And therefore it is mentioned also in the same history, that being in prison after he had deliuered by vertue of his office one of ÿ kepers daughters which was possessed of a diuel, he cōmitted her vnto the saied Marcellinus the Priest & felow

with

with him there in prison to be baptized, for
that the ministration of that high sacramēt
belonged not to the degree of an Exorcist,
but to the office of priesthod which is many
degres higher. For wheras there are seuen
degres in al of holy order ẏ Exorcist hath
foure aboue him, that is to saie ẏ Acolytus
who serueth at the altar , the Subdeacon,
Deacon & Priest: & two vnderneth him, the
Reader, & the Keper of the Church dores.
For in ẏ primitiue church euery one of these
seuen officers did their functions precisely &
separatly. & ẏ authoritie of euerie one is to
this day also seperately geuen vnto those
which do take orders: although ẏ same doth
not so particularly appeare to ẏ world, because men make more haste vnto ẏ highest
degres, which do obscure and take away ẏ
inferior names . Neuerthelesse the offices
remaine alwaies and are included in the
superior, so that whosoeuer is subdeacon,
deacō, or priest, he is also an exorcist, & hath
ẏ same power ouer the diuels, which the exorcist hath. but he which is an exorcist only
cā not likewise medle wᵗ their offices ẏ are
aboue him. The highest poīt of his office is
to deliuer possessed persons : which he doth
by such means as are allowed by ẏ church.
ẏ is to say , by calling on ẏ name of Iesus,
by vsing ẏ holy signe of ẏ crosse, & by saying
many deuote praiers apointed by ẏ church,
brin-

The 7. de-
grees of
holy O,-
ver.

bringing the party possessed vnto some
holy Sainctes tombe or into the pre=
sence of the blessed sacrament. whiche is
commonlie one of the laste and surest re=
fuges. And this coniuration is done pub-
likly, in the face of the world, and that by
the publike auctoritie of the church, which

Mar. 2.
& 6.

receaued the same as it appereth in the
Gospell by speciall wordes of Christe him
selfe, and therefore apointeth speciall mi=
nisters for it.   Neither are these menne
alowed to vse the seruice of the Deuill in
any temporall matter as those other false
coniurers do, but only to expell and banish
him as the deadly enemy of mankynde,
wheresoeuer thei shall finde him to vexe or
trouble ani person. Thus I trust, you vnderstand sufficiently the greate difference
which is betwene the lawfull coniuration
or Exorcisme of a Priest, & the wicked sor=
cery of a diuelish Coniurer. And therefore
now I wil go forward, to describe ye which
I haue sene done, by this lawful coniuratio.

In the yere of our Lord a thousand fiue
hundred syrtie three, on Midlent Sonday
being the 21 of March, there was brought
vnto a litle Church in Rome called the hos-
pital of ye Trinitie, a yong Gentlewoman
possessed with manie sprites. Her name
was Hortésia, her parétes whereof a wor=
shipfull family, & well estuned in the citie.

And

And therefore to auoyed the talke of the people, they endeuored so much as lay in them, to bring ẙ mayden vnto ẙ Church secretely: but ẙ euill sprites vnderstãding of like, ẙ she should be had thither to be deliuered of their dominion, then most of al raged in her body: in so much ẙ it was the labor of foure stronge men to kepe her in the coche or chariot, while she was caried therin, through the streates. But being at lẽgth brought into the Church and placed before the high altar, one poore Priest ruled those sindes a great deale better, by calling on the name of Iesus, sprinkling holy water in her face, putting a stole about her necke, & vsing such like deuout ceremonies, than those men could before wͪ al their strength. Neither yet were they so obedient to the Exorcist, but they would oftentymes shew them selues as they were stubborne & malicious diuels, and disobedient euẽ to God him self. Neuertplesse ẙ authority geuen of God vnto his minister in the end alwayes preuayled.

To come therefore nearer our purpose one of these chief deuils named him selfe Gradomarte & was at a time exceding stubborn, neither would by any meanes be brought to answer vnto such questiõs as ẙ Exorcist demãded, which were cõcerning ẙ occasion of his entring into ẙ body. And

E   there~

therefore the Exorcist vsed many godly
meanes to enforce him to cōfesse the truth.
I will recite you one notable one by the
way & so come vnto ẏ which cōcerneth the
blessed Sacramēt. He toke ẏ picture of our
blessed Lady w̄ Christ in her armes which
stode vpō the altar, & held it before the eyes
of ẏ party possessed, saying in this sense. Be
hold here ẏ wicked spirite the image of ẏ ho
ly virgin, in whose blessed womb he was
cōceaued, which hath triumphed ouer thee,
& al thy wicked cōpany. I commaund thee
therefore in ẏ name of her sonne Iesus, &
through her intercession, either to depart
straight way out of this body, which thou
doest vniustly possesse, either foorthwith to
make a true answer vnto my demaūd. He
desired the people also which were present
to pray w̄ him to ẏ end. wherevppon they
sang altogether kneeling on their knees ẏ
hymne of our Lady, Aue maris stella, & cæ.
And in ẏ meane season he did put the fore=
sayed picture nere to ẏ eyes of the possessed
bydding ẏ diuell to be cōfounded at ẏ sight
thereof. But ẏ diuel declared most euidētly
by geuing backe so much as he could, by
shutting & closing fast ẏ eyes which he pos=
sessed, by his terrible roring, great shaking
of al ẏ parts of ẏ body, & last of al by many
horrible shriches, how much he was dis=
contented and tormented therewith.

Now

Now to come to our principall matter, the diuel notwithstanding al this perseuering in his former obstinacie, the Prieste threatned him ⸢ that⸣ he would take the blessed Sacramēt into his hands: & by the vertue thereof (which is cōmonly one of ⸢ the⸣ vttermost refuges in such a case) torment him a great deale more, onlesse he would yeld & confesse the truth. To which wordes the diuell answered with a great scoffing and laughter. what care I for that, seing it is nothing els but farina & acqua, that is to say, wheaten meale and water? O thou blasphemous and hereticall sprite quod the Priest. But I will compell thee by ⸢ the⸣ vertue of the body of Christ here present which thou hast so shamfully blasphemed, not only to answer vnto my first question to thy own confusion, but also to recant this blasphemy which thou hast here vttered in the presence of so many Christen folke, & confesse that truth which thou knowest to be in this blessed Sacrament to the confusion of al thy wicked members the misbeleuers and heretikes.

And therewithal he toke the blessed Sacramēt into his hands the people kneeling al round about w great deuotion & reuerence. And after he had made his humble prayer together with the people desiring euery one to say with him a Pater noster

E ij   an⸗

and a Aue Maria, he turned to the party
possessed, & commaunded the diuel to geue
place vnto God there present. wherevnto
he answered stubbornly like him self. Non
voglio, non voglio, that is to say, I wil not
I will not. Then the Priest to auoyed all
inconueniences that might happen did put
the Sacrament into a chalice & so holding
it couered with a lynen cloth vpon the parties head, repeted often tymes these & such
like wordes. I beseche the good Lord to
torment this wycked sprite vntil he recant
his blasphemy and confesse the truth. I
commaund thee o wicked sprite to geue
place and yeld to thy Lord God. whereat
the diuell by diuerse tokens shewed him
self to be wōderfully tormēted, sometymes
roring & crying out, away with it, away w̄
it: sometymes shaking al partes of the body wrping the mouth, staring w̄ the eyes,
laying out the tōg, & tossing the head roūd
about the shoulders in such a terrible sort,
that I must nedes cōfesse it was one of the
most grysly sightes, that euer I beheld.
And no natural hart could I am sure with
out harty compassion geue thee looking
on.

I perceaued also afterward, by being
present at diuerse other like spectacles, that
the diuels when they are inwardly in dede
tormented them selues with hell paynes,
(through

(through the mighty power of God working by his minister oz by the presence of
some holy thing) doe vse to handle the bodies which they possesse after such an hoz-
rible sozt, euen of purpose: to moue as wel
the Priest, as the people standing there a-
bout to take pitie and compassion on the
partie, that they may the rather thereby be
let alone, and suffred to enioy quietly their
possessiō. And no doubt were not ƿ power
and mercy of God far passing their malice,
they would tozment the party euen vnto
death, rather then yeld one iote. But the
Exozcistes, which are practised in this
office, being accustomed to such their
gyles and deceites, and beleuing firmly on
the other side that without the permission
of God they can doe no harme, as the example of Job in holy scripture plainly wit
nesseth, are not moued by those sightes to
leaue of tozmēting them, but doe cal ernestly vppon God in such case by these oz like
wozds, absque lęsione membrorum in no-
mine Iesu: Beseching God, that although
he permit them to torment, wzest, & stretch
some parts of the body foz a space, & thereby to shew their malice yet ƿ they may not
haue power to hurte any membze. Neither
do I remēbze any harme done which cōtinued at any tyme, although I saw many
very soze panges : as once the diuell lay so
　　　　　　C iij　　　　　grea-

greueously a quarter of an houre together
at ÿ hart of an other womā which was likewise possessed, ÿ she semed to haue had ÿ
pāges of death. & the same womā at an o-
ther tyme was cast præsently into a shakig
feuer. And at this time this gentlewomās
necke was so pitifully turned & tossed a-
bout, ÿ it semed not possible for her selfe or
any other to doe the like without wrething
her necke a sunder.

But as the diuell both for the cause alleged, & also to declare his maliciouse nature
(which is to doe so much harme as he can
before he wilbe forced to doe any good) cōtinued in tormenting the pore body, as you
haue heard: so the good Priest ceassed not,
calling vpō God, that no member of hers
might take harme, and ÿ as the Catholike
Church beleued ÿ body of his sonne Iesus
Christ to be there truly present in ÿ cōsecra
ted host: so it might please him of his infinite goodnes, to torment ÿ wicked sprite,
vntil he had cōfessed ÿ truth. The diuel per
seuered as I haue declared in his stubbornesse crying sometymes: I wil not, I will
not, & sometyme again. Away wt it, away wt
it, meaning ÿ blessed Sacramēt, ÿ præsence
wherof did so much vexe him. And this en
dured for the space of a long halfe houre.

After which tyme ÿ diuel perceauing the
Priest to be so stedfast & ernest, ÿ he minded
not to

not to haue left tormenting him w̃ the pre=
sence of y̆ blessed Sacrament a long tyme,
onlesse he yelded, or as it is rather to be
thought, feling y̆ paynes of hell increasing
continually vpon him, through y̆ appoint=
ment of God whose power he could not re=
sist: being also still cõmaunded by y̆ Priest
to recãt his blasphemy, to confesse y̆ truth
which him self knew, & to tel opẽly what y̆
was in y̆ chalice, y̆ presẽce whereof so much
tormẽted him, he cried out at lẽgth with a
lowd voice, Il e mio creatore & tio, it is my
creator & thine, it is he y̆ created and made
both me & thee. And so he departed incõti=
nẽtly out of the head & vpper partes, and
descẽded down into her body, there to lye
priuy as the wont of them all is, after they
haue bene forced to say or doe any thing
which they would not.

Then the yong gentlewoman returned
also to her self after that long trance which
she endured so long as the diuell occupied
her senses. And so she rested herself a litle
for that she felt now all the partes of her
body meruellous wery, by reason of the
former tormenting & shaking, which she
then felt not, but as in a slepe or dreame.
& now she made vp her heare & did set her
garments in ordre, which the sprite occu=
pying her senses had tossed about her eares
& tombled out of al good frame & ordre. In

E iiij   this space

space also while she was come to her selfe,
the Priest willed her to make her humble
prayer vnto God, beseching him ẏ if it were
his pleasure she might be deliuered of those
fyndes tyranny. And he warned her more
ouer ẏ she should in no wise geue any consent to the deuill, but in hart & mind, resist
all his motions. After a while, the Priest
commaunded the deuill in the name of Iesus, to come again into the head, & answer
to his first question, which was to know
vpõ what occasion he entred into ẏ body.
And so although he obeyed not at the first
call as his maner is (thereby to shew that
stubborn nature of his own) yet being, as
it might seme well tamed with the former
torment, he was nothing so froward as at
the beginning, but came vp again into the
head quietly, & answered after a while, that
God suffered him & his cõpanie to possesse
that body for her excessiue pride. Then the
Priest commaunded him in the name of
God by whose permissiõ he possessed ẏ body, to depart therehence wͬ al his company,
out of hand. And vrged him therevnto by
many godly prayers & ceremonies, & specially by the presence of ẏ blessed Sacramẽt
vnto which he was so late cõpelled to yeld

Then he fel again sodenly into a great
rage & tormented ẏ body as before pitifully & in the end gaue a merueilous horrible
great

great shrich together wherewith the capi=
tain Deuil (as him self afterward being
commanded vnder a great penaulty to tell
truth confessed) did send away one of his
stoutest souldiars which he named Pôpida.
He sayd moreouer that him selfe was licen=
sed yet by God to abyde there a litle lôger,
& so he departed as before, down in to the
body. where vppon as well the exorcist, as
the standers by, & the party her selfe, being
not without iust cause very wery (for they
had bene there now more them foure long
howres) they concluded to remitte her
vntill the next day, thanking God hartely
for ý it had pleased him to geue ý capitain
Deuill such foiles: & to haue sent out one
of his company before hand. And I doubt
not but the capitaine him selfe was after=
ward likewise cast out although my for=
tune was not to be present there at. Thus
you haue one of those ensamples which I
promised and which was seen and heard
with these senses by the help of which I
write this vnto you. & thereby you haue
the practise of S. Chrysostoms wordes con
firmed where he saith that by the vertue of
the blessed Sacramêt the Diuels are made
to quake and fly away. you may also the=
reby considre the great goodnesse of God,
who euen as when the Jewes beleued not
that Christ was their true Messias, caused

E 5   the

the Diuels to crye out by the mouthes of the possessed persons and confesse the same to their great confusion: so now a dayes to confound the Sacramentaries which beleue not the same true Messias & sauiour to be truely present in the blessed Sacrament, he compelleth the Deuill him selfe to crye out and testifye that it is our creator & maker.

¶ Of that which happened in the Exorcisme at Padua.

The other example or experiment concerning this matter, J happened to see at Padua the moneth of July next ensuing, in ẙ famous Church of S. Anthony (not the Eremite but another) whose body lieth there buried, & euen to this day worketh many notable miracles. A pore yong maried wife called Iulia, being possessed of sundry sprites, was by her frindes brought thyther: vppon hope that through the intercession of that good Saynt, she should be the rather deliuered, as (if we may beleue the testimony of the whole city & country ther about) many before her haue bene. One of the religious men there taking compassion on her pitifull state, willed her frindes to send her dayly to the Church, promising that concerning the praiers & ceremonies appointed to be vsed in such a case, he would refuse no paines in applying them. And so after he
had

had taken her in hand, she resorted daily
vnto the Church for p space of sixe weeckes
before she was clean deliuered.neither was
she brought al this while by the force of mē
as in the example before recited, but went
to and fro accompained most commenly ꝯ
one other woman only, & was all the way
as quiet & sobre as any woman nead to be.
for although the exorcist did not at the first
time expell any of the Diuels, yet by ver=
tue of his office he bound them with the si=
gne of p crosse, after such sort in some one
parte of her body, where they might least
troble her (as in one of her fingers or
toes) that from the time the woman depar
ted from him, vntill she returned again &
that they were called for to come out, they
neuer comonly vexed or trobled her. which
thing must not be attributed to any vertue
or obedience that is in the wicked sprites
but to the infinite goodnes of God qui dedit talem potestatem hominibus, who hath
geuen such power vnto men.

Now although it perteineth more to my
purpose to declare foorthwith that point
which cōcerneth the glory of the blessed Sa
cramēt, yet for so much as I remēbre at my
last talke had with you of these matters,
you were very desirous to know many cir
cūstances & particulars, I will endeuour
first briefly to repete some of those which I
                                    my selfe

wrote from thence to a frind of myn more
at large, whē they were more freshe in my
memory. neither shal the same J trust seme
any vnprofitable digression, seing euery
particular thing setteth forth the glory of
God, together with the great auctority
which continueth in the catholike Chnrch:
and also cōdemneth wholy this new found
religion of the Sacramentaries, & sheweth
ý teachers thereof to be very malicious in
dispising those Godly Ceremonies, to the
vertue of which, the stubborn Diuels them
selues doe yeld. J wyshed truly with all
my hart both at this and that other spectacle
at Rome, that some of the most Zelons
and best learned new preachers of our con
try, had bene present. for if as they wil not
beleue some matters in religion, because
their senies teach them the contrary: so on
the other side any sensible thing may moue
thē, they should vndoubtedly hereby haue
perceaued most sensibly, their own foly &
ignorance.

But that you may vnderstand some of
those particulars which happened in this
exorcisme, when the religions man began
daily to expell those sprites, first of all he
vsed to cōmand thē in the name of Jhesus
to geue a signe or token by which it migh
appeare in what part of the body they lay.
The which being shewed of thē, either by
shaking

shaking and lifting vp that part, oz some
like meanes, then he neuer ceassed making
of the signe of the crosse and calling on the
name of Iesus, vntill he had forced one of
them to come vp in to the tonge. And many times we should see those partes of the
body by which he passed, to be shake oz lifted vp one after an nother, & specially whē
he was in the throte, you should see it swell
of a great bygnesse, and from hence sodenly you should euen sensibly perceaue,
how he started vp in to the tong, and occupied all other partes of the head. And then
it was easy to vnderstand, wherein a possessed person differed from an other, which
was not possessed. For this poze sely woman differed then so much from her self, &
from that she was befoze, both in talke,
lookes, gesture, & countenāce: that whereas befoze she was of few wozdes, sobze,
modest, fozowfull, &, to behold, rather pale
and sickly, then otherwise: so sone as the
spzite came vp into her head, she was altogether changed, her countenance became
malepert & wanton like a harlot, her eyes
rowling & gogling on euery side, her tong
alwaies pzatling some dishonesty oz other.
whereby it might euidently appeare, that
the Diuell spake, and not she, and that he
likewise abused al the rest of her senses.

For many times you should heare vile
mockes

mockes & schoffes against the holy Ceremo
nies & praiers which were vsed, much like
vnto those, with which our Protestantes &
new preachers are wont to stuf their sermons. And somtimes very greueous blasphemies were vttered. as for exaple once
I heard those horrible wordes: maledetto
sia il creatore del módo: cursed be y creator
of y world, which I suppose verely no crea
ture besides a find of hel in dede could haue
spoken. Also whereas y woman was altogether rude & ignorāt, the sprite possessing
her tonge & other senses, answered directly
very often to such thinges as were spoken
in Latin, or perteined to matter of learnig.
And albeit he himself spake alwaies y vulgar Italiā: yet by his scoffes as wel in wor
des as gesture he declared manifestly y he
vnderstode euery prayer, & all other sayinges, which were readen in Latin against
him out of y Ghospel. Now if you aske me
wherefore the exorcist did alwayes bring y
sprite in to y head, seing he played there so
many euill prākes: y was doen to cōfound
him y rather, being cōpelled by y senses of
that body which he possessed, to see & heare
those good thiges, which might cause hi to
be soner wery othis lodgig. Also by y meanes he was forced to answer vnto many
questions which gladly he would not. as
what cōpany he had there with him? who
                                                        was

was ẏ chief emongest thē? vpon what oc=
casiō they entred? what were their names?
Many other like questions were asked
whereby they were afterward one by one
more easely expelled.

For although ẏ diuel would (as his wōt
is) tel at ẏ first many fond lyes & stand also
somtimes a longe whyle in defence of thē,
yet i ẏ end he was alwais forced to declare
ẏ truth. And one special meanes which the
exorcist vsed to trye a truth from a falshode
was, to appoint a great encrease of his
paynes in hell, as for exāple twēty or forty
times so many more as he already suffered
& w al to recite a solemne othe wherein he
should desire God & all the holy cōpany of
Saints to take vengeance of him, & see his
paynes performed, onlesse ẏ which he then
should aswere were true. Neither doe they
cōmonly after this solēne othe dare to dif=
fer any lenger ẏ vttering of ẏ truth, where=
by it may appeare ẏ the diuels them selues
although they be alredy dāned, yet doe fear
much the increase of their paynes: & also of
what strēgth & efficacy those words are, by
which God his ministers doe worke here
in his name. for if any other mā threaten
thē by ẏ same wordes neuer so much, they
care not one rushe therefore. The exorcist
thē vsing this kind of cōiuration, which ta
keth his strēgh not by Sorcery & wtcraft, or
by the

by the power of Beelzebub the chief Diuel
but by the auctozity of the Church & name
of Jhesus, found ont within few dayes,
that there were a great nombze of spzites
gathered in to that body, as their maner
is, to gett in so many of their companions
as they can, to make their hold the strōger.
He found alss that certen of them were rulers and capitaines, in comparison of the
rest. The chief called him self by that generall name Sathan, but gaue vnto other his
pety capitaines certen particular strange
names, as Rampin, Panterin, Veronin, and
such like.

He learned furthermoze that the first entred in to the womā together with a great
feare, by ẏ speciall permission of God vnto
whom she called not foz helpe and succour
as she ought to haue doon in that case. many also (as J vnderstode by those which
had seen this oftē in pzactise) doe take possession often times, euen by the consent of
the party, and such are a great deale moze
hardly expelled, foz that God iustly suffereth them to haue moze power on such persons. Some also are thzough the infinite
mercy of God suffered to tozment the bodyes of certain folke in this life, that greater tozmentes may be auoyded in the life
to come. after which sozte, somt wzite that
i.Co.5. S. Paule deliuered certain offenders to be
vexed

vered of Sathan in their bodies for their greate offences to the ende their soules might be saued. And you shall finde in S. Chrysostom, that some possessed of diuells are in far better case than those which liue in deadly sinne, and secke not after true repentance. which seemeth to be ment of such as be penitent for their synnes committed, before they are possessed. For by y meanes they are allwaies in the state of saluation for so much as whatsoeuer they do whiles the diuell possesseth their witte that shall neuer be imputed vnto them.

we see very good folke also by y permission of God, to be troubled often times with these wicked spirites. And I my selfe haue seen it happen to young innocent children. In which case we must neds thinke y same is permitted of God, to th'end his glory may be setforth accordingly as we read of y blind man in y Ghospel, who is said to haue bene borne blind for no other cause, but y the glory of God might be shewed by restoring him to his sight. for he is likewise by this meanes glorified to this day in his holy Saintes, and in the ministers of his Church, at whose tombs, & by whose autority, the diuels are cast out, to the great cōfusiō of al heretiks. For what Christen man would not be moued to thinke wel of holy reliques, and praing to Saintes, when

*Chrys.
in Matt.
hom. 84.*

Ioan. 9

he should perceaue the Diuils our deadlie
enemies, to be vexed there with: when he
should see them, whiche lay quiet before in
some one extreme parte of the body possessed, so sone as thei were brought nere the
tombe of S. Anthonie, or anie other like
Saint, by and by to rage and make all shift
possible to get farther of, selig of like, some
speciall vertue in that place contrarie to
their disposition. And therefore vnder the
tôbe of S. Anthonie, there are Iron grates
made for the nonce, to kepe them there per-
force. It is wonderfull to se how sensiblie
thei declare by many tokens, that thei are
verie much tormented. And manie times
some by being there onlie, without anie
farther ceremonie or Exorcisme, haue bene
miraculouselie compelled to yeld vp their
possession.

Dow could any man also but think that
the blessed Saintes haue by God his appointment speciall care to help and succour
those, which at their tombes or otherwise
make intercession vnto them, if he should
heare as J did with my own eares a sprite
after long raging crye out at the tombe of
† S. Luke the Euagelist (which is there in
Padua also) Luca me brusa, Luca me brusa,
that is to say: Luke burneth me, Luke burneth me: we read a like historie in Abdias
of S. Bartelmew in whose presence the diuell

¶His body
was
brought
thither frô
Constâti-
nople by
one Urius
a holy mâ
to auoyde
the spoyle
whiche
Juiâ the
Apostata
made of al
suche holy
reliques.

uel cried out likewise in a possessed person, Apostole Bartholomæe incendunt me orationes tuæ.   O Apostle Bartlemew thy praiers burne me. Can any man therefore thinke ẏ the holy Saintes are not as readẏ & as well able to helpe men , as to torment diuels: especially whereas that was done also, to make the Diuell wery of his possession and consequẽtly to help the partẏ to be deliuered? Or did not God worke his glorẏ in this Sainct to the confusion of all heretikes, whereas the malicious diuell was forced to confesse that vertue in him & at his tomb which many who thinke them selues to be right honest men, are not ashamed to deny ? what shall I declare howe much God is glorified hereby , likewise in his ministers, & in the holy ceremonies of the Church by thẽ vsed? I had nede write a speciall treatise for this matter alone , if I should tell euery particular , whiche I my self saw and heard. But to speake generally, and yet most truely, there was no holy thing brought nere those sprites ; but theẏ shewed by some manifest token or other, that they were not pleased therewith . As whẽ any holy relique was shewed, or holy water sprikled on thẽ. likewise they would not by their wils be touched ŵ any stole, or any part of the halowed vestemẽts, which the priest vseth at Masse.

Abdias
in vita
Barth.
Apost.
fol. 97.

F 2   Theẏ

They were in like sort discontented hearing the wordes of the Gospell, but specially when any thing was readen concerning the incarnation and death of Christe, or casting out of diuels . In so much that many tymes they would stoppe the eares of the possessed, vntill her handes were by force kept donne. Now if they would not heare those holy wordes as it is likely, becanse of the vertue ef them, and because the exorcist and other that stode about, were thereby more animated and strengthened in faithe against them: why should we not thinke that they hated reliques, and other holy thinges for like cause also? For if those thinges were superstitious and naught, the diuels would not doutlesse be offended with the presence of thē, but would rather take greater comfort and strenght thereby to resiste those , which by suche vnlawfull meanes went about to expel them. Or if they pretended only to be offended with those reliqus to cause more superstitiō, how chaunce they vsed them selues in like manner toward the scripture and Gospell? For therby it appeareth that the vertue of those holy wordes vexed them, nd therefore we must nedes cōclude that the vertue of those other holy thinges did likewise in dede, torment them.

These wycked findes being then after
this

this sorte diuersly tormented, were com=
pelled at lengh by litle and litle to vtter all
their secrets and emongst other thinges to
confesse that they had conueied in to that
body whiche they possessed, much trumpry
and baggesse, to tormente the woman
withall at theyr pleasure more greueously.

And the same proued in the end also most
true. For they were compelled at lenghe
euery one to depart, and bring foorth part
of that fylth. One brought foorth with him
the shell of a fyshe, much like a snaples shel.
An other brought out an Iron naple about
foure inches long. A clout tied at both en=
des ful of il fauored earth was vomited vp
at an other tyme. Some also brought forth
diuerse little trifles immediatly one after
an other as a litle stone, the end of a bores
tuske, a pecce of brimestone. And an other
brough foorth a lesser naple then the first
was, wrapped about with filthy heare. If
a man would of purpose gather together
suche baggesse, he should very hardly (as
I suppose) match those iewells, which they
had there laied vp.

Now if you aske me, how those thinges
could possibly abide any whyle in the wo=
mans stomake, or any other parte of her
body, and not vtterly destroie her? I set
not what maie better be aunswered, then
that as God permitted those sprites vnder
F 3   this

this condition only to possesse that body,
that they should haue no power on her life:
so he might conditionally suffre them to
bring in such fylth into the body, that they
should notwithstanding mayntaine al partes thereof hole and sounde, as they were
before. which thing whether they are able
to doe by their naturall knowleg and experience or no, hauing all the humors of the
body at their commandement, I will not
here dispute. Hereof once I am sure, that
many men and women doe by meanes of
some singular complexion, or humor, de-
uoure glasse, cole, candels, and such like,
neither yet doe take much harme thereby.
And on the other side I am right well assured, that those thinges which this wemã
voyded, came truly out through her throte,
and were not fayned, neither deceaued the
eyes of the lookers on. For I handeled
and saw them many weekes after, and I
thinke whosoeuer goe to Padua, maie see
them yet. Also the woman returning to her
selfe, after that anie of the sprites was together with some of that filth cast foorthe,
complained allwaies, that shee felt some
token thereof in her throte, as a verie filthy
sauour of the earth and brimstone, & likewise a sorenesse, after those naiels & stones
had passed through. Again there is no reasõ
why the diuel should coũterfet such things
but

but rather great cause, considering his ma-
litious nature, why he should if God suffered him, deceaue men in the contrarie , and
secretly or inuisibly conueie them out of the
body. For nothing greueth him more thē by
so open and sensible an argumente to shew
him selfe ouercome and vanquished by the
minister of God.

But to come at lēgth vnto that particular thing whiche was wrought chiefly by
the vertue of ỹ blessed Sacrament, & in respect whereof I haue made all this longe
discourse: all the rest of the sprites being
now by diuerse meanes displaced , Sathan
the chiefe capitain remained, and the Exorcist had more to doe with him alone , then
with all the rest besides . He kept also with
him in the bodie a stone of a shreude big-
nesse as it appeared afterward. wherefore
the exorcist endeuored first to get out that
stone . But Sathan behauing him selfe ex-
cēding stubbornlie was brought on a time
before the blessed Sacrament , and commaunded by the vertue thereof to avoyde
that stone without delay and so him selfe
also to be packing . He being thus vrged a
prctie while was at length ouercome , & sodenly vomited vp a great stone, which was
thre square & about fiue inches in cōpasse: so
ỹ noīā wold thīk it could naturalli be swa-
lowed vp or downe wout tearing ỹ throte,

F 4　　　　onlesse

onlesse some find of hell in dede shuld help
to stretche the gorge. J my selfe stode hard
by when it happened together with diuerse
other, you might haue seen nature ther wo-
derfully strayned in bringing it vp, it made
also a great bunch in the throte, as it passed
through, and last of all it came foorth together with a great deale of fleme. The womā
returning incontinently to her self did put
her hand to her throte and complayned of
a great paine which she ther felt. And with
in few daies after ye great diuel himself was
expelled likewise in ye same place by vertue
of the same blessed sacrament. To declare
the circumstances whereof a litle more at
large, you shal vnderstand that as J saied
before he was more stubborn then al ye rest:
so in dede he played many false partes and
made many false promises, before he depar
ted. And once being very ernestly comaun
ded and vrged to departe out of hande, he
sayed his time was nere come in dede, and
that the next day without sayle he must nedes yeld, wherevpon the party was dimis-
sed for that present, and the deuill commaū
ded not to vexe at all any part of her body,
neither to remoue out of one other fingers,
vntill he departed. The next day she came
to the church after her accustomed maner,
and the Exorcist began to call for Sathan
vp into the tong, (as he was wont), for to
haue

haue him departe . But no token oz ſigne
would be geuen of hisbeing ther. wherup
pon euery man hoped well that ſhe had bē
thzoughly delyuered. And the Ezozciſt ho‑
ping well alſo went afterward to the poze
womās houſe, ſayed there many good pzai
ers, ſpzinkeled holy water rounde about,
willed her to be quiet, and to ſerue god di‑
ligently: but fearing withall ſome gyle pzo
nounced a ſolemne commaundement, that
if Sathan had any thig to do oz had left ani
thing behind him in that body, he ſhoulde
by the vertue of thoſe ſeuen laſt wozdes
which Chziſt pronoūced on the croſſe, whē
he redemed mankind from his tyzani, with
in ſeuen dayes next folowing geue ſome e‑
uident token therof. It happeued within
the compaſſe of thoſe dayes the woman
went up in to a blind loft, and immediatly
there appeared an euill fauozed old womā
appareled all in blacke, which ſight caſt her
in to a great feare, by reaſon wherof ſhe re
payzed again vnto the Ezozciſt. who vſiug
the accuſtomed ezozciſme of ỹ church made
Sathan come up into the tong as befoze,
and confeſſe all his craft and ſuttlety.

Emongeſt other things he ſayed he had
left a ſtone behind him together with cer‑
tayn of his ſoudiars , and therefoze he had
iuſt cauſe to returne. Then the Ezozciſt
neuer ceaſſed vexinge of him, vntill he had

F 5   ſent

sent forth those his companions together
rō the stone which was much lesse then the
former.

Last of al being brought before the blessed Sacrement on a fryday at Euening after he had ben him self by the vertue thereof much tormēted:(which thing he witnessed by tormenting ỹ pore body)at lenght he
went foorth with a merueilous great sigh,
whervppon the woman returning inconti
nently to herself,reported, that it semed vn
to her a great flame of fyre wēt at that time
out of her mouth. And therwithall she saw
also stādīng at the piller before her a terrible black felow, whereat she sodēly started
but being comforted by the exorcist & willed to make the signe of ỹ crosse , & to put
her trust in the blessed sacrament , it vani-
shed cleane away.And the pore woman be
ing thus at lengh throughly and perfitely
deliuered,receaued herself a few daies after
the blessed Sacramente, and was so comforted and strengthned thereby that to my
knowledge , whereas I remained there
more then sixe monethes afterward , she
was no more troubled with those, or any
other syndes.

So ỹ therby, S. Chrisostoms words are
most plainly confirmed wher he saieth that
by the presence hereof the diuells are put
to flyght:and they are lykewise euidently
con-

confounded, who neither esteme thys as
the true body of Christ, nor doe set by any
holy ceremony that is vsed in the Catho=
like Churche.

But that all such may be yet more confounded, and that you may geue more auctority & credite to these true miracles whiche god hath shewen in these dayes to con
firme you in the true faith: I thinke it not
amisse to adioyne briefly herevnto one or
two like miracles, which are witnessed by
that graue and anncient Father Saint Augustine: who in his bookes de Ciuitate **Lib. 22.**
Dei writeth, that a whole housholde of a **cap. 8.**
fermer in the country being much troubled
with sprits, one of the priests of his church
was sent for, to put them to flight by hys
prayers, wherevppon sayeth he: Perrexit
vnus, obtulit ibi sacrificiū corporis Christi
orans quantum potuit vt cessaret illa vexa-
tio: deo protinus miserante, cessauit. One
of the priestes went & offered there the sacrifice of the bodye of Christe, prayinge so
muche as lay in hym, that the same vexa-
tion might ceasse: and God by & by taking
mercy, it ceassed. By whiche wordes it is
euident, that in his dayes also the Christen people vsed the presence of the blessed
Sacramente of the Austar, as a mooste
assured remedie to displace the Diuelles
                                              when

when they molested any person . the same wordes also declare so playnly as it is possible, that masse was sayed ther by that priest. for the chiefest & most principall part of the masse is to offer vp that immaculat sacrifice of Christes body and blood: which thinge S. Augustin sayeth, this Prieste peeformed.

Ibidem.

He writeth moreouer in the same chapter of a yong man which being possessed of a diuell waas brought to a church wher ther was a memorial or monument of the holy martyrs S. Protasius and S. Geruatius, and so sone as the hymnes & other seruice were begun to be song, the diuell holding fast the altar as though he had bene tyed fast therbnto, cried out with a great shriching and howling, desiringe that he might be fauored: and confessing where and after what sort he inuaded the yong man. last of all he told that he would depart out of that body, but threatned withall that he would do some mischief to certain mēbers or partes thereof which he named, and together with those wordes departed in dede out of the body leaning one of the mans eyes hāging out by a litel vaine vppon his cheke. Then he which brought the yong man thither sayde. God who hath driuen the diuel away, is able also by the prayers of the Saintes to restore his sight, & so bound vp

hys

his eye with a stole, and would not lose the same before seuen dayes were expired. at the which time he founde that eye perfitly hole and sound as the other.

And thus you haue in few wordes many of those chief pointes which haue bene noted vnto you in the examples before recited, now stroogly confirmed by like histories out of S. Augustin. wherefore as I doute not but you wil credite these later, for his authority who wrote them, and those former vpon his word who faythfully reporteth only that which himself saw: so I hartely wish you through the depe consideration of a these verities which by euery of thē is sufficietly proued, ernestly to discredit al the doctrine and doinges of the Sacramentaries, whereby they wrongfully impugne the Catholike Religion.

¶ Testimonies takē out of S. Chrysostom vpon the xxvi. Chapter of S. Mathew.

After that place of the sixth Chapiter of S. Iohn, where Christe promised to geue his fleshe to be eaten, as you haue heard, those testimonies of the other Euangelistes folow next according to y order of time before prescribed, which declare, when, where, and after what sorte Christ fulfilled that promise whiche thing he did at his last supper, when as he instituted

The iiij. Chapiter.

ruted this blessed Sacrament. And there=
fore now you shall heare what the former
doctor S. Chrysostome saieth in that sermō
which he hath made vpon the xxvi chapter
of S. Mathew where that holy supper is
most plainly set foorth. And least it should
be ouer tedious for you to heare out the
whole sermon (specially wheras he talketh
there of many other things, and expoun=
deth diuerse other textes which apperteiu
not to ÿ supper) I will first note vnto you
those sentēces which in ÿ beginning of his
sermō do here & there touch ÿ poit,& after=
ward interpret wholy ÿ later part thereof,
which altogether belōgeth to this matter.

Emong many other saings in the begin=
ning which confirme the catholike faith,he
declareth why Christ did institute this bles=
sed sacrament a litle before his passion im=
mediatly after the eating of ÿ paschal lābe
and saith: ❧ For what cause did Christ de=
liuer this mysterie at ÿ time of his passion?
That we should know by al means ÿ ÿ old
law was also made by him,and ÿ al things
conteined therin were instituted as shado=
wes of ÿ new law : for this cause therefore
he adioyned ÿ truth vnto the figure.(And a
litle after.) If a figure (meaning that pas=
chal lamb of ÿ old law) deliuered from bō=
dage,much more shal ÿ truth make ÿ whole
worlde free. ❧ By which words it ap=
pereth not only ÿ the blessed sacrament is a

Chrys.
in Matt.
hom. 83.

truth and no bare figure as the Protestãts
would haue, who make it no better then ÿ
paschall lamb, which was in dede a figure
thereof: but also that it is such a truthe as
made the whole worlde free, that is to saÿ
ÿ true body of Christ which redemed vs. S.
Chrysostome goeth forward in confirming
the old and new testament together & saith
in effect this much. As the old testamēt had
ÿ blood of calues & shepe: euē so ÿ new testa
mēt doth possesse ÿ blood of our Lord. And
as the blood of the paschall lamb was sprikled on the postes for the sauegard of the
Jewes first begotten, whē the Angel stroke
the first begotten of euery house in Aegypt,
wher that blood was no sprinkled: euen so
this blood of Christ which is ÿ blessed sacra
ment was shed for the remission of ÿ sines
of the whole world. And a few lynes after
vpon those wordes, This is my blood which
is shed for the remission of sinnes, S. Chry=
sostoms own wordes are these.

“ Christ spake this to shew ÿ his death &
“ passion was a mystery, and to cõfort therby
“ his disciples, and as Moyses said this shal=
“ be an euerlasting memorial for you: so he hi
“ self said do it for ÿ cõmemoratiõ of me vntil
“ I come. for this cause he saith I haue great
“ ly desired to eat this passouer wt you ÿ is to
“ say to deliuer vnto you new thigs & to geue
“ a passouer to make you spirituall with all.

Deut. 16.

De

,, He him ſelf dranke alſo thereof, leaſt his
,, diſciples hearing thoſe words might ſay to
,, thē ſelues. what? do we then drinke blood,
,, and eate fleſh? and therefore be offended. for
,, before when Chriſt mētioned thoſe words,
,, many were offended for the words ſake
,, only. Leaſt therefore the like ſhould happē
,, at his ſupper, he did the ſame firſt him ſelfe
,, to induce thē to receaue the myſteries with
,, a quiet minde.

Ioan. 6.

By which few words it is very euidēt, ȳ
S. Chryſoſtom thought both that Chriſte
ment to geue his true body, fleſhe & blood
vnder the formes of bread & wine, and alſo ȳ
his diſciples ſo vnderſtode him. For other=
wiſe if Chriſt had ſignified by his words a
figure of his fleſh & blood only, thē neither
had there ben cauſe why he ſhould miſtruſt
his diſciples, nor any thing whereby they
might be moued to be offēded. It foloweth
immediatly after in S. Chryſoſtom.

,, But you wil ſay, what then? muſt we
,, celebrate ȳ old paſſouer alſo? no trulie. For
,, therfore he ſaid: do this to bring men frō ȳ
,, other. And again if this (ȳ is ȳ new paſſo-
,, uer) cauſeth remiſſiō of ſinnes, as in dede it
,, doth, thē ȳ other is altogether ſuperfluous.
,, Euē as i ȳ old teſtamēt, ſo likewiſe in ȳ new,
,, Chriſt hath for our benefite left behind him
,, & gathered together the memory of his my-
,, ſteries, brideling thereby the mouthes of
here=

heretikes. for whē they aſke how it is pro=
ued ẙ Chriſt was ſacrificed & put to death, "
beſides many other thinges to mouſell and "
ſtoppe their mouthes withal, we ſhew thē "
theſe myſteries. for if Chriſt died not, where "
of is this ſacrifice a pledge & token? Thus "
you ſee how diligēt Chriſt was & deſirous "
ẙ we ſhould haue continually his death in "
remēbrance. For wheras (thoſe Heretikes) "
Marciō Ualētinus, Manicheus & their di= "
ſciples ſhould deny this diſpenſation and "
work of God i fleſh: Chriſt by this myſtery "
ſo bringeth vs always in mind of his paſ= "
ſion, that no man onleſſe he be mad, can be "
ſeduced. And ſo by this moſt holy table he "
both ſaueth and teacheth vs: for this is the "
fontain or all goodneſſe. &

There are in theſe wordes three things
worthy to be noted, first in what great cre=
dite & eſtimation ẙ bleſſed Sacrament was
in S. Chryſoſtoms dayes, wheras by the
truth of Chriſtes body belieued therein to
be preſent Marchion Ualentinus & other
like heretiks were cōfounded, which ſayd
Chriſt had no true body in which he might
ſuffer on ẙ croſſe. for as it may be gathered
out of this place, ẙ Catholikes vſed againſt
ſuch kind of heretikes, this or the like ma=
ner of argumēt: Chriſt his true body is pre
ſent in the Sacramēt, to put vs in remem=
brāce of his true death & paſſion: wherefore

                              at his

B

at his true death and passion his true body was present & ther truly suffered. for otherwise, I see not how by these mysteries of y body and blood of Christ those heretikes mouthes might be stopped. for by saying y body of Christ to be here present only by a figure, nothing could haue bene concluded against them, but their heresy should rather by y meanes haue ben confirmed. for they denied not but it was figuratiuely also present on the crosse. & thus you may perceaue also how this new opinion of our Sacramentaries open the gappe to many old condemned heresies.

Secondarily it is much to be noted after what sort this Sacrament is a pledge or token, that is to say not as the Protestantes will wrest it, a pledge and token of the substance of Christe his body, which is therein truly present and not by a bare figure or token: but a pledge and token of his passion which is liuely there represented and brought to remembrance by the true presence of that selfe same body that suffered. And therefore Christ at the institution of this Sacrament after he had sayd: Take, eate, this is my body, adioned thereunto those other wordes: Doe this for the remembrance of me, which wordes S. Paule expoundeth very plainly saying: So

1. Co. 11. often as ye shall eate this bread and drinke

of his

of this chalice ye shall shew foorth our
Lordes death vntill he come. which thing
once well noted, one of the greatest foundations of the Protestantes opinion is
cleane ouerthrowen. For they as their
custome is do ground them selues vppon
the false meaning of those wordes of the
Ghospell: Doe this for the remembrance
of me endeuoring to proue thereby the it is
not Christes body but a signe and remembrance thereof only: as thoughe Christ
had ment in remembrance of his body, and
not rather of his death and passion as S.
Paule expoundeth, & as S. Chrysostome
here plainly witnesseth saying, ẏ hereby it
appeareth how desirous Christ was ẏ we
should haue cõtinually his death & passion
in remẽbrance. Note thirdly that he calleth
this blessed Sacrament the fontaine of all
goodnesse. for thereby to any reasonable mã
it may appeare, that God vnto whõ alone
these termes may be properly applied, is
therein specially present.

S. Chrysostome going forward in his
homely with the textes of the Ghospell
that doe folow cometh at lengthe to those **Math. 26**
wordes of Christ spoken to S. Peter:
Amen dico tibi quia in hac nocte antequã
cantet gallus, ter me negabis. Truly I say
vnto thee, that this night before the cock
crow thou shalt deny me thrise, after the

G 2   exposi-

exposition of which sentence, he retorneth again to the Sacrament as the principall matter of the whole homely, and maketh a very learned exhortation to the worthy receauing thereof, all which I will translate euen as it lieth together with a piece of his exposition vppon that text last rehersed, y you may better perceaue his whole discourse & drift therin, and thereby iudge also more persitly whether this holy father belieued of y blessed Sacramēt as y Protestātes now teach or no. his wordes are these.

Chrysos.
in Math.
Hom. 83
I.

we learne truly hereby this notable lesson y the will of man is by no meanes sufficient, onlesse it be strengthned by help from aboue : & also that we gayne nothing by that help from aboue, if our owne will resist the same. the one of which sainges is confirmed by the example of Peter, y other by the example of Iudas. for Iudas although Christ did bountefully ayde & helpe him, yet because he would not take hede & conferre that which was his owne part, nothing profited thereby. And Peter on the other side although he was stout and couragious, yet God his help being taken away, he was not able to stand. for of these

Of free
will.

two thinges vertue is made. wherefore I hartely pray & besech you that ye wil not so attribute all thinges to God, that ye thinke your selues must lye altogether shugging & sleping,

kepig : neither on the other side so watch & "
labour, that ye thinke the whole matter is "
brought to passe, by your owne trauel. For "
neither is it Gods will that we should lye "
like idle sluggards with out all how & care "
and therefore he requireth somwhat of vs: "
nor yet would he haue vs festred and cor- "
rupted with pride, & therefore he cōmitted "
not al vnto vs. so he worketh y̌, which is "
for vs profitable & necessary, putting away "
the inconuenience on ech side. And for thes "   2.
causes he suffered y̌ cheif or head of the Apo   Verticē
stles to fall, making him thereby more hum   Apostol.
ble & prouoking him to a greater charity. "
For (as Christ himself saith) He will loue   Luc. 7.
more, to whom more is forgeuen.   "

    Let vs therefore beleue God alwayes & "   3.
not repine against him allthough y̌ which "
he saith semeth absurd to our sense and vn= "
derstanding. Let his wordes surmount & "
passe both our sense & reason, which thing "
we ought to doe in all thinges, but chiefly "
in the mysteries: hauing more regard vnto "
his wordes, then to the thinges which lye "
before vs. for his wordes are infallible, but "
our sense may very easely be deceaued. thei "
cannot possibly be false, but this sense of "
ours is many & sūdry times begiled. Seig "
therefore he sayd, Hoc est corpus meū, this "
is my body, let vs haue no doubt, but be= "
lieue, & behold it with the eyes of our vn= "
         B 3   derstan=

" vnderstanding. for no sensible thing was
" deliuered vs of Christ, but vnder thinges
" sensible. but as for the things which he de-
" liuered, they are all out of the reach of our
" senses. So in Baptisme that excellent gift
" thereof is geuen by water, which water is
" a sensible thing: but that which is therein
" wrought(I mean the regeneration and re-
" nouation) that is to be conceiued by the vn
" derstanding. for if thou hadst ben without
" a body, he would haue deliuered the these
" giftes symply also and, without bodyes.
" But for so much as thy soule is coupled &
" ioyned to a body, therfor they are deliuered
" vnto thee in bodily and sensible thinges, ƿ
" they may be the better vnderstode.
"   O how many say now adayes, I would
" fayne see his forme & phisnomye, I would
" see his garmētes, I would see his shooes.
✦ " And behold thou seest himself: himself thou
" doest touch: himself thou doest eate. Thou
" desirest to see his garmentes: but he deli-
" uereth himself vnto the, not ƿ thou shuldest
" see him only, but touch him and haue him
" within thee. Let no man therefore come
" nere, whose stomake wambleth or riseth
" against it, nor any mā that is cold in deuo-
" tion, but let al such as approch hereunto,
" be styred vp, & feruently inflāmed. for if the
" Iewes did eate(their Paschal Lamb)with
Exod. 12 hast, standing on their feete w͡ their shooes
on, and

on, & holding their staues in their handes: "
how much moze must we watch & be dili= "
gēt? foz they were taking their iozney from "
Aegipt into Palestine, and therefoz they had "
on wayfaring and pilgrims apparel . but "
thou art going vp frō ẏ earth into heauē. "
wherfoze thou must watch and take good "
hede. foz it is no small punishmēt which re "
maineth foz such as cōmunicat vnwozthily. "
Considze ꝑ what indignation ẏ thy self art "
moued against the traitoz (Judas) & against "
those which crucified Chzist, & beware least "
ẏ also be made gilty of Chzist his body and "
blud. They did put his most holy body to a "
most bitter death : thou after so many & so "
great benefites, receauest it ꝑa filthy soule. "

For it did not satisfy him to be made mā "
only, to be scourged & crucified, but he bzin= "
geth vs again in to one masse oz lumpe (if "
I may so say) ꝑ himself, & maketh vs not   5.
by faith only, but in very dede his body.   "
what thing thē is ther so cleane, but ẏ man "
ought to be moze clean , which shal be par= "
taker of this sacrifice ? what sun beames "
shuld not that hand excede, which handleth "
this flesh? that mouth with is filled with "
this spirituall fyze : that tonge which is "
embzued with this miraculous & wonder= "
ful blood ? Call to thy mynd vnto what "
honoz thou art pzomoted, what table thou "
enioyest. Foz we are fead with that thing, "
B 4   at the

,, at the sight whereof the angels doe trem=
,, ble. Neither cã they without feare behold
,, it for the brightnes which frome thence re=
,, doundeth . and we are brought into one
,, masse with him, & are made one body with
Pſal. 105 Chriſt & one fleſh. Who ſhalbe able to vtter the powers of our Lord? Who ſhall
,, make al his prayſes to be heard? what ſhep=
7. herd euer nowriſhed his ſhepe with his
,, owne bodie? Many mothers after theye
,, are deliuered put foorth their children to be
,, nouriſhed of other, which thig Chriſt wold
,, not doe, but fedeth vs with his owne pro=
,, pre body, and thereby ioyneth, & coupleth
,, vs vnto him ſelf.

,, But let vs conſidre this a litle: he was
,, borne of our ſubſtãce. but that, you wil ſay,
,, belongeth not vnto al men. yes euen vnto
,, all. for if he came down to take our nature,
,, it appeareth he came to al: & if vnto al, then
,, vnto euery particular man alſo. But how
,, happeneth it thẽ (ſay you) ẙ al mẽ haue not
,, obteined cõmodity therby? truly ẙ cometh
,, not to paſſe through him, who moſt of all
,, wyſheth it were ſo: but through their faute
,, which wil not receaue hĩ. for by this my=
,, ſterie he ioyneth himſelf to euery faithfull
,, man. & thoſe whom he hath brought foorth
,, he deliuereth not to be nouriſhed of other,
,, but nouriſheth thẽ himſelf with al diligẽce,
,, hereby alſo perſuading thee, that he hath
taken

taken vppon him, thy self. wherefore let "
vs in no wise lye still like sluggers, seing "
we are so much both beloued and honored. "
Doe ye not see, with how gredy and cher= "
full a mind , the yong sucking babes doe "
reach after the pappes? How gredely, they "
presse downe the same with their lippes? "
Let vs come with no lesse gredinesse vnto "
this table , and to the spirituall pappe or "
brest of this chalice. Yea rather let vs with "
more ernest desire , sucke herehence like "
yong children, all heauenly and spirituall "
grace. Let that be our only sorow and "
heauinesse, to be depriued of this spirituall "
foode . "

These workes which he then wrought "   **8.**
at that supper, are not of mans power, he "
him selfe now also worketh them , he him "
self maketh them perfite, we occupy only "
the rome of ministers, but it is he him selfe "
that sanctifieth these thinges and changeth   Trāsmu-
them. Let no Judas therefore or couetous   tat.
man be present. He that is not a Disciple, "
let him depart, they which are not such, are "
excluded from this table. With my Disci-   Math.26
ples (sayeth he) I make my Passeouer. For "
this is that table and no other , this is no "
one iote inferior vnto that. Neither is it to "
be thought, ỹ Christ made ỹ, & some man "
maketh this , but he him self maketh both. "
This is that supping parlor, where Christ "

,, then was together wt his Disciples, from
,, hence he went foorth to the mount Oliuet,
,, let vs also goe from hence to the handes of
,, poore folke, for there is the hil of Olyues.
,, For the multitude of poore folke are the
,, Olyues planted in the house of God. From
,, hence that oyle droppeth downe, of which
,, we shall haue much nede in the later day.

Math.25 ,, This is that, which those fiue virgins
,, had, and for lacke of which the other pe-
,, rished. Hauing this oyle with vs, let vs
,, goe forward in our iorney with most
,, bright shyning lampes to meete the Bride-
,, grome.

,, Let no cruell, vnmercifull or vnclean
,, perso come hereunto by any meanes. And
,, this I speake, as well to you that doe cō-
,, municate, as vnto you which doe mini-
,, stre. For I must say the same vnto you, to
,, th'end ye distribute these giftes very care-
,, fully, and with great diligence. There
,, hangeth no small punishment ouer your
,, heades, if you permit one, whom you
,, know gilty of any wickednes, to be par-
,, taker of this table. For his blood shall be
,, required at your handes. If a Duke there-
,, fore, if the Consul himselfe, yea if he that
,, weareth the Croune come hereunto vn-

The hygh ,, worthely, forbyd him, kepe him backe.
dignitie of Thy auctority is greater then his. If so
Priesthod be that a fountayne of most pure water,
were

were committed to thy charge , to be kept "
clean for the flock : when thou shouldest "
see most stincking and filthy swyne draw "
nere,thou wouldest not suffre them , I am "
sure, to wallow in the streame,neither the "
welspring by thē to be troubled. And now "
whereas a most holy fountayne not of wa= "
ter, but of blood and spirite is committed "
vnto thee: if thou shalt see those men draw "
nere , which are most defiled with synne, "
wilt thou not take indignation thereat "
and forbid them ? what pardon els shalt "
thou obteyne for thy contempt ? Therefore "
God vouchsafed to endure you with such "
honor, to th'end you should most diligent= "
ly discerne these matters. Herein consi= "
steth your dignitie , herein your stay and "   9.
assurance. This is your chief Croune, Tunica
and garlond , and not to walke vp and induti
downe the Church arayed in a fayre white candidiſ
tunicle.   ſimam.

But you will say,how can I know "
what this or that man is ? I speake not "
this of such as are vnknowen , but of "
such as are noted and knowen. I will tell "
you one thinge , which is horrible and "
ought to make you quake for feare . It "
is not so euill to suffre such as are posſeſ= "
sed of Diuels to be within , as those "
whiche are polluted with synne : who "
                                        (as

Heb.10. (as S. Paul witnesseth) Doe tread Christ
„ vnder feete, doe esteme the biood of the
„ Testament vile and common, and doe re-
„ prochfully despise the grace of the holy
„ Ghost. He therefore that cometh herevnto
„ being gilty in his conscience of synne, is
„ much worse then one possessed w a Diuell.
„ For such possessed persons, because y diuel
„ tormenteth and vexeth them, are not pu-
„ nished: but such as come herevnto vnwor-
„ thely shalbe deliuered vnto euerlasting tor
„ mentes. Let vs therefore vtterly & with-
„ out exception thrust out all such as we per-
„ ceaue doe come vnworthely. Let none com
„ municat onlesse he be of the Disciples, let
„ none that hath an vnclean mind as Iudas
„ had receaue this bread, least he suffre like
„ payne.
„   This multitude (of faithfull people) is
„ also the body of Christ, & therefore y which
„ doest ministre these mysteries, must take
„ good hede, least if y purge not diligently
„ this body, thou prouoke our Lord to an-
„ ger, & least in stede of meate y geuest a shar
„ pe sword. But if any man come rashly and
„ vnaduisedly vnto this table cast him of w-
„ out all feare. Feare not man but God. For
„ if y feare man, y shalt be laughed to scorne
„ of him himself, whom y fearest. But if thou
„ feare God, thou shalt be reuerenced also of
„ men. And if thou darest not thrust him of
                                              thy

thy self, make relation thereof to me. I wil "
not suffre such thinges to be done. I will "
rather deliuer vp my life, than deliuer our "
Lordes body to any mā vnworthely. I wil "
rather suffre my own bloed to be shed all "
out, than I will geue that most holy bloed "   10.
to any other then such a one as is worthy. "
But if any man come in his fylth ignorāt= "
ly and you not ware thereof, if you vsed be "
fore much diligence, it is not your faute. "
For I haue spoken all this, concerning "
such as are noted and wel knowen. which "
if they were once amended, there is no "
doubt, God would quickly bring to light "
such also as are to vs vnknowen. But so "
longe as we admit open and knowen syn= "
ners, why should he reuele those which "
are secret? This much I haue sayed to "
th'end we should not restrayn only & cut "
of, but correct and bring into the right way "
again, and be carefull for all men. For by "
this meanes God wil be merciful vnto vs "
and multiply those which may communi= "
cate and receaue him worthely, ȳ we may "
receaue also the great rewardes as well of "
our own labor and diligence, as of the de= "
uout care which we haue of other, by the "
grace & mercy of our Lord Jesus Christ. ✲ "

  In this golden exhortation of S. Chry=
sostome, you shall first note those goodly
sentences in the beginninge, where he
                                    talketh

talketh of Peters presumption, and Iudas his desperation, warning vs diligently to auoyde these two most daungerous rockes. And although this matter belongeth not to that which I chiefly entreat of, yet doe I thinke the same most worthy to be noted vnto you by the way, as ỹ which may serue in stede of a sure anchore against many whurling windes of diuerse other pestiferous heresies, which are in the boisterous seas of this our miserable age blasted and blowen abrode. I meane against that venemous doctrine, which so setteth foorth predestination, that it taketh away mans freewill. Concerning which matter I am so much the gladder to note vnto you this holy and auncient Fathers mind, for that I remembre on a tyme your selfe moued vnto me some question belonging therevnto. But as I answered then according to this sense which you here finde: so now I ernestly require you, not to be hereafter ouer curious in such demaundes, but throughly to content your selfe with that which S. Chrysostome here teacheth you. His owne wordes are playne inough that I nede not repete them. Neuerthelesse to print the sense of thẽ better in your mind, they teach in effect this much, that we must not thinke, God worketh all by his predestination in such sort in vs, but that he lea-

usth

weth in our free wil to accept by his grace
always ready to concurre, or to refuse by
our own malice his benifites offered: nei=
ther yet y̆ any good thig cometh of our sel=
ues only, or by our own choyse, without
the grace of God preuenting ayding, and
assisting vs. But we must ioyne both to=
gether, and if we entend to attayne vnto
euerlasting saluation, we must put our
good will to worke together with God, &
vse that grace which he on his part neuer
fayleth liberally to offer.

S. Chrysostome maketh the matter ve=
ry playn, by those two examples of Peter
& Iudas. Of y̆ which, one trusted to much
to himself, & therefore stombled at y̆ rock of
presumption, but recouered himself again
afterward by acknowledgig his owne in=
firmitie, & trusting on y̆ mercy of God: the
other would conceaue no hope of mercy,
nether trust any whit in Gods goodnesse,
& there ore made a shipwracke at y̆ dange=
rous rocke of desperation, and was conse=
quently drowned in the depth of euerla=
sting damnation, because he would no=
thing helpe himself by asking mercy, which
was always ready for him. Note also by
the way how this auncient Doctor calleth
S. Peter head of the Apostles, because the
Protestants will not gladly heare there=
of: least if they confesse Sainct Peter,
to haue

to haue bene head of the Apostles, they
should be driuen also to confesse his successours the Bisshops of Rome for the chief
heads and rulers of the Church euer sense.
as generally they haue bene through out
all ages taken and allowed.

3.   He cometh immediatly to the matter of
the blessed Sacrament, and as it were in-
ferring vppon that which he sayed before
of the fall of Peter, because he trusted to
much in his owne stoutnesse, warneth vs
very wisely in this high mysterie, not to
trust therefore to much to our own sensual
iudgement, but to belieue the wordes of
Christ who calleth it his body. Nothing
can be sayed more plainly to declare the
true Catholike faith, then that which he
speaketh in this place, neither yet more
euident against the erroneous opinion of
the Protestants. For these men reason after this sort. I see bread, I tast bread, I
feale bread, ergo there is nothing but
bread. But S. Chrysostome teacheth a
clean contrary kind of argument, willing
vs not to credite our senses which may
easely be deceaued but y wordes of Christ
which are infallible. And therefore by his
verdit we must argue after this sort. Our
senses teache vs that in the Sacrament
there is nothing but bread, but we must
not credit our senses herein, ergo we must
                      not

not thinke it is bread. Again Christes wordes tell vs, it is his body, and they are necessarily to be credited, wherefore it must nedes folow that it is his body. Or if you will put both argumentes in one, then after this sort. Christes words are to be beleeued before our senses, but his wordes teach vs that the substance of this Sacrament is his body: And our senses teach vs by the outward formes, that it is stil bread as it was before: wherefore we must beleeue it is Christes body and not bread. And so by S. Chrysostome it is plainly proued that there is no bread, but the body of Christ vnder the forme of bread, accordingly as all Catholikes hartely doe beleeue.

what wordes also can be playner for this purpose then those which folow a litle after where he sayeth: we doe not see and touch his outward forme and physiomy or garmentes, but him selfe we see, touch, and eate? For in that we see and eate his substance vnder the formes of bread, we see him selfe, and eate him selfe. And if we haue not the inward substance there present, but a figure thereof only, as our Protestants affirme, then Chrysostome would rather haue sayed, that we touch and eate and see some externall garment or figure of him only, and not him selfe. wherefore

4.

D these

these his wordes doe plainly ouerthrow
5. their false assertion. Fiftbly note that as be
sayed before vppon the sirth of S. Jhon,
through this Sacrament we are made one
with Christ not by loue only but in dede:
so here he sayeth in like maner that not by
faith only, but euen in dede we are made
one body with him. For this place is some=
what more directly against the Protestāts
who affirme that we receaue him only by
faith and no otherwise.

6. Note also that we are nourished with y
in this blessed Sacrament, which the An=
gels do behold, with trembling and great
reuerence. whereby it appeareth most ma=
nifestly that it is not bread, but God him
selfe that here is present, and which we doe
receaue: onlesse you will make the Angels
The reall   also to be Idolators and to reuerēce a piece
presence   of bread. To signifye likewise the true real
euidently   presence of Christes blood, he sayeth a litle
proued.   before y our tonge is imbrued, & as it were
made bloody w receauing this Sacramēt,
not y our tonge or lippes are in dede made
redde w the outward colour of blood, but
because they receaue as truly the inward
substance of blood, which is there miracu=
lously vnder the forme & colour of wine, as
if they receaued therewithall the outward
forme of blood also, & were in dede made
redde and bloody therewith.

You

You may note moreouer what great force
y̆ comparison of y̆ shepherd & y̆ mother hath
to proue y̆ Christes true body, is truly present, & not by a figure only. For although
neither y̆ shepherd feedeth his shepe w̆ his
own body, nor y̆ mother always her infāt,
w̆ her own milke., yet both the one and the
other are fed of them w̆ true meat, & not w̆
figures, as our Protestantes would haue
Christ fede vs, & so geue vs much lesse then
either the mother geueth her child, or the
shepherd geueth his flocke. But to put all
out of question, & make the comparison most
perfite Chrysostome himselfe sayeth that
Christ feedeth vs with his own members
and with his own propre body.

7.

Note furthermore y̆ Christ worketh cōtinually y̆ same effect in this blessed Sacramēt of the altar by y̆ mouth of his Priestes
as he did at his last supper himselfe. And
that the Priestes are only as instruments
to pronounce those words vnto which he
gaue y̆ vertue, & together w̆ which being
orderly pronounced by his lawfull ministre he continually worketh. Neither doth
the Priest take vpō him by his own power
to make God at his pleasure, as some blasphemously haue reported, but it is God
him selfe that sanctifieth these thinges as
S. Chrysostome sayeth, and causeth this
wonderfull transmutation, and change.

8.

D 2 The

Tranſub=
ſtantiatiõ
proued
out of S.
Chryſo=
ſtome.

The which one word is ſufficient to ſtoppe
the mouthes of al Sacramentaries, which
wil haue herein no chãge at al to be made.
For þ word traſmutat, which I haue there
fore noted in the margent, ſignifieth þ kind
of change, whereby one nature is changed
into an other: & thereby proueth moſt eui=
dently, þ tranſubſtantiation, which they ſo
much impugne. Alſo whereas þ accidents
& outward formes remayne the ſame in þ
bleſſed Sacramẽt after conſecration, which
they were before, & yet a change therein is
wrought, as S. Chryſoſtom here teacheth:
þ muſt nedes be the change of one ſubſtãce
into an other, which is no other beſides þ
change of the ſubſtance of bread into þ ſub
ſtance of the fleſh of Chriſt. And ſo howſo=
euer this chãge which S. Chryſoſtom ſpea
keth of be taken, it muſt nedes confirme þ
traſubſtantiatiõ which þ Catholikes mean.

9.
Churche
veſte=
ments
vſed in S.
Chryſo=
ſtomes
tyme.

Now you ſhall doe well to note alſo by
the way for our diſordered miniſters ſake
þ ſentence a litle after, where S. Chryſo=
ſtome declareth þ the Prieſtes vſed in his
tyme, to weere in the Churche at ſeruice
tyme a ſolẽne whyte veſtement. For as the
Sacramentaries can not away with his
Catholike doctrine, being in dede cleane
cõtrarie to theirs: ſo likewiſe they wil not
gladly allow any ſuch papiſtical ceremonie
ſpecially thoſe which wil be coũted perfite
in that

in ye secte, & which therefore cal them selues
Puritãs. Note last of all how ernestly he
exhorteth all men in ye later part of his ser=
mon, to be carefull in receauing these holy
mysteries, & specially what great charge he
geueth vnto al Priestes ye they admit ther=
vnto no open or notorious synners but ye
they repell all such, of what so euer state &
degree they be of. For this great reuerence
which is declared hereby to be due vnto
this hygh Sacramẽt, proueth ye there is cõ
teined therein a far greater thing thã bare
bread & wine. And what ye is, those wordes
doe most plainly witnesse where he sayeth
toward ye very end, ye he would rather suf=
fre his own blood to be drawen all out of
his own body, than geue wittingly ye most
holy blood of Christ to an vnworthy per=
son. For ye blood of Christ being geuen by
ye Priest ye deliuereth ye Sacrament, it must
nedes folow ye the same is there really con
teined vnder ye forme & in that Sacrament
which is geuen. And then it dependeth not
vpon the faith of the receauer, as the faith=
les Sacramentaries most falsely imagin.

¶ Testimonies out of S. Chrysost. vpon
the first Epistle to the Corinth.

The fifth
Chapiter.

FOr so much as I find this holy Do=
ctor S. Chrysostome to haue writen
somewhat cõcerning ye blessed Sacra=
mẽt not only vpon ye sixth of S. Ihon
H iij where

where Chꝛist pꝛomised it, ⁊ the.xrvi.of S.
Mathew where he instituted it: but also
vpon ỹ firstEpistle to ỹ Coꝛinthiās,where
S. Paul ỹ chosen vessell of God,was moued by ỹ holy Ghost to witnesse ỹ same: J
haue thought good to translat some part of
ỹ which he hath wꝛiten there also,to th'end
you may see how vnifoꝛmely he wꝛiteth of
this matter in those places, where he had
occasiō directly ⁊ pꝛincipally to treat there
of: trusting ỹ you will thereby take occasiō
also ỹ rather, both to embꝛace hartely this
truth, ⁊ tō a firme ⁊ stedfast faith cōtinually manteyn ⁊ belieue ỹ same. That which
J mind here to trāslate out of S. Chꝛyso-
stome is not wꝛiten vpon ỹ place of ỹ. ri.
to ỹ Coꝛinthians which J haue in the first
chapiter set befoꝛe your eyes, but vpō one
part of ỹ chap.next befoꝛe,where S.Paule
taketh occasiō to speake of this matter, foꝛ
ỹ ỹ Coꝛinth.being then conuersant emōgst
ỹ heathen Jdolatoꝛs,oftentymes toke part
wittingly of ỹ meat which was offered vp
to their ydols. By this meanes therefoꝛe
he rebuketh them sharply declaring how
absurd ⁊ abhominable thing it was, to eat
meate ỹ was offered to Jdols ⁊ diuels, after they had receaued ỹ pꝛetious body and
blood of Chꝛist. Oꝛ as S. Chꝛysostom saith
after they had receaued ỹ Eucharist ⁊ Sacrament of thanksgeuing, whereby they
than-

thanked God for deliuering them from I=
dols, incontinētly to runne again to ȳ ta=
ble of Idols. S.Paul emōgst many other,
hath thesewordes.The chalice or cup which　　1.Cor.10
we blesse is it not the communicating of the
blood of Christ? wherevppon S. Chryso=
stome writeth on this wise.

S.Paul vseth in thesewordes a vehemēt " Chry-
kind of persuasiō ⁊ causeth the Corinthiās " sost. in
greatly to quake for feare. The meaning " 1.Cor.
whereof is this.That which is in ȳ chalice " Hom.
is ȳ, which flowed out of his side, ⁊ thereof " 24.
we are partakers. But he calleth it ȳ cha- " 1.
lice of blessing, because ȳ when we haue it "
before vs, we doe wᵗ a certen admiration, ⁊ "
horror, of ȳ vnspeakable gift, praise ⁊ blesse "
him, for ȳ he did shedde his blood, to thᵉ end "
we should not continew in errour, neither "
did shed it only but made vs all partakers "
thereof. And therefore if thou desirest blood "
(saith he) sprinkle not ȳ altar of Idols, by "
killing brute beastes, but sprinkle my altar "
wᵗ my blood. what could be sayd more wō "
derfull then this? what I pray you could "
be said more loueingly? Such as are in "
loue vse this practise. when they see those, "
whome they loue to be affectioned vnto "
any thing, that belongeth to other folke, "
⁊ to set litle by their giftes: to draw thē frō "
ȳ affection, they geue vnto them somewhat "
of their own. Now mē ȳ are in loue vse to "
　　　　　　H 4　　　　signifie

2.

" signifie this good will by many garmētes,
" possessions, and such like. No man euer
" shewed it by his owne proper blood. But
" Christ euen hereby hath declared his exce=
" ding great loue toward vs. And in the old
" Testament when men were more imper=
" fite, he of his vnspeakable louing kindnesse
" to turne them from Idols, vouchsafed him
" self to accept ye blood at their hands which
" they offered vnto Idols. But here (in the
" new Testament) he hath prouided a great
" deale more wonderfull and royal sacrifice,
" both for that he hath changed the sacrifice,

3.

" and also for that in stede of killing beastes,
" he hath commaunded him selfe to be offe=
" red. ❧

1.

You shall note in these few wordes before you goe any farther: first ye Christ maketh vs partakers in this Sacrament of ye
which flowed out of his side. If then Christ
his true blood flowed out of his side, how
cā it be auoyded but his true blood is like=
wise here present? For by saying in the cha
lice he declareth that to be present within
that compasse and vnder the forme of wine
there conteyned. whereby their false po=
sition is perfitely refelled, who teach that
Christ is present only to the mind of the re
ceauer by faith, and not vnder those visi=
ble formes of bread and wine.

2.

Note secondly that Christ in leauing
behind

behind him these hyghe mysteries, passeth the common sort of wooers and louiers. for they (saith Chrysostom) to testifie their great good will, leaue with such as they loue some garment, piece of mony, ring or other like token of their owne: but Christ to witnesse his exceding great loue, leaueth with vs his own propre blood. Now if he leaue with vs but a signe and token of his blood only, as the Protestantes imagine: then iudge you how these wordes of S. Chrysostom may be verified, or how Christ passeth the common sort of woers, whereas they leaue behind them tokens and signes also. Note thirdly that in stede of kylling beastes which was daily vsed in the old law, Christ hath commaunded him selfe here in this Sacrament and sacrifice of the new law to be offered. for those wordes doe not only import y Christ him selfe is present in the blessed Sacrament, but also that he commaunded himselfe there to be offered. which thing the Protestants can not abyde to heare, becaufe thereby they are constrayned to confesse this Sacramet to be also a sacrifice: that is to say, therein the body of Christ to be daily offered vnto God the Father, for the synnes of the people, in remembrance of that singular sacrifice on the crosse, where the same was once only and once for al bloodely and painfully

H 5 offered

3.

offered for the whole world. And this is ȳ
only cause why the Protestantes rayle so
much at ȳ holy sacrifice of the masse which
is so called. for that the body of Christ is
therein offered : for if they should graunt
Christ his body to be a sacrifice and to be
there offered as Chrysostome here plainly
teacheth, then they should be forced to con=
fesse , the same body to be there also truly
present . For otherwise it could not be so
offered.

But to returne to S. Chrysost. he goeth
forward in expounding the text of S. Paul
and at the end maketh a long discourse as
he is wont vpon the worthy receauing of
the Sacrament. which because it conteineth many good lessens to confute the
Protestants , and also hangeth together
without interruption, I haue gladly ioyned the same hereunto . his wordes are
these.

Chrysos.
in 1. Co.
Hom. 24

1.

2.

Math. 24

&ᴐ Seing now we vnderstãd these things
let vs endeuour to manteine vnity and
loue one with an other . for hereunto we
are prouoked by that dreadfull and won=
derful sacrifice, which cõmaundeth vs with
great concorde & charitie to approch vnto
it: that being as it were Egles in this life
we may flye vp into heauen it selfe, or ra=
ther aboue heauen. for where the carkas is
(sayeth Christ) there are the Egles. The
body

body of our Lord is through death become
the carkas. for onlesse he had fallen we had
not risen. He vseth the name of Egles, to
declare that it behoueth him who shall approch vnto this body, to seeke for highe
thinges and not to meadle with the earth,
neither to be drawen or crepe vnto earthly
matters wich are a low, but to flye alwayes
vp to higher matters, and behold the sonne
of righteousnes, and haue the eye of the
mynd quicke of sight: for this is the table
of Egles, and not of Jayes. And so after
this sorte such as worthely take the benefite thereof, shall meete him coming down
out of heauen: as contrariwise such as vnworthely receaue the same, shall suffre extreme punishment.

For what would be sayd if a man should
behaue him self vnsemely in receauing or
intertayning a kinge? what speake I of a
kyng? if a man should but hädle a princes
garment with foule and vncleane handes,
yea althoug he were alone in some solitary
place? And yet the garment is nothing but
wormes threed. And if ye wondre at y purp-
pie dye, that also is no better then y blood
of a dead fishe. Neuerthelesse a man would
not dare to touch that garment with defiled handes. If then no man will rashly
handle another mans garment, how dare
we with so great shame and reproch
　　　　　　　　　　　　receaue

Of the worthy receuig of y Sacramét.

„ receaue the pure & immaculat body of him
„ who is Lord of all? to receaue J ſay that
„ body which is partaker of the diuine na=
„ ture, through which we haue our being &
„ liuing, by which the gates of hell are bro=
„ ken downe and the gates of heauen ſet
„ wyde open? Let vs not J beſech you, let
„ vs not impudently kill our ſelues, but let
„ vs come vnto God with all reuerence and
„ puritty. And when thou ſeeſt that ſet befoꝛe
„ the, ſay with thy ſelfe, by meanes of this
„ body J am no moꝛe earth and aſhes, J am
„ no lenger bonde, but free and at liberty:
„ thꝛough this J hope to enioy heauen, all
„ ſuch good things as ther are, & life euer=
„ laſting, together with the ſeat of Angels &
„ company of Chꝛiſt.

4.

„　This body being nailed & beaten was
„ not ouer come by death. The ſonne behol=
„ ding this body crucified, turned away his
„ beames. foꝛ this the vele of the temple and
„ the ſtones were rent a ſondꝛe, & the whole

Hoc idē
corpus.

earth trembled and quaked. this ſelfeſame
body being al ſpotted with blood, & woun=
ded with a ſpeare, powꝛed out holſom fon=
„ taynes of water and blood, to the whole
„ woꝛld. wil you by ſome other meanes vn=
„ derſtand the vertue & power hereof? Aſke
„ of her that had the bloody flire, who tou=
„ ched not Iheſus but his garment: neither
„ yet all that, but the hem thereof only. Aſke
　　　　　　　　　　　　　　　the

the sea,on whose backe it was caried. Aske "
the Diuel, and say vnto him: where tokest "
thou thy incurable wound? how didst thou "
leese thy strengh? how art thou taken cap= "
tiue? of whō art thou kept prisoner? frome "
whom fleest thou? He wil answer no other "
thing,but from that crucified body, where= "
by his stinge was broken, his head troden "
vnder fote,his dominion and power quite "
destroyed.for Christ (as it is written) spoy- Colos. 2.
ling dominiōs and powers lead them cap- "
tiue triumphing ouer them in him selfe o- "
penly and valiantly. "

　　Aske death saying: how hast thou lost "
thy sting? how is thy conquest come to "
naught? how are thy synowes cut? & thou "
who before tyme hast bene terrible vnto "
great princes,and all iust men,art now lau "
ghed to scorne of boyes and gyrls? And it "
wil confesse this body to be cause of al these "
thinges. which when it was crucified then "
the dead were raysed to life: then that pri- "
son together with the brasen gates was "
broken downe: the dead rose vp, and al the "
partes of hell were put to flyght. But and "
if he had bene one of the common sort, it "
must needes haue come to passe otherwise, "
& death must needes haue preuayled,which "
now is ouerthrowen . for he was not like "
the reste , and therefore he was free from "
death. And euen as they which eate some "
　　　　　　　　　　　　　　　　meate

,, meate which they can not digest, doe for ý
,, morsels sake, vomit vp again such meate as
,, they haue eaten before: so it came to passe in
,, ý death of Christ. for death hauing receaued
,, a body which could not take corruption did
,, cast forth such bodyes also on which it
,, had power before. for it was in great paine
,, & trauaile so long as it held Christ vntill it
,, had cast him vp again: And therfore ý Apo=
Act. 2. & ,, stle (speaking of Christ) saith: He loosed the
Rom. 6. sorowes of death. for truly no woman was
,, euer so greued and tormented in her tra=
,, uell, as death was vexed and torne so long
,, as it kept the body of our Lord. And that
,, which chaunced to the dragon of Babilon,
Dan. 14. which hauing receaued meat did burst a=
,, sondre in the midst, the same happened her=
,, by to death. For Christ brake not out again
,, by the mouth of death, but tearing & ren=
,, ting a sondre the dragons bely, brake with
,, great glory out of the entrailles & inward
,, partes thereof: & did send foorth his shy=
,, ning beames, not vnto this skye, but vnto
,, the very heauenly throne aboue.
5. ,, For thyther he caried vp the same which
,, also he gaue vnto vs both to kepe and to
,, eate. which is a singular token of loue. for
,, we sticke not often tymes euen to bite such
,, as we loue. And therefore Iob to expresse
,, the loue of his seruants towardes him re=
porteth

Iob. 31.

porteth that many tymes vppon that exce= "
ding vehement affection they sayd : Who "
t hal geue vs his flesh, wherewith we may be "
filled? And so Christ gaue vs his flesh that "
we should be filled w̃ it, & allured thereby "
very much to loue him . Let vs therefore "
come vnto Christ with a feruent zeale and "
vehement affection, least we be more grea= "
ueously punished. for looke how greater "
the benefit is, so much more greuous pu "
nishment must we looke for, if we shall ap= "
peare vnworthy thereof. "

6.

The wise me̅ of the East being so̅mtime "
wicked and barbarous, worshipped this "
body in the manger, & after a long viage, "
adored it with much feare and trembling. "
Let vs therfore which are citizens of hea= "
uen at least take ensample of those barba= "
rous men . for they seing none of those "
thinges which thou now seest, but only a "
manger and a pore litle cotage, came yet "
with great reuerence and horrour . But "
thou seest it not in a manger, but vppon "
an aultar, thou beholdest not a woman hol "
ding it in her armes, but seest a priest ther "
present, and the holy Ghost abundantly "
spred vpon y̅ sacrifice there set foorth. Nei= "
ther dost thou as they did behold a simple "
body, but therewithall knowest his power "
& all the dispe̅sation which he vsed in flesh. "

neither

>> dispensation which he vsed in flesh. neither
>> art ignozant of any thing that is made by
>> him but art perfytly instructed in all poin=
>> tes. Let vs then be stirred vp & quake foz
>> feare, let vs endenour to excede the deuo=
>> tion of those barbarous men, least by co=
>> ming therevnto rudely and coldly without
>> deuotion, we put our selues in danger of a
>> greater fyze.
>> I speake not this, to discomfozt any man
>> frome approching thereunto : but to then=
>> tent we should not come thereunto rashe=
>> ly. foz as it is dangerous to come with
>> colde deuotion: so not to be at all partaker
>> of that mysticall supper, it is very pestilent
>> and deadly. foz that same table is y strengh
>> and fozce of our soule and mind , the bond
>> of our trust and confidence. it is our soun=
>> dation, hope, healh, lyght, and life. if we de=
>> part out of this wozld strengthned with
>> this sacrifice we shal with great confidence
>> and as it were clothed with golden gar=
>> mēts ascend vnto the holy pozch: but what
>> speake I of thinges to come ? foz while we
7. >> are here liuing, this mystery causeth the
>> earth to be vnto vs heauen. Clyme vp
>> therefoze vnto the gates of heauē & marke
>> diligently, I say not of heauen but of the
>> heauen of heauens. & then shalt thou be=
>> hold that which we talke of. foz that which
8. >> is wozthy of highest honoz that wil I shew
                                    the in

thee in the earth.   For as in the courtes of   "
princes not the walles, not the golden roof   "
or couering, but the princes body sitting in   "
his seat of maiesty, far passeth and excelleth: "
so also the kinges body in heauen, whiche   "
now is set foorth to be seen of thee in earth.   "
Neither doe I shew vnto thee Angels or   "
Archangels, heauen or heauens of heaues,   "
but I shew vnto thee him who is Lord of   "
all these.   "

Doest thou consydere after what sorte   "
thou dost not only behold on the earth, that   "
which is of al thigs ye chiefest & most worthi   "
but dost also touch it, neither doest only   "
touch it, but also eate it, and hauing eaten it   "
returnest home to thi house? Make therefore   "
thy soule cleane from all fylth, prepare thy   "
mind to the receauing of these mysteries.   "
If a yong prince decked with his purple   "
robe and croun on his head were commit-   "
ted vnto thee to be borne any whither, wol   "
dest thou not cast all other thinges in the   "
ground, and take him in to thy armes? And   "
now seing thou receauest not a yong prince   "
begotten of any man, but the only begottē   "
sonne of God: tel me I praie thee dost thou   "
not tremble and quake, laying a side the   "
loue of all worldly thinges, and thinke thy   "
selfe adorned sufficiently with that only?   "

But if thou lookest yet towardes the   "
ground setting thy mind alltogether vpon   "

10

,, richesse and geuing thy selfe wholy to the
,, earth, what pardō canst thou aske oꝛ what
,, excuse canst thou make? Doest thou not see
,, our Loꝛd and master vtterly to haue aba=
,, doned and foꝛsaken all woꝛldly pōpe? was
,, he not therfoꝛe at his first cōming into the
,, woꝛld layed in a manger, & did he not ther=
,, foꝛe chose a poꝛe woman to his mother? did
,, he not therefore say vnto him ẙ had respect

Luc.9. vnto his loging, The sonne of mā hath not
,, where to lay his head? what did his disci=
,, ples? obserued they not ẙ saine kind of life
,, entring alwaies into poꝛe mens houses,
,, one to a shoomakers house, another to a
,, tētmakers, & some other to a womās house
,, ẙ sold purple die? foꝛ thei sought not ẙ ma=
,, iesty of houses but the vertue of soules. Let

Act. 16. vs thē desire such thigs, & cōtemne the beu=
,, ty of pillers & of marble, sekig only to haue
,, mansion places in heauen, & treding vnder
,, fete al woꝛldly pꝛyde, together wẙ isatiable
,, gredines of mony, let vs lift vp our minds
,, to higher maters. Foꝛ there can be no other
,, oꝛnamēt, poꝛch oꝛ walkig place meeter foꝛ
,, vs, thē to liue in sobꝛiety. wherfoꝛe my de=
,, sire is, ẙ we deck & adoꝛn our soule, & onely
,, pꝛepare it, as ẙ which only shal accōpanie
,, vs, whē we shal depart hence to enioy ẙ e=
,, uerlasting tabernacles, through ẙ fauour &
,. mercy of our loꝛd Iesus Chꝛist. to whōbe ho
,, noꝛ & gloꝛy woꝛld without end. Amen.

Although S. Chꝛysostōs woꝛdes in this

place be so playne & euident, that they nede
not any farther to be discussed & are so ma=
ny also in number which make for the reall
presence of Christ his body and bloud in y͏͏e
blessed Sacrament, y͏͏t I can not well iudge
which principally to note : yet seing that a
good thing (as the prouerbe sayth) can not
be to often repeted, and the repeting of one
thing ofte, causeth the same to sticke better
in the memory, euen as the second chewing
of meates causeth in certain beastes a more
perfite digestion : I will be bold here also,
as I haue bene before vpon your patience.
wherfore I beseeh you turne backe again
ouer the leaf , according as my notes leade
you, & ponder in your own conscience betwixt
god & your self, whether al good folke haue
not iust cause to lament the great myserie
of our time, in which there are found men so
impudēt, that not withstāding al y͏͏s this ho=
ly doctor writeth, both here & in other pla=
ces so plainly against thē, yet will vaunt &
crake, yea in open pulpets also, themselues
only to haue truth, & al old writers so to be
on their side, y͏͏t there cānot be found in al their
writings one word or syllable against thē.

But to come to S. Chrysostome and to
signify vnto you which sentēces you ought
here chiefly to ruminate, if you did consider
well but those three wordes in the begin=
ning , where he calleth this Sacramēt that
                              I 2   dread=

dreadful & wonderfull sacrifice you should
find that euery one of thē vtterly confoun-
deth the Protestants damnable heresie. For
first the name sacrifice as I told you before,
is not for naught so spited of them. For the
same declareth it to be the true body of
Christ, which was our true and only sacrifice vpon the Crosse, and so remaineth continually both in heauen and in the blessed
Sacramēt, offering him self dayly & houre-
ly, to appeace the wrath of God the Father
for our sinnes. Albeit in heauen he offereth
him selfe without intermission in the same
visible forme & shape, as he ascended, & shal
come to iudge the world, shewing ÿ woūds
of his syde, hands & feete, which he suffered
for our sake. But in the blessed Sacrament
he doth both offer him self, and is offered of
the priest his ministre, and by the hartes of
al deuoute people, inuisibly & vnder another forme, that is to say of bread & wine: so
often as those creatures are changed by
due cōsecration into his most precious body & blood. And therefore I pray you, note
once for all that so often as you shall finde
this worde sacrifice attributed to the blessed Sacrament either in this doctor or any
other, so often the true presence of Christes
body is confirmed, & the Protestants opinion by those mens censure vtterly condē-
ned. The word dreadfull likewise how can
they

I.

This
word sacri-
fice attri-
buted to
ÿ Sacra-
ment pro-
ueth ÿ real
presence.

they abyde which deny any honor or wor=
ship to be done vnto it?and in what respect
can they call it wonderfull, if there bee no
miraculous mutation at all, & nothing els
besides naked bread and simple wine?

There doe solowe certein wordes in S.
Chrysostom of whiche some Protestantes
haue taken holdfast making the world be=
lieue that this auncient doctor maketh for
them, whereas in dede he ment nothing
lesse. wherefore I would wishe you did
marke them diligently, conferring thē wi h
those that solow & go before. for it skilleth
as muche or more, to know how litle those
places whiche they them selues allege doe
make for their purpose, as to vnderstand
how much other places make against thē.
The words which they bring for their side
are those where he saith, that we must be=
come like vnto Egles by sleing high in our
vnderstanding, and being quicke of sight
when we come to be partakers of Christes
body. for so muche as this is the table of
Egles & not of Iayes,wherby thei would
conclude that we must slee vp i our mind
to Christ in heauen, and feed on him spiri=
tuailie,& by faith only,and not belieue that
his body is here preset on the earth. which
kind of reasonig is very simple God kno=
weth,if you cōsider either wherof S. Chry=
sostom here speaketh or what he saieth sone

I 3   after

2.

This wre
sting of S.
Chryso=
stoms
words, is
vsed in ꝫ
late con=
futed
Apologis.

after. For he talketh not here of ẙ maner of Chriſtes being in the ſacrament, but of the manner of receauing the ſame worthely, as his own words do witneſſe before, ſaying: by this name of Egles we are warned how it behoueth vs to approche vnto this body. And therefore he willeth vs not to crepe alow, by geuing our ſelues to earthly thinges as al ſinners do, and ſuch as come vnworthely: but to flie vp to heauen with the Egles and haue our minds fixed vpon the ſonne of righteouſnes, who ſhal endue vs with al vertue and godlineſſe.

And howſoeuer a man take the flying vp into heauē by cōſidering the diuine power and maieſtie of God, or otherwiſe, that nothing proueth that God is not here truely preſent in the ſacramēt. For that place may be called after a ſorte heauen whereſoeuer Chriſte is preſent, accordingly as the holy doctors do expoūd that, where Chriſt ſaid to the theſe, This day thou ſhalt be with me in Paradiſe. For that promiſe was performed when as the ſoule of ẙ theef accōpained the bleſſed ſoule of Chriſt, which brought ſuch ioy to euery place wher it came, that it was for the tyme a perfite Paradiſe. And therefore S. Chryſoſtō alſo ſaith not long after in this very place, that by this ſacramēt the earth is made heauē: doing vs therby to vnderſtand ẙ that we may flie vp like Egles euen

Luc.23.

euen to heaue it self, if we do but throughly
& deeply côsidre ÿ diuine maiesty which is
here preset vpô earth in ÿ blessed sacramêt.
wherefore you see to what narrow shyftes
thei are driue which to make a shew of so m̄
auctoritie, allege such slender places. but ÿ
you may see most clerely how far their in=
terpretation of this holy doctor is from his
meanig, as thê selues also might haue per=
ceued if thei wold haue readê alitle farther:
Note thirdly where he saith we receaue in
this sacramêt ÿ pure & imaculat body of him
who is Lord of al, & which is partaker of ÿ
diuine nature, & by whô we haue our beig.

Note also how many circûstâces he vseth
to declare this to be his most true & natural
body. For he saith it is ÿ body which was
crucified, torne with whippes, & wounded
with a speare, & to expresse his mind most
plainly he saith moreouer, hoc idem corpus
this self same body. wherby he taketh awai
al maner of tropes & figures, if by any wor
des a man may plainly signifie ÿ whiche he
meaneth. And so you find many lines toge
ther, where he maketh no differêce at al cô=
cernig ÿ truth & substâce, betwixt ÿ body of
Christ in ÿ sacramêt, & ÿ which walked in ÿ
earth & suffred on ÿ crosse; but attributeth al
together as much to one as to ÿ other, as ÿ
walkig ô ÿ sea, ÿ healig of maladies, ÿ redêp
tiô of mã, côquerig ÿ diuel & rãsackig of hel.

The selfe
same body
is in the
sacrament
which
was cru-
cified.

J 4   But

But if the Protestantes wyll styll flee & lowe by the ground like Iayes, or rather Iack dawes, and cleue altogether to their grosse and sensuall imagination, if they wil alwayes vse that folyshe argumente and say: the same body of Christ which was crucified and ascended into heauen cannot be in the blessed sacrament, because one body cannot be in diuerse places at once, nether will any whit endeuour to flee alofte with the egles, and considre the omnipotency of almighty God: Note you fifthly to stop al such iangling & iarring Iaies mouthes that Chrisostom sayeth: for a singular token of loue he gaue vs bothe to eate and kepe that same body which he caried also vp in to heauen. wherby it euidently appeareth that to the fayth of this holy father it semed nothing absurd that the same body should be in heauen and eaten of vs on ye earth.

Note a litle after that singular place for the adoration of the blessed sacramet. which thinge because it employeth so necessarily the true presence of Christ his true body the Protestants most of al abhorre, calling it plain Idolatrie. But S. Chrisostom his verdit is, that we haue muche more cause to adore Christ here vppon the aultar then the Magi had whe they saw him lyinge in the manger. wherby a ma may worthily coiecture ye these men who so spitefully rayle against

5.
The same body is in the Sacrament which is asceded into heaue

6.
That body is on the altar to be adored, which was adored in the manger.

againſt him here, would haue of likelyhod
doon ſmall reuerence to him if they had liued in thoſe dayes with the Magi and ſeen
him there in that pore cotage, but would
rather haue ſought his death to cruel He-
rode &y̆ wicked Iewes. I wil not ſtād long
in vrging this place any farther ſeing the
wordes of themſelues are ſo plain . Note
well alſo that place where he ſaith, this mi-
ſterie cauſeth the earth to be vnto vs heauen, becauſe hereby I proued befoze that
place of y̆ Egles not to be ment that Chriſt
is only to be ſought aboue in ſuch ſort, that
he is not alſo to be ſought here alow in the
bleſſed ſacrament: but to be chiefly ment of
ſeeking him by a pure and heauenly life, or
els by cōceuing this hygh myſtery by faith
and not by ſenſuall reaſon.

   Note furthermore that Chriſoſtom pro-
miſethe to ſhew that on the earth , whiche
is worthy of higheſt honour. for thereby it
foloweth, not onlie that god who onlie is
worthie of the higheſte honor , is truely
preſent in the ſacrament (for by promiſing
to ſhew it he declareth y̆ it is in ſome particular place wher it maie be pointed vnto)
but alſo that he is there to be worſhiped w̄
all reuerence . And to vtter his minde yet
more plainlie, a litle after he ſaith, for your
ninthe note: that we doe not onlie here on
ths earth (meaning in the bleſſed ſacramēt)
                     beholde

7.

8.

9.

beholde ÿ which is worthy of most honor,
but also touch and eat it. So that not only
to our fayth, but euē to our senses the true
body of Chriſt is here truely preſent: al=
though not vnder ÿ forme and thoſe pro=
per accidēts by which it ſhould be ſenſibly
perceaued, for thē our faith ſhould lack that
merite which therfore is due vnto it. But
by ſaying ÿ we touch & feele it, he meaneth
ÿ ÿ ſubſtance thereof is no leſſe truly preſēt
to our ſenſes vnder thoſe ſtrange accidēts.
thē if we ſaw & felt it vnder ÿ proper form.

10.

Note alſo ÿ goodly ſimilitude, whereby
we are taught ÿ in receuing this high miſ=
tery, not ÿ yong prince of any earthly king
but ÿ only begottē ſonne of god is deliuered
vnto vs. Laſt of al note diligently & beare
wel away ÿ later end of this exhortation, &
thinke in dede earneſtly vpon your ſoules
health. For frinds, riches, glory of ÿ world,
fauor of Princes, together wᵗal other ſuch
worldy toies ſhal in ÿ end come to naught,
as thei do daily vaniſh & paſſe away, ÿ pore
ſoule only muſte ſticke by you to make a=
ſtraight account to God in that dreadfull
iudgement of all miſdedes & miſbeliefe.

¶ A few Teſtimonis out of S. Chryſoſtōs other
works, & namely out of his Maſſe or Liturgie.

The ſixth
Chapiter.
Now that you haue hearde this aun=
cient Doctors minde, vppon thoſe
places of holy ſcripture, where this matter

of

of ꝑ blessed sacramēt is chiefly mētioned: I
haue thought good to adde thereto two oɔ
three places moe taken out of other partes
of his works, where he hath incidētly talked herof, to thēd you shuld throughly vnderstād how wel this holy father agreth tō
him self, & how far he disagreth euery wher
from ꝑ protestants of our time, whiche yet
would seme in al poits & in this especially
of ꝑ supper of our Loɔd, to agree w̄ ꝑ primi
tiue church. In his thirde boke, De Sacer-
dotio of Priesthode, wherin he declareth ꝑ
high dignitie of ꝑ office, he maketh not far
frō ꝑ begining a cōparisō betwene those oɔ
namentes, which cōmēded ꝑ priestes of ꝑ
old Law, & those things which do set foɔth
ꝑ priesthode instituted by Chɔist in the new
law: pɔouing therby how much our priests
of this time of grace are to be preferred befoɔe those other. I will translate the whole
cōparison ꝑ you may perceaue I allege not
halfe sentences, as ꝑ Protestants do. And
therfoɔe I pɔay you beare with me as wel
befoɔe as hereafter, if in this behalfe I seme
somwhat tedious, cōsidering that I do the
same only vpō an eruest desire to make the
truth plainli appeare. his woɔds are thɔee:

As we vnderstande many thinges were
vsed befoɔe the tyme of grace whiche moued to great feare and reuerence, as foɔ example the litle bels, ꝑ pomgranets of gold,
the

Lib. 3. de
sacer.

" y pretious stones which were set, some in y
" priestes brest, some aboute his shoulders,
" the miter, y Ephod the long garmet donne
" to his feet, the plate of gold, the sancta san-
" ctorum, the great quiet and silence whiche
" was there within. But if a man examine
" these things which the tyme of grace hath
" brought, he will iudge those other which I
" said before did moue great feare and reue-
" rence, to be very light and litle worth. And
" he shall find those words of S. Paule to be
" verified where he saieth: That which was

2. Cor. 3. glorified and much estemed, was nothinge
" glorious in respect of this far passing glory.
" For whiles thou doest behold our Lord sa-

2. crificed, y priest attending the sacrifice, and
" saying the praiers, & then the people round
" about to be died and made redde with that
" pretious blood, doest thou yet thinke thy
" selfe to be on the earth and amongest mor-
" tall men? or rather art thou not imediatly
" transferred in to heauen? And doest thou
" not rather cast away all fleshly cogitation,
" and with a cleane soule and pure mind be-

2. hold those thinges which are in heauen? O
" miracle, o bountifulnes of God. He y sit-
" teth aboue with his father in the selfe same
" moment is handled in euery mans handes
" and deliuereth him selfe to all that are wil-
" ling to embrace and receaue him. Neither
" is that brought to passe by any iuglinge or
                                            witch-

wichcrafte, but in the open sight of al ꝑ stand "
about. Do these things seme vnto thee such "
as may be contēned & despised? or such , as "
against which any man may rise vp and in "
sult ?(and a litle after) This mysterie there= "
fore of al mysteries is most of al to be trēm= "
bled at & reuerenced. ⸺ wherupon he cōclu "
deth also his purpose ꝑ the priests of ꝑ new
testament are therefor merueilously to be
estemed, seing through their working as by
instrumentes, these holy mysteries are my=
stically begon and ended .　Note first the
worde sacrifice here repeted, the strength of
which I haue alredie noted vnto you. And
then note also what plaine words he vseth
to expresse the true presēce of Christs blood,
doing vs to vnderstād(as before) ꝑ we haue
it here no lesse truly present vnder ꝑ forme
of wine, thē if we were died & made red by
propre form thereof. If you marke well the
exclamatiō also toward ꝑ end of this place ,
you may vnderstand therby ꝑ in the blessed
sacramēt there is wrought a great miracle,
to their great cōfusiō which seeke by natu=
ral reason to proue it to be bread only . For
where a miracle is cōfessed, what sondnesse
is it to vse agaist ꝑ same any natural reasō?
wheras a miracle signifieth ꝑ which is to be
wōdred at, for beig aboue reasō, & therefore
ought in no wise by reason to be tried , but
of a true Christē mā by faith to be beleeued.

In

In the next sentence of S. Chrysostō you
find ÿ folish argumēt refelled. Christ sitteth
at ÿ right hād of his father: ergo he is not in
ÿ sacramēt of ÿ altar. For at one instāt (saith
he) Christ is both in heauen, & in the handes
of all ÿ doe receaue him. You may note here
by ÿ way ÿ in ÿ primitiue church (as many
other also do witnesse) ÿ christens receaued
ÿ blessed sacramēt first in their hāds. which
custō was afterwards chāged vpō iust occa
sion, many lewed people being found by ÿ
meanes to haue abused oftē times this holy
mystery. Now I dout not but if a protestāt
happē vpō this place, he wil note diligētly
for his purpose those words next before ÿ ex
clamation, wher S. Chrysostom willeth vs
in the presēce of those mysteries to haue our
minds lifted vp to heauē. But cōsider how
litle hold ÿ Protestāt hath, if he take all together as the Catholike doth. who neuer
affirmeth Christ to be so in the Sacrament,
that he mindeth thereby to diminishe any
iote of his being in heauen, neither dissua-
deth any mā frō lifting his mid vp to heauē
but wisheth with S. Chrysostō euery mā ÿ
approcheth herunto, to thinke only on heauē
ly thinges, which he must nedes doe if he
thinke on the blessed sacramēt and Christes
body therein cōteined. for (as I noted vnto
you before out of this same doctor) there is
heuē wheresoeuer Christ is, but ÿ Protestāts
contrariwise would so bind Christes body

to one place ẙ the same should by no meanꝛ
be able to be in any other beside, and therfor
if thei fide any half woꝛd in scripture oꝛ doc
toꝛ, which teacheth ẙ we must seek Chꝛist in
heauē, ẙ thei make much of & set foꝛth to ẙ
vttermost: but be ther neuerso many which
teach ẙ he is also in ẙ blessed sacramēt, those
thei wil not heare of, but either wꝛig & wꝛest
thē to their figuratiue meanig, oꝛ vtterly de
nie thē. And therefoꝛe it may happē ẙ some
wil canil vpō those plain woꝛds also which
do folow saing ẙ he which sitteth in heauen
may be here at ẙ same momēt spiritually, &
so nothig therby to be cōcluded against thē.
which interpꝛetatiō whether ẙ woꝛds wout
plai violēce cā beare, I thinke I may bold=
ly leaue to your owne discretion, specially
wheras you haue heard alredy this doctoꝛs
mid most plaily vttered against this theyꝛ
spiritish imaginatiō. But to assure you here
of moꝛe perfitly, I wil recite an other place
which you haue not yet heard, taken out of
the latter end of his secōd sermō made toẙ
people of Antioche. There speakig against ẙ
couetousnes of rich mē& cōmēding pouertꝓ,
he applieth to his purpose ẙ stoꝛi of Helias ẙ
pꝛophet, who beig lifted vp in a firi chariot
into heauē least his cloke behind him vnto
his disciple Heliseus, wishing him therby
(as S. Chꝛysostom expoūdeth) to cōtinue
in ẙ pouerty which he befoꝛe had pꝛofessed.
wheres

wheruppon S. Chrysostom taketh occasiō also to declare how Christ when he ascended in to heauen far passed Elias leauinge with vs behind in the blessed sacramēt not his cloke or garment, but himself his owne precious body and blood. But hearkē now to S. Chrysostōs words which are as here soloweth. ❧ What wil ye say thē if I shew you, that so many of vs as be partakers of

,, the holy mysteries do receaue a thinge far
,, greater then that which Elias gaue? For
,, Elias left vnto his disciple his cloke, but
,, the sonne of god ascending in to heauē left
,, with vs his flesh. And again Elias went
,, himself, without his cloke: but Christ both
,, left his fleshe with vs, and ascēded hauing
,, with him the selfsame flesh. Let vs not ther
,, fore be discomforted neither bewayle nor
,, dread the difficulties of ỹ troublous times.
,, For he which refused not to shed his blood
,, for vs al, and hath also made vs partakers
,, of his flesh and of the selfsame bloud, he I
,, say wyll refuse nothing that may be for the
,, furtherance of our saluation. ❧

Hitherto S. Chrisostome. Whereby you maie perceaue how perfitly he agreeth with him selfe, wher he hath so often before saied, that the self same fleshe whiche was borne of the blessed virgin, and was crucified on the crosse, is receaued in these holy mysteries. And you see also howe to confounde

Chry. ad po. Anti. hom. 2.

found all such as by their tropes & figures
peruersly interpret any other place of his.
He sayeth here most plainly that Christ left
ye selfe same flesh behind him which he toke
with him into heauen. And it is also most
euident, that the Protestantes cannot possibly manteyn the blessed Sacrament to be
a remembrance only of Christes flesh , if
they admit this mans auctoritie , which
they can not deny onlesse they be vtterly
past all shame. For Elias left a remem-
brāce also of hiinself, when he left his cloke
behind him. But herein standeth the force
of this comparison, that Christ far passed
Elias. And therefore sayeth Chrysostome,
he did not only leaue a far more excellent
thing, that is to say, his own flesh: but also
toke that same with him into heauē which
he left behind him. So that the same flesh
of Christ, and not a figure thereof is in the
Sacrament, which ascended into heauen.

    I doe not vrge that later sentēce where
he sayeth we are made partakers of the self
same blood which Christ shed for vs. Only I besech you note once for all how often
tymes you haue already in these few places found words of like efficacy & strēgth.
And thereby enforme your selfe throughly
what you ought to belieue in this matter:
considering that this is ye Catholike faith,
which is not only by this one Doctor ap=

An inuin-
cible argu
ment for ye
reall pre-
sence.

                   K   proued

proued, but as it may appeare by his writing, both was in his tyme, & before, & hath bene euer sence of al Christē men generally receaued. For had he either taught then in his opē sermōs (out of which al these places are takē) cōtrarie to ỹ which was then cōmonly beliued euē from the Apostles, or had there bene at any tyme since any thing found in his bokes, cōtrary to ỹ which all other good Doctors taught, & al Christendome professed: no doubt he should at some tyme or other haue bene noted for an heretike, or at ỹ least, his doctrine should haue bene noted in this point as not agreable to scripture. wherefore seing his wordes are so plaine, seing there is not foūd any good man or generall Councell of any age to haue reproued him therefore: but rather contrariewise all men haue embraced him as a most holy Doctor of the Churche, it must nedes folow that his doctrine hath bene in all ages generally allowed, as receaued euen from the Apostles and Christ himselfe. Likewise on the other side, that which the Protestantes now teach, contrarie to this, must nedes be a new inuention of their owne braynes, or whensoeuer it was inuented, false, erroneous, & heretical. And therefore it ought of all such as looke to enioy any part with Christ in heauen, together with those holy Apostles & blessed

fed fathers of the primitiue Church, vt=
terly to be difcredited, detefted, & abhorred.

And if there had bene no place at all, ex=
tant in S. Chrysoftoms workes for the
profe hereof (as there are thankes be to
God, a great many moe then I haue or cã
well traflat, onlesse I should make a great
volume thereof) yet there would not lacke
sufficient argumēt to proue vnto any rea=
sonable man, what both he & all Christens
of his tyme belieued concerning this mat=
ter. For y̆ Grecians which haue euer more
had in great reuerence thefe holy mysteries
haue vfed cõtinually since S. Chrysoftoms
tyme in the adminiftration of them, thofe
prayers & ceremonies which he him selfe
did vfe: Hauing made a great nombre of
his own deuotion and auctoritie, as being
Archebishop of Cõftãtinople, & hauing re=
ceaued also a great nõbre (as it is moft eui=
dēt) by traditiõ frõ his forefathers. Now
as thofe Grecians vfe S. Chrysoft. Masse:
so they professe that same faith concerning
y̆ mysterie there wrought, which their fa=
thers learned of him, as he learned it of his
auncesters y̆ Apostles Scholers. For in all
their Chronicles they find not y̆ any other
faith in this matter hath bene taught any
tyme synce, disagreing from that which
Chrysoft. left them, but y̆ they hold y̆ same
ftyll together w̃ his prayers & ceremonies
                                    K 2   Also

Also if any man demaund what their be
lief is at this present he shall find them to
agree herein with the Catholikes of ý La=
tin Church and to defend most ernestly the
reall presence of Christes body in the bles=
sed Sacrament, which thing they witnesse
also to euery man that beholdeth them at
their seruice, by the great reuerence & ado=
ration which they yeld therevnto. Neither
can the Protestantes escape here and say
that these men learned this faith of ý Pope
and Papistes of the Latin Church. Both
for that there hath not ben commonly suche
humilitie on the Grekes behalfe, that they
would vouchsafe to learne of the Latins:
And also for that the contrary appeareth
by their somewhat diuerse ordre in ceremo
nies, by their own report, and by al bokes
writen in that behalf. So that hereby it ap
peareth, that the very tradition of ý Gre=
cians conuinceth what S. Chrysostom his
mind was of the blessed Sacrament, al=
though he had writen neuer a word in the
matter.

But now what will you say if not only
ý seruice which ý Grecians vse to this day
beareth witnesse what S. Chrysostome be=
lieued: but also S. Chrysostom witnesseth
by his workes which are in print, ý kind
of Masse which they vse, to haue ben re=
ceaued fro him? That you may better vn=
derstand

stand my meaning: emongst S. Chrysostomes workes, those prayers & ceremonies are found which himselfe vsed at ye ad
ministration of ye blessed Sacrament, & are
traslated out of Greke into Latin by Erasmus Rotrodamus whom ye Protestantes
I am sure take for one of their welwillers
at the least. And the very same haue ben
continually, & are to this day most generally vsed throughout the Greke Church.
So ye whereas noma doubteth of S. Chry
sostoms other workes set foorth together
w this part, how much better is this proued to be of good auctoritie, being not only
set foorth vnder his name together w the
rest of his workes: but also cotinually practised vnder his name, emongest all the
Grecians.

If then these prayers & ceremonies so
well auctorised all maner of ways doe declare the Grecians agreemet w the Catholikes of the Latin Church, as well in the
principall point, which is the real presence
of Christes body, as also in many other
principal ceremonies vsed in ye holy Masse:
ye same must nedes geue a great ouerthrow
to our Protestantes, which are so much offended both w the principall matter & all
other good ceremonies vsed at the admini-
stratio thereof, ye they cãnot abyde to heare
so much as ye name Masse only, which yet

K 3   of it

of it self is as other names be a thing indif
ferēt. Now to proue this agreemēt I will
truly report vnto you ẏ only which my self
haue heard & seen emōgst them at their ser=
uice time in ẏ worthy citie of Uenice where
they haue a Church by thē selues & weekly
faile not therein deuoutly to serue God.

But to bring somewhat first there hence
before I goe any farther for ẏ cōfirmation
of my principal matter which is already so
well proued, you shall vnderstād, ẏ as it is
most euidēt ẏ they receaued most part of ẏ
prayers & ceremonies of this their Masse,
frō S. Chrysostome & his ancestours : so ẏ
name thereof which is in their tōge Liturgia, they receaued euē from ẏ Apostles thē
selues. For besides ẏ all ẏ Greke Fathers
from S. Chrysost. tyme vpward vse much
this word when they write of this matter,
ẏ holy Euāgelist S. Luke also mentioning
in ẏ Actes of ẏ Apostles ẏ vse of this holy
Sacrament, vseth ẏ same. And in ẏ begin=
ning of his Ghospell where he speaketh of
ẏ office of Zacharias, which was to offer sa
crifice for ẏ people he hath this word like=
wise. so that it is most probable ẏ as in his
Ghospel he signifieth thereby ẏ office of of=
fering sacrifices according to ẏ old law : so
in ẏ Actes of the Apostles he vsed the same
speaking of this holy Sacramēt , vpō spe=
ciall cōsideration ẏ it succedeth all ẏ sacrifi=
ces of ẏ Iewes, & is ẏ only sacrifice of the

λειτουρ=
γία.

λειτουρ=
γούντ δ'
αὐτ.
Act. 13.
αἱ ἡμέραι
τῆς λει=
τουργίας
αὐτοῦ.
Luc. I.

new law. And therfore although this word
Liturgia signifieth generally emõgst prophane writers, any publike functiõ, or ministerie: yet y̌ Christiãs folowing y̌ exãple
of S. Luke haue specially applyed it to signifie y̌ celebration of this holy mysterie, as
being y̌ only publike sacrifice offered for y̌
synnes of y̌ world, wherein al sortes of mẽ
are comeded vnto God, & y̌ functiõ whereof, is y̌ chiefest & highest in all Christẽ religion. Now hereby sufficient argument is
geuẽ to vnderstãd what y̌ Grecians belief
hath euer bene concerning y̌ reall presence.
For onlesse Christ be there really presẽt to
be offered, they could not haue called it a sa
crifice, for so much as he alone is y̌ only sacrifice of y̌ new law as it is alredy declared

But whether y̌ name Liturgia were vsed
chiefly vpon this respect or no, it shall not
much skill for y̌ word sacrifice it selfe is so
oftẽ applied to this Sacramẽt throughout
y̌ prayers of y̌ sayd Liturgie y̌ a man may
euery where find sufficiẽt grosñ for y̌ argu
ment. And to geue you a few places which
may be in stede of many, hearkẽ now vnto
this one prayer which I shal trãslate, wher
in it is not only called a sacrifice, but also a
vnbloody sacrifice, as differing in y̌ maner
of being only, frõ y̌ one sacrifice which was
once for al bludely offered on y̌ crosse. You
shal find also i plain words y̌ Christ is both

he that there offereth by his minister and
is the sacrifice which is offered, and more=
ouer that his true body & blood are there
by the mighty power of the holy Ghost,
truly consecrated, and made present. This
prayer is writen in S. Chrysostoms Masse
or Liturgie and vsed continually in the
Greke Church betwene the Ghospell and
the Crede. And it is in English this much.

In Litur.
Chrysof.

    None of those which are entagled w
" fleshly lustes and pleasurs, is worthy to
" come neare, to stand by, or ministre vnto
" thee o King of glorie. For to serue thee it
" is a great and dreadfull thing, euen for the
" heauenly powers them selues. Neuerthe=
" lesse throught thy vnspeakable and infini=
" tie mercy thou wast without any change
" or alteration in thy selfe made man, and
" become our Priest, and as Lord of all didst
" deliuer vnto vs the celebration of this mi=
" nisterie, and vnbloody sacrifice. For thou
" alone o Lord our God art ruler of all that
" are in heauen & in earth. who sittest vpon
" the throne of Cherubin, who art Lord of
" Seraphin, and King of Israell: who on=
" ly art holy and dost rest in those which are
" holy. Thee therefore, I beseche who alone
" art good and ready to geue eare, looke
" downe vppon me a synner, and thy vn=
" profitable seruant. And cleanse my soule
" and harte from an euil & wicked conscience.
                 And

& make me being endewed with the grace "
of priesthod, meete by the power of thy ho= "
ly spirite to stand at this thy holy table, & "
consecrate thy holy and immaculate body "
and precious blood. For I come vnto thee "
bowing downe my necke, and thee I be= "
sech that thou turne not thy face from me, "
and refuse me not for one of thy children: "
but vouchsafe to accept these gyftes to be "
offered vnto thee, by me a synner and thy "
vnworthy seruant. for thou art both the "
offerer, and he that is offered, the receauer, "
& he that is receaued or distributed Christ "
our God: and to thee we geue glory toge= "
ther with the Father who is without be= "
ginning, and to thy most holy and blessed "
spirite the geuer of life, now and euer more "
world without end. Amen. & "

Thus you see in most plain wordes not
only y this is an vnbloody sacrifice, but al=
so that Christ our God is he who therin is
both offered and offereth by meanes of the
Priest his minister: that be both receaueth
the sacrifice as being true God, and is re=
ceaued of al that communicate, as being
there both in his humanity and Godhead
most truly present. Also you heare in the
midst of the prayer y Priest beseching God
to assist him with his power that he may
consecrat his holy body and blood. so that
you see it most euident before your ieyes

how ŷ Grecians frō S. Chrysost. time vnto
this day haue always professed ŷ faith con
cerning this holy mistery which the Catho
likes in ŷ Latin Church doe defend. which
thig they witnesse also by their whole beha
uour al their Masse, & specially at ŷ time of
cōsecration & Eleuation, for then they bow
down with their whole body euen in ma=
ner to the ground merueilous reuerently.
But now you shall heare also one of those
prayers which the Priest saith after the con
secration . it is thus.

Ibid.

” Looke down frō thy holy tabernacle &
” from the glorious throne of thy Kingdome
” & come to sāctifie vs O Lord Iesus Christ
” our God, which sittest aboue w̄ thy Father
” & art here with vs inuisibly presēt. vouch=
” safe by thy mighty power to make vs & by
” vs all thy people partakers of thy imma=
” culate body & blood. In which few
” wordes you may note how wel S. Chryso
stom agreeth with himself where he sayd a
litle before ŷ Christ is in one moment pre=
sent both in the handes of all that receaue
this holy Sacramēt, & in heauen at ŷ right
hād of God ŷ Father. for so likwise by this
prayer it is manifest ŷ the selfe same Christ
is inuisibly present here after consecration
vnder the formes of bread & wyne , which
remaineth cōtinually visible in heauen.

But because my desire was to be throu̅g-
ghly

ghly instructed of their belife in this point,
after their seruice was doon, J communed
with some that were learned amongst thē
and desired to vnderstand what they belei=
ued generally concerning the same . who
answered me that accordingly as they had
receaued of their forefathers , so they belei=
ued most constantly, ẙ real presence of Chri
stes true body & blood vnder the formes of
bread and wine. And they tolde me moreo=
uer in farther talke that if any man was
found amongest thē to discredite the same,
he was, if he cōtinued in that error, accoun
ted for an heretike, & finally also excommu
nicated , so ẙ no honest man would eate or
drinke iu his company . By all which eui=
dent argumentes ẙ beliefe of S. Chrysost.&
of ẙ whole primitiue Church is most mani
festly proued vnto you to be one wᵗ ẙ which
is by ẙ Catholikes so ernestly defended. for
here not only S. Chrysostōs plaine wor=
des doe as in ẙ placesbefore alleaged wit=
nesse what his meaning was, but also the
continuall practise & open confession of the
whole Greke Church cōfirmeth ẙ same.

The which being espied by ẙ Sacramen
taries to be as it is in dede , an inuincible
confirmation against them of the catho=
like truth : one of the Ringleaders there
emongst them hath of late endeuored to the
vttermost of his power to discredite it,
affirming

affirming the saied liturgie oz Masse neuer
to haue bene ozdeined noz vsed by S. Chzy
softom in his time, but inuented long time
sence. But the pzofes which he vseth in that
behalfe are so exceding slender, that he doth
nothig thereby in effect, but discredite him
selfe in al the rest of his doctrine. My foz=
tune was to heare of them, euen as I was
handling this place, & therefoze I thought
it my part to say somewhat in defence both
of my selfe hauinge vsed ẙ same already as
a strong argumẽt, & of the truth whiche no
good harte can chose but lament to see so
impudẽtly impugned. I wil therfoze shew
first how vaine those surmises are by which
he would discredite the saied Liturgie, and
afterward geue you some most euident to=
kens, by whiche it may yet better appere
to be the selfe same which S. Chzysostome
vsed in his time. And therewithall I will
take occasion to perfozme my fozmer pzo=
mise, and bziefly to set befoze, your eyes
some of those ceremonies also, whiche
I saw vsed ther in Venice of the Gre=
cians, accozdingly as they haue
receaued them together with
those pzayers from
S. Chzysostome.

The

¶ S. Chrysostoms Masse or Liturgie defended against ẏ false surmises of M. Iuel in his Reply to D. Harding pag. 10. & therewithall many Ceremonies vsed to this day in the Greke Churche are declared.

THe surmises which are brought to discredit this holy Liturgie, are grounded vpon one praier only, wherein one Pope Nicholas called there vniuersalis Papa, and the Patriarches of Alexandria, Antioche, Hierusalem, together with Alexius somtime Emperour of ẏ East, are prayed for, that they might liue long and rule peaceably on the earth. Now all these men liued many yeres synce Chrysostom : for Pope Nicolas (saith this surmiser) liued in the yere of our Lorde 857. & was second Pope of Rome after Pope Ione, (who is noted in the margent of his boke with great letters, for good will I warrant you to make that false fable the better remembred.) Also Alexius the Emperour liued in the yere 1080, that is to say many hūdred yeres after Chrysostō, whereuppon he concludeth that for him to haue prayed so long before for them, had ben rather prophesing than praying', and therefore this to be none of S. Chrysostoms Liturgie.

But will you see how much his great malice against the truth appeareth hereby, and

The vij. Chapter.

and howe litle he hath proued his purpose:
First it is most euident that the name Ni=
cholas can not be ment of that Pope Ni=
cholas of Rome which he mentioneth, be=
cause ỹ man liued aboue two hūdred yeres
before the Emperour Alexius, as him selfe
confesseth, but those which are here prayed
for, were liuing altogether at one time, as
the wordes of the prayer do plainly declare.
The same reason proueth also that it can
be ment of no Pope of Rome at all, for so
much as none of that name was Bishop
of Rome in that Alexius daies. And which
confirmeth the matter a greate deal more
the Grecians in Alexius time did not bere
anie suche reuerence to the See of Rome,
that they would pray for that Bishoppe
by name, and leue out the name of their
owne Patriarche. Whiche they must nedes
haue done if the name, Pope Nicholas,
be referred to any Bishoppe of Rome. For
there is no name lefte besyde for the Pa=
triarche of Constantinople, and yet the
other three Patriarches of Alexandria, An=
tioche and Hierusalem, are specially na=
med. Nowe as for the worde Pope, al=
though the same may deceaue some simple
man, supposing that no Bishoppe was
euer called by that name, besydes the Bis=
shop of Rome: yet the Surmiser him selfe
can not be ignorant, that the worde Papa
in la

in Latin is and hath ben commonly vsed of many good wꝛiters, to signifie any other Bishope aswell as the Bishope of Rome: and that it is attributed vnto him in common talke by reason of excellency only, as the woꝛde Byble signifieth with vs one certen boke, whereas the same in Greke signifieth euery boke indifferently.

The woꝛde vniuersalis also ioyned vnto Papa, whereby the sayd Nicholas is called in the pꝛaier, vniuersall Pope oꝛ Bishop, maketh very litle, oꝛ rather much lesse foꝛ his purpose. Yea I should say that woꝛde alone pꝛoueth the rest not to be ment at all of any Bishop of Rome, but of some Bishop of Constantinople. foꝛ ẏ Bishopes of this See only haue both chalenged, and vsed wꝛongfully that title, as it appeareth by chose Epistles of S. Gregoꝛie which are so famous amongst the Pꝛotestants. And therefoꝛe they of all men are most vnlikely to haue yelded the same to the Pope of Rome. who also neuer chalended noꝛ vsed that title, although it may and hath ben in ryght good sense geuen him, as in respect that he is of the vniuersall Church the chiefe Bishop. So that the woꝛd, vniuersall declareth manifestly the name whereunto it is ioyned,
                              to be

to belong rather to the Bishope of Constantinople, than of Rome. But what vse we coniectures in this matter which is of it self so plaine? for Zonoras a writer of the greke histories putteth al out of doubt, witnessing vnto vs, that there was one Nicholas Bishop of Constantinople euen in that Alexius dayes which is mentioned in the prayer, and that they liued many yeres together. whereupon it must nedes folow, that whereas both the Bishop and Emperour are prayed for as liuing together, those wordes of Nicholas vniuersal pope, are to be vnderstode of Nicolas Bishope of Constantinople and not of Nicholas Pope of Rome, named second after the feined Pope Ione. Albeit in some sense this surmiser may be sayd here to tell truth against his will. as if those wordes Pope Ione be vnderstode (as they ought to be) to stand for Pope None or Pope Nunquá. for so it is true in dede that the forsayd Nicholas was second Pope of Rome after Pope Ione. But perchaunce he will say I haue gained litle hereby toward prouing the Liturgie to be S. Chrysostoms, seing this Nicholas of Constantinople is farther of from Chrysostoms daies thã that other. Yeas truly this much I haue gayned, that he is proued thereby a false surmiser in one point, and that he ought therefore without

any

Lib.3. de Alexio Cómen.

Pope Ione. Pope None.

any further profe likewise to be suspected in the rest. But let vs goe forward & detect all the iugling and falsedealing which he vseth in this matter.

There are three copies of this Liturgie printed in diuerse places and translated by diuerse men, which I my selfe haue seen : & two of those three lacke altogether al those names, vpō which his surmises are groun ded. For neither y copie which was tran= slated & printed at Venice in the yere. 28. nor that which was traslated by Erasmus & printed both in Paris and diuerse other places, maketh any mention of them. So y if by his argument the third copie which hath those names be improued, yet nothig is sayed against the other two, but they re mayne still true copies, & the same which is in them may be still truly accounted S. Chrysostoms Liturgie. And so the drift of his whole argument is not in dede against the thing it self, but against one copie ther= of only, & yet it is such as maketh very litle or nothig at al against y neither. For what is y third copie, which hath y prayer to all those names in it? Forsoth it is the trensla tion of one Leo Tuscus, which was set foorth of late together with the Greke by Claudius de Sainctes Doctor of Paris, and printed by Morelius at that tyme the Kinges printer there.

L   Now

Now that Leo Tuscus (as it appeareth by his owne Epistle set before his translation) did translate the sayd Liturgie, at Constantinople in the tyme of Emanuel ỹ Emperour, who was secõd after ỹ forsayd Alexius. whereof it may be very probable gathered, ỹ this Leo translated the sayed Liturgie, out of some copie which was writ ten there at Constantinople in Alexius tyme, and therefore might haue in it his name together with the names of ỹ foure Patriarches then lyuing. For what absur= ditie is it that a Masse boke or any other prayer boke, made many hundred yeres be fore, should at what tyme it is new writen or printed haue the chief Bisshops, ỹ Em= perour or Prince then gouerning, special= ly named in some one Collect? Is that a sufficient surmise to proue the whole order of the Masse & prayers to be no older than those names or ỹ Collect? Truly the same may stand perchaunce for a strong argu= mēt if respect be had to the new Commun= nion of England only, or some other such like. For thereof it may be truly said, King Edward the sixth was named therein, er= go before his days that seruice was neuer heard of: because vnder him the same was first set vp. But otherwise in all Catholike prayers and ceremonies I doubt not but euery mean witted man perceaueth how

fonde

fonde a coniecture it is. For we may dayly
see both prymmers & Masse bokes where=
in the name of some Prince of our tyme is
expressed, and yet by other old parchment
bokes of the same sorte, those selfsame suf=
frages & ceremonies are proued to be ma=
ny score yeres elder. And that it is euen so
in this matter, what better profe can any
man aske, than that copie of Erasmus tra=
slation, which is commonly ioyned vnto
S. Chrysostoms other workes? Or than
the Greke copies them selues printed both
at Uenice & Paris? None of which make
any mentiō of Pope Nicholas, or Alexius,
or any such. But they haue in stede of those
names, certen Greke wordes which im=
porte the same as this letter. N. doth with
vs, to signifie that Bishop and Emperour
always to be named in the Collect which
are for the tyme lyuing.

The
Greke
wordes
are these,
ὅςις ἄμ ᾖ.
ὁ δεῖνος.

And therefore a great deale more im=
pudence appeareth in this aduersarie, who
knowing that very Greke copie, which
was printed at Paris together w⁹ ỹ Latin
translation of Leo Tuscus, which he alle=
geth & vseth for his vātage, to haue no such
names mentioned therein, would not with
stāding ground his argumēt vpō ỹ Latin,
& cōtemne ỹ Greke, wherby this case ought
chiefly to be tried. Especially ỹ same Greke
copie being so perfite, that as Morelius

L 2   the

the printer testifieth, it was confirmed by most autentike old copies both out of the library of our King of England, and out of the French Kings Librarie. For it had ben his parte that would haue dealt vprightly, first of all to haue regarded the Greke copies, and next to haue conferred the Latin translations, and so to haue argued vppon those places wherein they all agree: and not to haue picked out one or two wordes only which no common Greke copie, nor any moe than one Latin translation hath. For what other thing may this be deemed, but either an extreme and detestable malice against the knowen truth: either an exceding grosse and shamfull ignorance of the truth. Both which faultes be very vndecent for one of his profession, and most vnsemely for a man of such knowledge and learnig as he would seme to be.

And now because I thinke his wrongfull reproofe of S. Chrysostoms Liturgie to be in these few lynes sufficiently disproued: You shall heare briefly also what my simple learning can shew for the profe and confirmation thereof. First therefore as y̌ bruit commonly proueth true which being somewhat diuersly from diuerse costes reported, agreeth wholy in y̌ pricipal poits: euen so this is no small argument for the

auctoritie

auctoritie of the sayed Liturgie, y̌ the same
in all copies which were taken as it may
appeare out of diuerse libraries, agreeth
still with it selfe in the chief matters, & is
generally ascribed to S. Chrysostome. Yea
& as the lawyers say, Exceptio confirmat
regulá: so I may say most truly in this case
y̌ those small differences of a few names or
some one collect, doe much more strongly
confirme the rest wherein there is no disa-
greement to be S. Chrysostoms, than if no
difference at all had bene found. For thereby it appeareth that although diuersitie of
tyme & place, might cause some particular
things therein to be altered, added, or demi-
nished, yet the whole was always & euery
where so côstantly ascribed vnto S. Chrysostom, y̌ noman could bring in any alteration or change thereof. Furthermore all
y̌ haue writen any thing touching this Liturgie, and namely those Grecians which
haue writen expositions thereuppon, doe
all agree y̌ it is the same which S. Chrysostome appointed to be vsed.

And if yet you require more euident pro
se, Proclus who was Bishop of Constantinople not long after S. Chrysostome, &
was also by Nicephorus report sometyme
a yong scholer vnder him, witnesseth y̌ S.
Chrysostome traueyled in this matter, and
y̌ he after S. Iames & S. Basil brought in

Ni. li. 14.
cap. 38.
Proclus
in prefat.
Liturg.

L 3   to a

to a more cōpedius ordre those prayers &
ceremonies, which were before his tyme
vsed at ẙ administratiō of this holy Sacra
mēt. whereby it came to passe ẙ his Liturgie hath ben euer synce through out Grece
most cōmōli vsed. But becanse now a days
inē are much more ready to destroy & discre
dite, thā to build vp and belieue, allthough
there is not ẙ worst of these last proses, but
counterpaiseth & also ouerpaiseth far, that
surmised reprose before confuted, yet I wil
not cōtēt my self therwith. But I wil now
briefly proue vnto you out of S. Chrysost.
workes ẙ most of those prayers & ceremonies vsed to this day of ẙ Grecians. in this
Masse or Liturgie, were vsed also in his
tyme. whereby it must nedes appeare ẙ the
same was appointed either by S. Chrysostom or by his auncestours which for our
purpose to witnesse ẙ vse of the primitiue
Church is all one. And here you shall haue
all those ceremonies according to promise
set before your eyes, which I being presēt
in Uenice at this their Masse, either noted
presently or learned of them. wherefore I
besech you also note diligently how ẙ same
are vnlike ẙ orders vsed in our new ministers religiō. & thereafter iudge as i these so
m ẙ principall matter of ẙ blessed sacramēt
& in their whole faith, how far wide they
are frō ẙ primitiue Church, of which they
make so many vaine crakes.

To begin therefore wᵗ ẏ form of ẏ Church it self ẏ you may vnderstãd som other thigs hereafter ẏ better. The same is deuided prĩcipally into two parts as it was wõt to be wᵗ vs in Englãd: ẏ is to say into ẏ chaũcell & ẏ body of ẏ Church. Yet this oddes there is, ẏ their chaũcel is much lesse thẽ ours as made to serue only for ẏ Priest, and those which assist him at ẏ altar. For they which sing & answer ẏ Priest, doe stãd wout ẏ partition. The body of ẏ Church is according to ẏ order of ẏ peoples standing, to be subdiuided into three partes. The vppermost part next ẏ chaũcel is occupied on eche side of those which singe ẏ antymes, Psalmes, & hymnes, & may therefore well be called ẏ Quyre. In ẏ secõd or midle place ẏ cõmon people doth stãd. Last of all in ẏ third place al ẏ womẽ stãd together very deuoutly by thẽselues. And generally in ẏ Churches of Grece there is a partitiõ of bordes made betwixt ẏ mẽ & womã: so ẏ ẏ womẽ may loke out through latises only. And this custom appeareth manifestly to haue bene obserued in S. Chrysost. days & before also. For he hath in one of his sermõs these wordes. Men should truly be se parated from womẽ by the inward wall of the mynd, but seing you wil not so be separated, our forefathers haue thought good to separate you at the least by these wodden walles.

Hom. 74
in Math.

L 4   But

But to returne to the chauncel, you shal vnderstand, ý therewithin are two altars, one bigger & an other lesse, the bigger stan deth iust in the midst, & hath a faire brode dore answering vnto it in the midst of the partition which is betwene the chauncell and the body of the Church. And this altar serueth for the chief celebration of their Masse or Liturgie. The other lesser altar standeth on the north & left side of ý chaun cell. And hath also a lesser dore answering it in the partition, to come from thence straight into the body of the Church. And it serueth only for the Priest to prepare him selfe to Masse & for the bread & wine being prepared & made ready before Masse is be gon to stand thereupon, vntill the same be after the Ghospell solemnly brought from thence into ý midst of ý body of ý Church, & so t through the great dore vnto the highe altar, as you shal heare more plainly here after. Now it is worthy to be noted, ý al though ý high altar is most truly called of S, Chrysost. & others ý table of our Lord, yet both ý name altar is vsed also of him, & the thing it selfe made of stones, like those which are throwe down in Englãd, remai neth still amõgst ý Greciãs as it hath ben, receaued from ý primitiue Church. For be sides those places of S. Chrysostom before translated, where you shall find this word
altar

altar now, and then mentioned: what can
be more playner then that where he saith
on this wise, If a man should take fyre to
destroy this house (the Church) and should
digge vp this aultar, would not euery man
ouerwhelme him with stones as a prophane
and wycked man? By which wordes you
may plainly perceaue not only that there
were in S. Chrysostoms time aultars of
stone, far vnlike our Communion tables,
but also what a wycked & prophane thing
it was then counted to digge vp and ouerthrow aultars, as many haue doen in our
dayes and in our Countrie, to their great
shame & confusion. Especially for so much
as S. Chrysostom witnesseth in an other
place, that euen in his time aultars were
erected vnto God in our Jle of Brytanie.
If you aske me how these aultars of the
Grecians doe stande, therein they declare
also y the remoueable Communio table is
far vnlike the order of y primitiue Church.
for they stande alwayes after one sorte, as
our hygh aultars were wont to stand, at the
vpper end of the Chauncel toward y East,
so y y priest turning his face toward y altar
hath his backe alwayes toward the people.

There are moreouer in that partition
which is betwene the Chauncell and the
Quyre, many very faire painted Images
of Christ and our Ladie, together with di-

Hom. 53.
ad pop.
Antioch.

In demõ
strat. ad-
uers. gen
til. quòd
Christus
sit Deus.

uerse other, of S. Jhon Baptist, S. Nicolas, S. George. S. Spiridion &c. Many
denoute folke also both at their entring in
to the Church, and going out, doe come reuerently & kisse them. whereby J would
haue you note ƥ Images are not only vsed
of the Papistes of the latin Church nor by
ƥ ordonaunces of the Pope of Rome only
as some Protestantes imagin: but also of
those which these later yeres haue ben com
monly at variāce to the Bishope of Rome,
& therefore kept not these ceremonies for
his sake, but for ƥ they receaued them from
their owne aunciēt Fathers. And which is
more, they kepe images, in their Churches,
who had sometime the same controuersie
about images, which is now amōgst vs. for
thereby al Jmagebreakers are cōfounded,
& ƥ truth which in th'end alwayes preuay-
leth, is most euidently confirmed. whether
that ceremonie of kissing the images were
vsed in S. Chrysostoms time or no, it shall
not much skill. Of this once we are assured
that both in his time & before his time ima
ges were both kept of the Christians & reuerenced. for so Eusebius reporteth that the
images of our Sauiour Christ & of S. Peter & S. Paul were kept, in token of honor
dew vnto them & in tokē of Christen mens
loue towardes them. Nicephorus also witnesseth, that S. Luke the Euangelist made
himself

Euseb.li.
7.cap. 14
Niceph.li.
14.cap.2.

him selfe diuerse picturs of our blessed La=
die, of which some are yet extant to be sene
both in Rome and other places.

And as for the kissing of thē why should
that seme more absurde, than to kisse p̄ hād
or garment of any noble personage, when
he is saluted, or to kisse a letter, or booke,
and whatsoeuer els is deliuered him? Also
what superstition can be feared in shewing
this toke of reuerēce to the blessed Saints,
which we are sure are in heauen & do wish
vs wel,seing many without reprehension.
kisse & embrace the pictures of their tem=
porall frinds, whose soules lie perchaunce
amongst the wicked sprites in hell? And
that this kinde of reuer ence was lawfully
vsed in S. Chrysostomes time toward the
very bare stones of the Church,whiche are
nothing so lyuely a representation of any
good thing, as Images of Saints are,her=
ke I pray you how plainly it is proued by
his own words where he saith: See ye not
how some kisse the grises or entrance of p̄
Churche, some bowing down thereunto,
some touching them w̄ their hands & after
ward putting their hand to their mouth?
whiche manner is vsed of deuout folke to
this day throughout all Italie, when they
come nere any holy places,as to the tōbe of
any Sainte. For some kisse p̄ tombe it selfe,
some touche it only with their hande, and
after=

So P.
Martir in
Oxford
kyssed &
colled Bu
cers pi=
cture.

Hom. 30
in 2. Co.
"
"
"
"

afterward kiste their hande . And in like
sort doe the Grecians behaue them selues
toward the foozesayd Images. so that it ap
peareth manifestly the same is no superstitious ceremonie noz obserued of late only
but receaued frō their auncient forefathers.

Another Ceremonie vsed of them at
their first entrie in to ỹ Church much moze
generally than the former, (which will no
lesse mislike the Protestants) is, that euery
man cometh into the midle of the Church,
and there to shew himselfe not ashamed of
his Christianitie blesseth hiself thzee times
solemnly making thzee longe signes of the
crosse , from his head downwarde, & from
the right shoulder 'to the left. and therewithal he boweth his whole body in maner downe to the ground. which signe of
obeisance they vse commōly in stede of our
kneeling. And if it be demaunded whether
this crossing and blessing was vsed also in
S. Chrysostoms dayes, that is so euident
by sundzie places of his wozkes, that it appeareth al Christen men vsed it not only at
their coming to Church , but whensoeuer
they went about any good thinge oz ende-
nozed to repell any euill. I wil recite you
one notable sentence foz example, where he
warning men to auoyde all kinde of Soz-
cerie and wichcraft, and against all trobles
to vse this holy signe , hath these wozdes:

Art

Art thou a Christen man? vse the signe of
the Crosse. Say this only is my shilde and
buckler, this only is my medicine, I know
nonother. I might translate likewise out
of another place twentie lines together,
where he doth nothing els but commend
this holy signe, declarig how it was in his
time to the great glory of Christes religion
set vp in all places, as Churches, houses
streates, highwayes, vsed at all times, and
of al sortes of Christē men, for anoyding of
tediousnes, take these few wordes which
are as good as a hundred. All mē (saith he)
blesse them selues often with the signe of
the Crosse, making it vpon the most noble
andworthy parte of our body. for it is
dayly signed on our forehead as on a piller.

Hom. 8.
in Colos.

In demō
strat ad-
uers. gen
til. quód
Christus
sit Deus.

But to come at length to the Ceremonies vsed in the Liturgie it selfe : you shall
vnderstād first that the apparel which the
Priest weareth at the celebration therof, is
not much vnlike that which the Priestes
of the Latin Churche doe vse likewise at
Masse. when I was last present in Venice
at their seruice which was in ye yere of our
Lord 1564 on the first sonday after Ester
cōmonly called dominica in albis, ye priestes
vpper garment was of white taffety in
fashion somwhat like a cope, & vnder ye he
had a long vestimēt down to his feete very
like

Φελώνι
ου casula

Φορχάριον
tunica.
ἐπιροχχ κ
λιου stola
ἐπιμχνί-
κιχ
manipuli
ζώνη
cyngulú
ὑπογουνά
Τιου
fubgenia
le.

like that which we cal an Albe, sauing that
it was there of very faire sylke of diuerse
colours and most mengled w̄ redde. he had
vpon this vestmēt a very faire brode Stole
of y̆ same kind of silke, which hong about
his necke on ech side all most down to the
groond. Also on eche arme a Maniple
much shorter then the stole but of the very
same kid of silke. He had also a gyrdle wherewith the vnder vestiment was gyrded
vnto him, & therat there honge downe by a
strēg to his right knee, a square piece of the
former silke of diuerse colours, about two
hādes brode. y̆ which was lined & starched
in y̆ inner side wherby it was made somwhat stiffe. And this one thing semeth to be
peculiar to the Grecians, for I remēbre not
any such ceremonie vsed omōg the Latins.

But euery one of these which are vsed either of the Grekes or latins were ordained
as an ornament of y̆ high office which the
priest ther executeth, & to represēt mistically
some good thing. which is performed therby diuerse wayes. you may applie euery
particular thing to signifie some particular
vertue belonging to the priest him selfe,
who ought specially at those holy misteries
to be voyde of sinne and indued with holy
nesse: accordingly as the praiers & verses
which he saith at the puttinge on of those
robes doe particularly put him in minde.
You may also apply them no lesse aptly to

represent vnto you many particular thin=
ges which happened vnto Christ about his
passion. which must nedes be not the least
cause why they were instituted seing the
Sacrament it selfe was ordeined of Christ
to that end. As for example the vppermost
garmēt representeth that cloke wherewith
the souldiars mockt Christ whē they crou=
ned him with thorne, the next longe gar=
ment representeth that long robe wherein
he was sent backe ꝛ derision fromHerode.
ꝛ it is with the Greciās somtime of diuerse
colours to represēt it al spotted with blood
by reason y̌ his holy body wasbefore al to
torne ꝛ rent with whippes, the Maniples
about y̌ priests armes signifie those cordes
wherwith his innocēt handes were bound
both whē he was sent to Caiphas ꝛ when
he was tyed to be scourged. That lōg stole
about y̌ priests necke ꝛ y̌ gyrdle do signifie
y̌ other long cordes wherewith they drew
most villanoussyChristes whole body toge
ther ꝛ the crosse on his shoulders vnto the
hill of Caluarie. And y̌ last square piece of
sylke which(as I sayd)is peculiar to y̌ Gre=
cians hanging downe vpon y̌ priests right
thygh,representeth y̌ valiēt sword ꝛ myghty
power whereby Christ in this great bale=
nesse ꝛ humility of his death and passion,
triumphed ouer death and conquered the
deuill our great enemye, and therefore the
                                                        the

the Priesse who in this whole function representeth the person of Christe , when he
rieth that vnto his gyrdle saith very apte-
ly that verse of the Psalme , Accingere gla-
dio tuo super femur tuum potentissimè. Be
gyrded with thy sworde on thy thygh O
thou most mightie.

Now what honest man can pretend any
iust quarel against these so Godly represen-
tations, or against the vestiments whereby
so many good thinges are set forth both to
the eye and vnderstanding . If no Prince
cometh into parlament , no iudge sitteth in
iudgement , no maior mainteineth his
maioraltie, without maces, robes , longe
gownes, cappes of maintenāce & such like,
to represent secretely some politike vertues
which belong vnto them selues , & withall
to represent the great authority cōmitted to
them by God whose person in those offices they susteine: yea if the new named bisshops thēselues be not ashamed although
they lyue moste vnchastely, yet for ŷ names
sake to weare white rochets in token of pu
ritie of life whiche they should haue : what
reason is it that the Priesse who presenteth
Gods owne person in this most high function of al functiōs that are committed vnto men vpon earth, should not be adorned
also with comoely garments mete for the
same? Or if certein be alowed as the cope &
the

the surplesse, why may not many moe by the same raison be thought lawful, seing all were instituted of like sorte to one good intent and propose: that is to say to the glory and honor of God and to put the people in minde of good thinges: And concerning the antiquitie of the vse of these vestiments both amongst the Grekes and Latins, as the same might be proued diuerse wayes: so by that place of S. Chrysostome vpõ the xxvj. of S. Mathew which I haue noted vnto you before, it may euidently appeare that some such speciall apparell was worne of the priest in ȳ Church in his time.

Emongst other ceremonies which are vsed in the beginning of this Liturgie, one of the first is that the priest cometh frõ the high aultar vnto the great dore right before it & ther senseth the people, praying, that as the perfume by the heate of the fyre sendeth vp a swete sauour into the ayer, so through their feruent deuotion, both his & their praier may ascend & be acceptable in the sight of God. Afterward the Quire singeth many Godly Psalmes, Antines, versicles and respons while the priest standeth within at ȳ aultar saying to himself many praiers, a courtein being alwayes drawen ouer the chauncell dore, vntill those speciall times which I shall note vnto you hereafter in order, The priest also singeth out w a

         M   loud

loud voyce sundrie tymes, certain Colleets and other verses, wherunto the Quier answereth. then the epistle is readen in the body of the Church about the midst of that place which I sayd before may be called the Quire. After y̆ epistle, there are song a few other very swete Hymnes and versicles, & so to the Ghospell, at the reading whereof many torches are lighted, which were in this Church very faire and great, of white virgin waxe, set all in a rancke ouer the breadth of the Church before the partition of the chauncell. And hereat the courtein also of the great doze is drawen open. there solow immediatly after the Ghospel many goodly praiers emong which that is one which I haue before translated. and at this time as before also and afterward, al states & sortes of men as well liuing as departed out of this lyfe are prayed for. which thing is very agreable to y̆ which S. Chrysost. witnesseth to haue bẽ dõ in his time sayig.

Lib.6.de Sacerd. The priest as an ambassadeur or legate maketh intercessiõ and sueth vnto God for all the whole world, that he may remitte the synnes of all men not only which lyue, but also which are departed this lyfe.

After these praiers the priest (who in this place at Venice whẽ I was preset supplied also the rome of the deacõ, & therfore did all y̆ himself which S. Chrysost. assigneth vnto the deacõ) cometh forth solemnly out of the

lesser doꝛe answering as I sayd to the lesser
aultar wheron the bꝛead & wine was pꝛe=
pared, & holdeth vpon his head the chalice
couered together with the bꝛead and wine
hauing a towell of fine lawne about his
shoulders. I should haue told you first ẏ
against his coming foorth all the toꝛches
are lighted again the second time: and so he
cometh as it were in solemne pꝛocession in
to the midst of ẏ Quire & ther hauing made
alow obeissance towards the high aultar,
entreth in at ẏ great doꝛe (& setteth down ẏ
bꝛead & wyne w̄ great reuerēce vpon ẏ aul
tar. thē ẏ channcel doꝛes are closed vp accoꝛ
dingly as S. Chꝛysost. wꝛiteth in an home=
lie. Mysteria clausis ianuis celebramus, we
celebrate the mysteries the dores beīg shut. ┆ Hom. 24 in Math.
So ẏ they in ẏ Quire may heare only what
the pꝛiest saith when he singeth out, but not
see him vntill the doꝛes be opened again.

　　After shutting of the doꝛes the Crede is
song. after that the pꝛiest supplying here as
I sayd the Deacons place also, warneth ẏ
people to attend the holy mysteries w̄ these
woꝛdes: Stemus honeste cum timore &c.
Let vs stand soberly with feare and reue=
rēce. which woꝛdes I doe ẏ rather note be= ┆ Hom. 4. de Deĭ nat. & 2. in 2. Co.
cause S. Chꝛys. i an other place maketh mē
tiō of ẏ very same woꝛdes saying. Therfore
we are cōmāded to stād soberly at the tyme
of the diuine sacrifice to th'end we should

vp our cogitations, which as earthly crepe
low on the ground. The there folowe those
other admonitions which are vsed also in
the latin Church. Sursum teneamus corda,
let vs lift vp our hartes , whereunto the
Quire answereth, habemus ad dominū, we
haue thē lifted vp vnto our Lord. vnto that
succedeth the preface of thanks geuing,
whiche endeth in praysinge God together
with the Angels, the Cherubim, and Seraphim singing, Sanctus sanctus sanctus do
minus Deus Sabaoth. Holy holy holy Lord
God of Ostes. Of al which particulars S.
Chrysostome maketh in other places very
particular mētion. As for exāple in one ser
Hom. de   mon he hath these words. What doest thou
Euchar.   o man ? when the Priest saied vp with our
hartes & minds , didst not thou promise &
say vnto him, we haue them lifted vnto our
Lord? And in an other sermon he speaketh
Hom. 14   likewise of that holy Hymne , Sanctus san-
in epist.   ctus, &c. saying. Thinke to thēd thou maist
adEphe.   forgeue thy enemies what words thi mouth
hath spokē, what it toucheth & tasteth, what
fode it enioyeth , with whom thou standest
at the tyme of the misteries . With Cherubim, with Seraphim. The Seraphim do speke
ill of no man, but their mouthes are filled
with one custome & máner, that is to say of
praysing & glorifying God. how canst thou

s.v

say with thē holy holy holy, which doest ab
use thy mouth to disprasing and bakbiting?

Not long after foloweth the cōsecration
of the most blessed body & blood of Christ
which thing is brought passe (as you haue
often before heard) principally by ẏ mighty
and miraculously power of God, & seconda
rily by the ministerie of his holy priest pro-
nounceing ther those holy wordes of Christ
this is my body. to confirme which thing
you shal heare one plain place of S. Chrysostom which you haue not yet heard. his
wordes are these. It is not ẏ mā which
maketh the body & blood of Christ, but it is
that Christ which was crucified for vs. the
wordes are pronounced by the mouth of ẏ
priest, & the thinges proponed or set before,
are cōsecrated by ẏ vertue & grace of God.
for This (saith he) is my body : with this
worde the thinges set before vs are consecrated. And as that worde, wherby it was
sayd, Increase & multiplie & fylle the earth
was spoken once, but hath his effect euery
time that nature worketh to generation:
euen so ẏ worde also was spoken once but
geueth strength to this sacrifice through all
the tables or aultars of the Church euen to
this day & euē vntil ẏ coming of Christ.
After consecration the priest commendeth
again all sortes of men vnto the mercy of
God aswel the soules departed as ẏ liuing

Hom. 81
in Math.
"
"
"
"
"
"
"
"
"
"
"

　　M 3　　　　and in

and in this parte that praier is vsed one of which the cauilles before refuted are taken.

But becaufe prayer for the dead vfed in this Liturgie is one caufe why the Proteſtantes will not allow the fame to be S. Chryſoſtoms, I will alleage you one place moe for ỹ matter wherby it may plainly appeare that therfore the rather it is his, or at leaſt was lawfully vfed in his time. for he faith in two diuerfe homelies on this wife, It was not without caufe decreed by the Apoſtles that in the celebration of the reuerend myſteries, memorie ſhould be made of thofe which are departed this lyfe . they knew much commoditie ſhould be brought vnto them therby and much profite . for

„ whereas the whole people together with
„ the company of Prieſtes ſtãdeth holding vp
„ their handes vnto heauen, and the reuerẽd
„ ſacrifice is ſet before vs, how ſhould we
„ not appeaſe Gods wrath praying for thẽ?

So that by thefe wordes it is manifeſt that S. Chryſoſtom meaneth that very prayer wherin after confecration, when as the ſacrifice of the body and blood of Chriſt is vppon the auſtar, ſpecial mention is made of the departed.

Not long after foloweth the Pater noſter in maner euen as in the Latin Maſſe, And with in a litle while liſter that, the

great

Hom. 3. in epiſt. adPhi.& Ho.69. ad pop. Antioch.

great dore of the chancell which al this whi
le synce the crede stode shut is set wide open
and the courtenics are drawen, the torches
also are lighted and then the priest cometh
solemly to the chancel dore holding the
holy misteries together with the chalice as
high as his head and sheweth them to the
people to be adored of them, and to inuite
the to comunicate with him saying alowd
these wordes . Sancta Sanctis holy thinges
for the holy: wherunto they answere with
al tokens of adoration and reuerence, One
holy one Lord Iesus Christ in the glory of
god the father. The which very wordes to
haue bene vsed in S . Chrysostoms dayes
also, him selfe witnesseth in that Sermon
wher he saieth: when the priest sayeth holy
thinges for the holy , he meaneth this,
That if any man be not holy, he presume
not to come therunto.

Hom. 61.
ad pop.
Ant.

The shewing and Adoration of the
holy misteries are lykewyse by him in o=
ther diuerse places approued . The ado=
ration you haue harde alredy sufficiently
proued in that place vppon S . Paull
to the Corinthians. And as for the she=
wing therof vnto the people hearken vnto
these his playne wordes whyche are also
in the former Sermon . whyles the Sa=   "
crament is brought fourthe, and Christ   "
M 4   that

,, that is ſacrificed , & the lambe of our Lord:
,, when thou heareſt, let vs pray all in com-
,, munc, when thou ſeeſt the courteines dra-
,, wen back , then think heauen aboue to be
opened and the Angels to come downe.&

Hom. 36
in 1. Cor.

in an other place. Thinke who it is here
ẙ cometh forth and before his coming forth
thou wilt tremble & quake for feare . hear-
,, ken alſo to the third place where he chy-
deth thoſe in his ſermon which departed
out of ẙ Church before the Sacramēt was
,, ſhewed. it is thus. Whē I preach who am
,, your felow ſeruant, you apply al diligence
,, & wytt, one thruſteth an other that he may

Hom. 3.
de Dei
natura.

ſtand neare . when Chriſt himſelf who is
maſter & Lorde of vs all ſhall ſhew himſelf
in the holy myſteries , the Churche is left
voyd & deſolat. By which plain wordes he
,, rebuketh thoſe ẙ departed, out of ẙ Church
before the eleuatiō time, which is not immediatly after cōſecratiō, as in ẙ Latin Maſſe,
but neare the end a litle before the cōmuni-
on. whereunto the Prieſt hauing inuited
the people by thoſe wordes, holy thinges
for the holy , if any be diſpoſed , they receaue with him, but otherwiſe the prieſt receaueth alone, as it may appeare it happened ſundrie times in S. Chryſoſtoms own
dayes by ẙ he reproueth thē ſo often in his
ſermons for not preparing them ſelues.

And now it is moſt certain ẙ the Greciās
through

through lacke of deuotion in the people
haue on common Sondayes & Holydayes
as few communicating with them as the
Latins. For I was present at their seruice
from the beginnig to y end diuerse tymes,
and then I am sure none communicated
but the Priest alone. And therefore if that
be priuate Masse, the Grecians haue priuate Masse also. But they doe great wrōg
to the truth, who call any Masse priuate in
this respect. For it is called priuate only in
respect that it is doon priuately and not
solemnly. For otherwise the Greke worde
Liturgia proueth manifestly, that no Masse
may properly be called priuate seing it is
of it self in his own nature always, whersoeuer it be sayd or songe a publike functiō
and sacrifice. And the nature of a thing is
not wont to be changed by reason of any
circumstance. Neither is it called a Communion, because many receaue in one place
or at one tyme, but because he that receaueth that mysterie receaueth one thing vn
many, be they in tyme or place neuer so far
distant: and because he is thereby if he receaue it worthely most perfitely vnited vnto Christ in whom all true Christens are
one mysticall body, and therefore by receauing his naturall body doe most perfitely
communicate together.

　For otherwise if it be called Communiō

How the
Grecians
vse at
their Maſ
se sole re-
ceauing.

because three at the least receaue together in one place. J pray aske this question of those especially which together herewith doe defend that the euil man receaueth not at all by any meanes the body of Christ, what if of six persons which receaue toge-ther in one Church and at one tyme, fyue receaue vnworthely, is there any true Cō-munion or no? Jf there be a Communion then euery breakfast, dynner, and supper is likewise a Communion whersoeuer a like nombre is gathered together to eate and drinke. For euill men being without true faith doe by their owne doctrine receaue at the Communion no other thing then they doe at common meales. Again if it be a Communion then they all communicate together in some one thing. But that one thing by their doctrine is neither the reall body of Christ, nor the spirituall feeding thereon by faith: for so much as the vn-worthy receauers lacke the same. where-fore it remaineth that this one thing is the bread only, which they eat, and so the same absurditie foloweth, that likewise where-soeuer so many men eate bread together, there is a true Communion. And if it be no Communion then they must nedes cōfesse that the numbre receauing together at one tyme and in one place maketh not ý Com-munion: because they may haue all those

circum=

circumstances & yet not be sure of a Communion. For so much as they can not be
sure of so many worthy receauers which
may faithfully or by faith only according
to their doctrine communicat together.

But to returne againe from whence I
digressed, let it be inough for you to remembre, that the Grecians vse sole receauing also at their Masse, when as no
other be disposed to receaue with them.
And if you desire to know also what ceremonie is vsed when any of the lay people
receaueth: My fortune was to come into their Church one Sonday morning before their seruice was begoon, when as
one of the lay sorte receaued after this maner. He went to the Chauncell dore and
there stode very reuerently, bowing his
whole body towardes the ground, and attending for the Priest: who brought immediatly from the highe altar in a chalice,
parte of that which was consecrated the
Sonday before, and so with a litle spone
which had a Crosse at one end, deliuered
the Sacrament vnder both kyndes into
the parties mouth. which being receaued, the partie after humble and lowly o-
beissance, returned backe againe into his
place.

Now there is no doubt but a Protestāt
will triumphe here, & demaund, wherefore
the lay

the lay people of the Latin Church is not
suffered to receaue vnder both kindes like
wise: seing the Grecians receaued this cu=
stome of all lykelyhode from their forefa=
thers also. wherevnto I answere that as
the Catholikes denye not but both kindes
were in the old tyme commonly ministred
vnto most men: so they know right well
that some euen in the primitiue Church re=
ceaued vnder one kinde also, without any
derogation to Christes institution, as di=
nerse Hystories doe plainly witnesse. And
which is most of all, they know that the
Catholike Church hath supreme authori=
tie in earth, for to appoint the administra=
tion and vse of the Sacramentes: and that
by the same authoritie this order hath bene
taken of late yeres in the Latin Churche,
vppon many good considerations, & for
the auoyding of sundrie inconueniences.
Neither can the same mislike any Catho=
like who is assured y he hath lost nothing
therby, for so much as he belieueth y whole
substance of Christes true body and blood
to be not only vnder ech kinde, but vnder
euery portion and parte thereof, most per=
fitely conteined. But seing we are entred
so far into this matter, I pray make this
one demaund again vnto the Protestant
which misliketh this order. How it happe=
neth that they of his sect blame the Catho=
                                              likes

likes therefore, seing they them selues by
their own doctrine geue no moze than the
Catholikes doe. For know they not that
the Catholikes geue vnto the lay people
vnconsecrated wine also? And why should
not that be as good oz better than their
Communion table wine, if their doctrine
be true, that the wozdes of consecration
wozke nothing, and that the substance of
wine remayneth still vnchanged? Oz if
faith only doth all why may not one aswel
belieue and remembze the passion of Christ
by dzinking ÿ wine, as by dzinking theirs?
wherefore if they will speake against the
Catholike Church, for not ministring vn=
der both kindes, let them first belieue the
reall pzesence of Christes body and blood
vnder ech kinde, for otherwise they say no=
thing.

It is tyme now to make an end of the
Grecians Masse, and therefore to cōfound
the Protestantes yet in one point moze, let
vs conclude as the Grecians doe, calling
for help by the intercession of our blessed
Lady the mother of God, and of all other
good Saintes. which thing is vsed in S.
Chzysostoms Liturgie moze then once oz
twise, but for example take you this one
prayer which is vsed toward the later end
after the blessed Sacrament is receaued. Chry. in
It is thus. We rendre thee thankes o most Liturg.
                merci-

mercifull Lord and redemer of our soules, for that thou hast vouchsafed to make vs this present day partakers of thy heauenly and immortall mysteries. Direct thou our way. Kepe vs in thy feare, defend our lyfe, make sure our steppes through the prayers and intercession of the glorious mother of God, and perpetuall virgin Mary, and of all Saintes. And to confirme this kynde of prayer to be agreable to the doctrine of the same S. Chrysostom in other places, what can be in few wordes brought better for this purpose, then that where he sayeth: Dauid mortuus est, & merita eius vrgent. O rem mirabilem, ô ineffabilis clementia Dei, homo mortuus viuo patrocinatur. Dauid is dead, and yet his merites haue their force and strength. O wonderfull thing, o vnspeakable mercy of God. A dead man becometh patron for the liue. And in an other place talking of the persecutions which some of the Apostles suffered, he sayeth: Credimus iuuari nos illorum meritis. We beleue that we are holpen by their merites. So that there can be no doubt, but S. Chrysostome thought alwayes of the prayers & merites of Saintes departed this lyfe, as al Catholikes now doe.

And therefore now you haue not only my principall purpose concerning the reall presence,

Hom. 2.
in Ps. 50.

Ho. post
red. ab
exilio.

presence, diuerse wayes confirmed: but to
confirme you throughly in the whole Catholike faith, you haue a numbre of other
verities briefly proued. You haue his fond
cauilles and surmises who denied this Liturgie to be S. Chrysostoms perfitely refelled: and euery matter which is therein
of any weyght or controuersie witnessed
by other parts of his workes, to be agreable to his doctrine. You haue also by the
way many other Ceremonies declared,
which the Grecians vse to this day, as receaued not of the Pope of Rome, but from
their own fathers. Neither yet haue I told
you of holy bread, and holy water, which
they vse likewise, nor of the great differēce
which is betwene y learnedGreke wherein their seruice is song, and the vulgar
speach which only is vsed & vnderstode of
the commō people. I pray you note chiefly those which are so euidently proued to
haue bene deliuered them of S. Chrysostom together with his Liturgie, and
consider whether the order thereof agreeth more with the old
Masse or the new Com-
munion.

❧ Testimonies taken out of that which S. Cyrille, Bisshop of Alexandria hath writ= ten vppon the sixth of S. Ihon.

The viij. Chapiter.

YOu haue heard now the true Catho like beliefe cōcerning the blessed Sa= crament sufficiently proued out of ƴ holy and auncient Father S. Chry= sostom, and his doctrine also sufficiently cō firmed by the tradition and vse of ƴ Greke Church continuing vnto this day. Yet for so much as the holy Scripture sayeth all truth is perfitely tried by two or thre wit= **Math. 18** nesses, and to th'intent you may perceaue how well the auncient Doctors agree to= gether in this truth, and thereby through= ly persuade your selfe, laying a syde all sen= suall reason to sticke vnto the true Catho= like faith: I haue thought good not to con tent my self with S. Chrysostom alone, as I might haue don full wel, but to adioyne vnto him some other. And therefore now you shall first heare the verdit of an other auncient Grecian named S. Cyrille, who liuing immediatly after S. Chrysostoms days, doth not only him self confirme that which you haue bene already taught by S. Chrysostome, but declareth also the same faith to haue bene generally receaned in his days, as well in Alexandria in Aegipt where him selfe was Bisshop, as in Con= stantinople and other partes of the East where

where S. Chrysostom preached. Moreouer iudge your selfe what credit his wordes ought to haue, seing for his great learning he was in Celestinus y Bishop of Romes stede appointed President of that worthy generall Councell kept at Ephesus, one of those fower which the Protestantes them selues are forced to allow euen for antiquitie sake, and which also are of late yeres in our Actes of parlement, named and approued to be of good auctoritie. Hearken you therefore diligently what the Presidēt of that generall Council writeth vpon the sixth chapiter of S. Ihon, & in effect vpon the same wordes, wherevppon you haue heard already S. Chrysostoms exposition. The wordes of the Euangelist which moued S. Cyrille to write that which I shall translate vnto you are these. Then the lewes fell at variance amongst them selues Ioan. 6. saying: How can this man geue vs his flesh Cyril. li. to eate? wherevpon S. Cyrille writeth as 4 cap 13. here foloweth. in Ioan.

All things are plaine and euident vnto " those which (as the Scripture sayth) haue Prou. 8. found knowledge. But vnto fooles suche " things as are most easy seme darke and ob " scure. For the wise & discrete hearer stayeth " not vpon the vnderstanding of that he hea- " reth, but committeth al faithfully to his me " morie, and if any thing seemeth hard, by ᴄ

N diligent

„ diligent serching and often asking, he at=
„ teyneth to the knowledge thereof: folow=
„ ing very wel in that point y good hound,
„ which runneth vp and downe after his
„ game. And that the wise man is thus
„ affectioned , the Prophete witnesseth in
„ those wordes saying in the person of God:

Esaie 21. „ Seeke out diligently and dwell with me.
„ For we must allwayes so seeke, that we
„ dwell with him , and that we be not ca=
„ ried away with strange opinions. But
„ the malicious and wicked mind doth not
„ so. For whatsoeuer is not vnderstode,
„ he reiecteth straight way vppon a pride,
„ as vayne and false. Neither will he geue
„ place to any other , or thinke any thing
„ true , which is aboue his owne capaci=
„ tie. And suche we shall find the Jewes
„ in this place. For whereas they haning
„ now perceaued by those miraculous sig=
„ nes Christes diuine power , should of
„ right haue allowed that which he sayed,
„ and haue sought the solution afterward
„ if any thing had seemed difficile : they
„ clean contrariewise say : How can this
1. „ man geue vs his flesh? They crye out
„ blasphemously vppon God , not calling
„ to mind that with him nothing is vnpos=
1.Cor. 2. „ sible. For being (as S. Paule sayeth)
„ sensuall and carnall, they could not vn=
„ derstand spirituall things : but this great
mysterie

mysterie seemeth vnto them peeuishnes "
and foly. But let vs, I beseech you, take "
great profite of other mens synnes, and "
beleining stedfastly those mysteries, let vs "
neuer vtter with our mouth, or so much "
as thinke with our hart that same How. "
For it is a Iewish word, and deserueth "
extreme punishment. And Nicodemus "
therefore when he sayed: How may these "
things be brought to passe? was an- "
swered as he well was worthy: Art thou Ioan. 3.
a Master in Israell, and ignorant here- "
of? "

Seing therefore we are so well taught "
by other mens faultes, let vs not de- "
maunde when God worketh any thing, "
how, or which way, he doth it: but let "
vs leaue vnto him selfe the knowledge "
and way of his owne working. "

For euen as although no man know- "
eth what thing God is in his owne na- "
ture, yet a man is iustified by faith, when "
he beleiueth that God will reward all such "
as seeke him: so though a man knowe not "
the reason of Gods workes, yet when "
through faith he doubteth not but God is "
able to doe all thinges, he shall receaue "
for this good mind, no small rewardes. "
And y we should be of this mind our Lord "
him self exhorteth vs by the Prophet Esay. "
For my deuices be not as your deuices be, "

N 2   neither

Esai. 55. neither are my wayes suche as your wayes
,, are, sayth our Lord : but as the heauen is ex
,, alted from the earth, so are my wayes exal-
,, ted aboue your wayes, and my deuices a-
,, boue your deuices. He then who by his
,, Godhead so far excelleth in wisedom and
,, power , how can it be but he shall worke
,, so wonderfully , that the reason of his
,, workes , may easely escape our vnder-
,, standing and capacitie? Doest thou not
,, see what handy craftesmen often tymes
,, doe? Sometymes they tell vs thinges
,, incredible , and yet because we haue seen
,, them doe the like before , we easely be-
,, leue they can doe those thinges also. How
,, can it be therefore but that they deserue ex-
,, treme tormentes which so contemne all-
,, mighty God, the worker of all thinges,
,, that they dare in his workes say, how,
,, whereas they know him to be the geuer of
,, all wisedom , and whom the Scripture
,, hath taught vs , to be able to doe all
,, thinges?

2.   ,,   But now thou Jewe if thou wilt yet
,, crie out, and aske how , then will I imi-
,, tating this thy foolishnes, gladly aske of
,, thee , how thou camst out of Aegipte?
Exod. 4. How Moyses rodde was turned into a
,, serpent? How the hand strooken with a
,, lepre was in a moment restored to his
,, former state again? How the waters tur-
,,   ned

ned into the nature of blood? How thy
forefathers escaped through the midde seas
as though they had walked vppon drye
land? How the bitter waters were chan=
ged swete by the tree? How fountaines
of water flowed out of the stone? How
the running riuer of Jordan stode still?
How Jericho otherwise inuincible with
a bare noyse and clamour only fell to the
ground? There are innumerable things,
in whiche if thou aske how, thou must
nedes ouerthrow the Scripture, set at
naught the doctrine of the Prophetes, and
Moyses owne writings. Wherefore ye
Jewes ye should haue belieued Christ,
and if any thing seemed hard, haue de=
maunded him humbly, rather then like
drunken folke crie out: How can this man
geue vs his flesh? Doe ye not perceaue
that when ye say these thinges there ap=
peareth anon a great arrogance in ẙ word
it selfe?

Exod. 7.
Exod. 14
Exod. 15
Exod. 17
Iosue. 3.
Iosue. 6.
"
"
"
"
"
"
"
"
"
"
"
"
"
"
"

Hitherto S. Cyrille. In which dis=
course of his, I would wishe you to note
two thinges. First that in blaming the
Jewes for their incredulitie, he warneth
vs of the omnipotent power of God,
willing vs to be guyded by the beliefe
thereof as by a most sure stay vnto the
stedfast and true beliefe of these mysteries.
Which proueth that him self belieued some

1,

N 3   wonder=

wonderfull worke of God to be shewed
in them far exceding the common course of
nature. For els what neded the omnipotency of God to be called for to helpe the
beliuer thereof. As for example if there
be but a bare figure and remembraunce of
Christ as the Protestantes would haue it,
what thing were there to be merueiled or
wondered at? what nede the extraordinarie power of God to bring that to passe?
Doe not men when they goe into far countries, or depart out of this world, leaue
tokens and signes to their frindes to be
remembred of them also? wherefore you
must nedes conclude, that seing there is in
this blessed Sacramēt a miraculous worke
of God, belonging to his omnipotency,
there must nedes be much more than a naked figure. Secondarily note as I warned you before in S. Chrysostom, that the
Protestantes doe not only agree with the
Iewes in asking that Iewishe question
how, but also that if the Iewes were
then blameworthy, these men ought
now a thousand tymes more both to be
blamed and vtterly ashamed.

For besides that they beliue all those
miracles which S. Cyrille rekoneth vp
to confound the Iewes, what a numbre
is there of those which euery Christian
man beliueth, concerning Christ him
selfe,

selfe , which those Iewes neuer acknow-
ledged?

And therefore hereafter when you shall
heare any Protestantes aske those Iudai-
call questions , how the body of Christ
can be conteined vnder the forme of bread?
How one body of Christ can be in a thousand places at once? How it can be dayly eaten and neuer consumed? How ther
can be true flesh and blood seing the same
is neither seen , felt , nor tasted , with
a numbre of suche like : put vnto them a-
gain like interrogatories as S. Cyril putteth vnto the Iewe. And aske them how
one woman could be both a mother and a
virgin? How one litle babe could be both
God and man? How he which was before
all tyme could take his beginning of time?
And how he whom all the wyde world
was not able to comprehend, could lye closed forty weekes within the compasse of
a yong virgins wombe? Aske how Christ
being but twelue yeres old confounded the
auncient and learned Doctors? How he
fasted forty dayes without meat or drinke?
How he turned water into wine? How
he walked on the sea without drowning?
How the Sonne of God could be put to
death? And how the Sonne of man could
rise again from death? How he came forth
of y̆ sepulchre the same being closed fast vp?

By such howes as the Prote-stants vse al Christs religion many be called in doubt.

N 4   How

How he entred in amongst his Disciples, the dores being fast shutt? How man ascended vp to heauen, and sitteth in equall glorie with God? How pore fishers became sodenly great Doctors, and with their wordes and shadowes healed all diseases? How twelue poore men without any materiall sword or shilde ouercame all the world? And how so many Emperours, Kinges, and Princes without violence or compulsion haue embraced ỹ faith, which so much repugneth to all sense and reason?

Aske them last of all how those bodies, which are so many hundred yeres synce dead and rotten, some deuoured of wild beastes, some consumed with fyre, some cast into the bottome of the mayn sea, shall at the later day rise again with ỹ selfe same flesh, blood, and benes, which they had here on the earth? And when you shall finde that they can not by naturall reason answere to any of these questions, but be forced to allege the omnipotent power of God, then conclude with S. Cyrill that they shew them selues not only cupshotte & dronke by vsing that kind of questioning in this high miracle of ỹ blessed Sacramēt, which may as easely ouerthrow the whole Christē faith: but also ỹ those their demaūdes proced of a proud, lofty, & arrogāt spirit,
                                                which

which will not suffre them to submitt their natural reason in this one point to faith, & confesse herein the omnipotent power of God: wheras they must of force allow the same for a chief ground in al other marters of religion. There are many other thinges in this place of S. Cyrille worthy to be noted, which I leaue to your owne discretion and iudgement.

Now you shall heare an other chapter of the same S. Cyrill vppon the wordes of Christ which folow in S. Jhons Ghospel. Marke diligently I pray you how plainly he wryreth herein of the true presence of Christes true fleshe & blood in the blessed Sacrament, and considre withall whether as the other before, so these wordes which he speaketh here against the Jewes, and all misbelieuers concerning these mysteries, may not most truly be spoken in these our dayes, against the Protestantes. Christ his wordes folowing in the sirt of S. Jhon are these: Verely verely I say vnto you, onlesse ye eate the flesh of the sonne of man and drinke his blood, ye shall not haue lyfe in you: wherevpon S. Cyrille writeth on this wise.

❧ Christ is very mercifull and mild as the thinges them selues doe declare. for he answereth not here sharply to the Jewes stubbornesse, neither falleth at contention

Cyril. li. 4. ca. 14. in Ioan. "

N 5   with

,, with the. but endeuoreth to imprint againe
,, and again in their mindes the liuely know-
,, lege of this misterie. And as for how & in
,, what maner he shall geue them his flesh to
,, eate, that he teacheth them not, because they
,, were not able to vnderstand it. But how
,, great good they should gette if they eate it
,, with faith, that he declareth more then once
,, or twise : to the end they should be driuen
,, to faith, by the desire of life euerlasting, &
,, faith once hadde they should be then more
,, easy to be taught. For so Esay saith, for if
,, ye belieue not (saith he) neither shal ye vn-
Esaiæ 7. derstande. First therfore they should haue
,, fastened the rootes of faith in their mind,
,, & afterward aske those questions, meet for
,, men to aske. But they asked out of season
,, their importune questiōs befor they would
,, belieue:& therfor our Lord did not expound
,, how it might be doon, but exhorteth thē to
,, seeke it out by faith. So on the other side to
,, his disciples which belieued, he deliuered y
,, pieces of bread saying: Take and eate, this is
,, my body, he gaue about y chalice likewise
,, saying: drinke ye all of this, this is the cha-
,, lice of my blood which shal be shed for ma-
,, ny in the remission of sinnes. Here thou
,, seest y vnto thē which asked without faith
,, he opened not y maner of this mystery or
,, Sacramēt : but vnto them which belieued
,, he expounded it although they asked not.

Let

Let them herken herevnto which of "
pride and arrogance will not as yet re= "
ceaue the faith of Chꝛist. Onlesse ye eate "
(saith he) the flesh of the sonne of man "
and drinke his blood ye shall not haue "
lyfe in you. foꝛ they can not be sanctified "
and be made partakers of the heauenly "
lyfe, which by the misticall benediction oꝛ "
consecration haue not receaued Iesus. Foꝛ "
he is naturally true lyfe who is begotten "
of his liuing Father, and his body also "
geueth life euen no lesse. Foꝛ that is after "
an vnspeakable maner vnited vnto the "
Sonne of God by whom all thinges haue "
life.& therfoꝛe it is called his body & he is "
one with it. Foꝛ synce the incarnatiõ he is "
one, & continueth one without any diui= "
siõ,this only excepted ẙ ẙ woꝛd of god ẙ Fa= "
ther,& ẙ temple oꝛ body which ẙ woꝛd toke "
of ẙ virgin are not one in nature.Foꝛ man "
being assumpted to ẙ woꝛd of God is not "
of one substance oꝛ nature w it, & yet it is "
one therwith by an vnspeakable vnion. "
Seing therfoꝛe ẙ flesh of our sauiour ioy= "
ned vnto ẙ woꝛd of God which naturally "
is life,therby hath power to geue life vnto "
other: whẽ we eate that flesh then we haue "
life in vs, foꝛ somuch as we are ioyned "
vnto that which is made life. And foꝛ this "
cause in raysing, vp the dead to lyfe "
Chꝛist

2.

,, Christ did not only as God vse his word &
,, commaundment, but ioyned thervnto now
,, and then his flesh to worke together with
,, him: to declare in dede that his flesh be-
,, cause it was ioyned vnto him, had power
,, to geue life: and to teache the faithfull that
,, it was his owne and no other mans body.

,, For whē he raysed the Prince of the Sy-
Math. 9. nagogs daughter, He toke her by the hād
,, (as it is written) and lyfted her vp saying:
,, Mayd arise. so that God raysed her to life
,, by his word, and by the touch of his flesh,
,, shewing foorth one operation frō himselfe
,, one Christ both God and man. Likewise
Lucæ. 7. when he entred into the city called Naim
,, and a deade man was brought vnto him,
,, which was ỹ only begotten of his mother,
,, he touched the body saying: Yong mā I say
,, vnto the arise. And therfore it is euident (as
,, I sayd before) that he did not raise vp dead
,, men alwayes by his worde only, but by
,, touching thē also, to declare that his body
,, also was able to quicken and geue life. If
,, then by his touche only, thinges alredy
,, gone and perished, were restored to their
,, former state: how can it be but we shall liue
5. ,, which doe tast and eate that flesh? for he
,, shall geue throughly a new forme & shape
,, of his immortality to such as are parta-
,, kers of him. Neither doe thou here play
,, the Iew, and aske how this may be? but
remem-

remembre that water is naturally some=
what colde, yet by putting fyre thervnto, it
boyleth and leaseth his coldnesse. For euen
in like maner we although by the nature
of our owne flesh, we are corruptible and
mortal: yet by taking part of life we are
deliuered from that imbecillity and weak=
nesse, & are framed after a new sorte vnto
life, according to his propriety. for it was
very necessary that not only our soule by
meanes of the holy Ghoost should ascend
into euerlasting life, but also ỹ this grosse
and earthly body should be brought to im=
mortality by a tast, a touching, and a meate
like it selfe and of the same kinde.

Neither let the Iew thinke because of
the dulnesse of his own minde and vnder=
standing, that such mysteries are inuented
by vs as neuer were before heard of: for he
shal perceaue if he marke well that the selfe
same thing was by a figure don very often
in Moises time. for what deliuered their
forefathers from the fury of the Aegiptiãs,
when death raged vppon the firstbegotten
of Aegipt? Is it not well knowen vnto all
men that because they did, accordingly as
they were taught by Gods appointment,
eat the Lambes flesh, and anoynt the po=
stes of their dores with the blood, therfore
death auoyded them? for destruction, that
is to say the death of this flesh, raged

                                        against

4.

Exod. 12

,, agaïnst mankind for the transgression of
,, the first man. for by reason of sinne it was
Gen. 3. ,, then sayd vnto vs, earth thou art and to
,, earth thou shalt returne. But because Christ
,, should by his flesh ouerthrow this cruell
,, tyran therfore that mistery was geuen to
,, the old Fathers in a shadow or figure,
,, and they beinge sanctified by the flesh and
,, blood of a Lamb (because God would
,, haue it so)therby eschaped death. why art
,, thou therfore o Iew disquieted and tro-
i. ,, bled when thou seest now the verity and
,, truth which was before figured : why art
,, thou, I say, discomforted if Christ saieth,
,, onlesse ye eate the flesh of the sonne of man
,, and drinke his blood ye shall not haue lyfe
,, in you, whereas thou being instructed by
,, Moyses and taught sufficiently to belieue
,, by the old figures and shadowes, shouldest
,, of dewty haue ben most apte to vnderstand
,, these misteries?

S. Cyrill as in the place before alleaged, warned you by crediting the omnipotent power of God to detest all maner of
Iewishe and doubtfull questions in al his
workes, and consequently to belieue his
miraculous worke in the blessed Sacrament: so in this place he first teacheth you
i. that the way to come to the knowlege of
this truth and to haue all doutes dissolu-
ed, is to belieue first of all Christ his
wordes

wordes to be most true . For to this purpose he allegeth those wordes of the Prophet, onlesse ye belieue, ye shall not vnderstand. whereby it appereth how our Protestants alwayes like the faithlesse Iewes
must nedes be farre wyde from the truth.
For they cleane contrary to this rule first
goe about to discusse the matter by naturall reason, and afterward belieue no more
then their sense teacheth them. But I must
exhort you as S. Cyril doth, first to belieue
ỹ Christ is able to do whatsoeuer he saith,
and secondarily to credite those wordes,
which he speaketh, & namely these where
he saieth .   Onlesse ye eate the flesh of the
sonne of man and drinke his blood, ye shall
not haue life in you . whiche wordes that
they are ment of Christ his true and naturall fleshe , S. Cyrill doth not only constantly affirme : but also confirmeth and
proueth the same by a stronge argument.
For he saieth in effect this muche. the fleshe
of Christ being vnited & made one with the
person of his Godhed, hath power to geue
life vnto vs, by reason of ỹ Godhead. And
therefore to ỹ end our bodies should ryse at
the latter day to life euerlasting together
with our soules , he hath geuē vs his body
to eate in ỹ blessed Sacramēt by the vertue
wherof our bodies should be raysed to life
euen as our soules are through ỹ vertue &
grace

grace of the holy ghost raysed from sinne in this world & in the other which is to come vnto euerlasting blysse. And therefore after he had proued by the miracles at which Christ touched ý ded bodies ý his flesh hath power to geue lyfe, he concludeth that the same must nedes worke the like effect in vs who do not only touch it but receaue it in to our mouthes and eate it, wherby he meaneth not that we tast the qualities of flesh, but sheweth plainly that the substance of ý same flesh which touched the dead bodies doth passe really through ý sense of tasting and is no lesse truely present vnto the tast, then if it were tasted vnder his owne proper qualities & accidentes. For if we receaued not as truely in to our mouthes ý substance of his fleshe as it truely touched the princes Daughter, and the wydows sonne, how would it folow that our bodies much more shal therby be reuiued and made immortall?

Note furthermore that if accordinge to the Protestantes doctrin our soule only receaueth Christ his body by faith & spirite, so that our body receaue nothing besides bare bread, then they may conclud by . S. Cyrill, that our soule only also shall enioy euerlasting life, and that there shalbe at al no resurrection of the fleshe. For S. Cyrill saieth it is as necessary for the body & fleshe

of

of man to be fed with an immortall meate
like it selfe (which is no other besides the
flesh of Christ) by the vertue whereof it
may come into heauen, as for the soule to
be fed with the heauenly gyftes of the holy
Ghoost. In which place he vseth those
wordes again of tast, & touching, whereby
a real presence is alwayes confirmed. But
to shew more plainly, that the true resur=
rection of our fleshe dependeth vpon this
true eating of Christes fleshe, he saith in
another chapiter, that where Christ sayd
he that eateth my fleshe and drinketh my
blood hath life euerlasting, & I shall rayse
him vp in the last day: by saying, I shall
rayse him, he ment that his owne body
which should be eaten, should rayse him.
And it appeareth in dede by ye very wordes
of the Ghospell now recited, that Christ
ment by the vertue of this Sacrament to
rayse vp our bodies. For wherfore should
he adioyne vnto these wordes of eating his
fleshe, those other of raysing vs at the later
day, onlesse he ment that the one should be
in dede cause of the other? And therefore
I may worthely conclude with S. Cyrill,
that they which deny the receauing of his
true flesh into our bodies, doe in effect de=
ny the true resurrection of our fleshe and
bodies. But what will you say, if as their
whole doctrine tendeth vnto that & many
                    D   other

4.

Lib. 4.
cap. 15.
in Ioan.
"
"
"

other like absurdities (all which I trust shalbe through rotten before they be full ripe):so god of his goodnesse to warne vs thereof, hath suffered some of that sect by their opē factes and dedes to bewray this myschief before hand?

Villagagnon a worthy knight of Rodes writeth, that one Richerus a minister of Geneua , being sent of Caluin into the contries late founde out toward the west partes of the world(wher his fortune was then to be Gouerner)vnder pretence of cōuerting Infidels , sowed there together with his Sacramentary doctrine many other detestable heresies. Amongst which this was one,that the Resurrectiō should not perteyne properly to our fleshe and bodies: but vnto our soules only , & from thē should be deriued secōdarily vnto our bodies. And this he vsed as a meanes to cōfirme his other doctrine against ye Sacrament,saying that therefore it was not necessary, our bodies should receaue at all the flesh of Christ: because they had no nede thereby to be raysed,but our soules only.whereas the truth is,that the resurrection belōgeth in dede accordingly (as our Crede teacheth vs) moste properly of all to the fleshe: for that alone rotteth & perisheth,and therefore moste truely riseth again , where vnto it nedeth specially the

helps

helpe & vertue of the incorruptible fleshe
of Christ : whereby it may be made an
apt instrument again for the soule. But
the foresayed Richerus had besides this,
many other great heresies also : as that
Christes humanitie was not to be ado=
red , and that Christ should not come in
his owne person to iudge the world. all
which he did professe that he learned out of
Caluins writings. Now whether all Sa=
cramentaries will confesse likewise & de=
fend the same, I know not, let it be suffici=
ent to note by this one exaple, where vnto
theyr Sacramentary religion tendeth : &
how some of them haue openly professed
that foule absurditie of denying the resur=
rection of the fleshe, which by this auncie=
ent father S. Cyrill his iudgement is in ef=
fect plainely included in theyr whole doc=
trine.

You shall note farther in S . Cyrille   5.
for the profe of the reall presence, that place
towardes th'end, where he exhorteth the
Jew not to discredite this veritie, neyther
to thinke it strange: seing he hath bene al=
redie accustomed to the figure there of, in
eating the fleshe of the paschall Lambe. for
if S. Cyrille had thought hereof as the Sa=
cramentaries doe, he might haue vsed a far
more easy kinde of persuasion, and haue
sayd vnto the Jew, that it is a bare figure
D ij   only

only as that was in the old law, & therefore no cause to remayne why any of them shonld sticke thereat. But he telleth a cleane contrary tale, and putteth vs out of doubt that it is no bare figure but the trueth it selfe foresignified and presigured by the Paschall Lamb: which being true flesh & blood was a most liuely signe of Christes flesh torne, and his blood shed on the crosse for our sakes. And therefore seing this Sacrament conteineth the trueth presigured by that Lambes flesh, it must nedes folow that it conteineth the true flesh and blood of Christ. I would wishe you to note generally also in this whole discourse of S. Cyrille, that whereas he proueth, the flesh of Christ being ioyned in one person with his Godhead to haue power to quicken & gene life, thereby the true meaning is declared of those wordes of the Ghospell. The spirite is that which quikneth the flesh auayleth nothing: and the false glose also which the Sacramentaries make there vppon is confuted. For by S. Cyrille it appeareth plainly, that the worde flesh can not stande in that sentence for the flesh of Christ, seing the same auayleth very much and geueth life to the whole worlde : but must nedes be vnderstode of the Iewes grosse & fleshly vnderstanding. And therefore they are confounded which hereupon

doe

doe ground most wrongfully their heresie,
saying that hereby it is proued the reall
presence of Christes flesh in the Sacramēt
can nothing profit vs. But because the Sa
cramentaries make this one of the chiefe
places to proue their false doctrine, you
shall heare what S. Cyrille himself saith
particularly thereuppon. First to repete
again the words of the Ghospell, they are
these: The spirite is that which quickneth
the flesh auaileth nothing. Where vppon
S. Cyrill writeth on this wise.

Ye do not vnwisely deny (saith he) ỹ ỹ
flesh hath altogether power to quickē and
geue life. For if you take fleshe alone by it
selfe, it can nothing at all quicken, as the
which lacketh that which should quicken
it. But if you will search with such diligēce
as may be praysworthy, the mystery of the
incarnation, and will know him that dwel
leth in fleshe: although fleshe by it selfe be
able to doe nothing, yet then you will be=
leue that it is made able and of power to
quicken, onlesse you wil contend also, that
the holy ghost hath not power to quicken.
For whereas fleshe was ioyned with that
word which quickneth and geueth life, ther
by it was made also wholy of power to
quicken, and geue life. For it did not draw
vnto his corruptible nature the worde of
god which was ioyned vnto it, but it selfe

Cyril. li.
4.ca.23.
"
"
"
"
"
"
"
"
"
"
"
"
"
"
"
"
"
"

D iij　was

,, was lifted vp vnto the power of a better
,, nature. Although therefore the nature of
,, flesh as it is fleshe cannot quicken or geue
,, life, yet it worketh that now because it hath
,, receaued the whole operatiō of the worde.
,, For this body, the flesh whereof may som-
,, what auayle, is not the body of euery man.
,, For it is nether the bodye of Peter, nor of
,, Paule, nor of any such lyke: But the bodis
,, of the life it selfe & of our Sauiour Jesus

Coloss. 2 Christ, in whom ȳ fulnesse of the godhead
,, corporally dwelleth, is able to do this. For
,, if hony whereas it is naturally swete, ma-
,, keth those thinges swete with whiche it is
,, mengled, shal it not be very folish to think
,, ȳ the liuely & quickning nature of ȳ word
,, did not geue vnto that man in whome it
,, dwelleth power also to quicken and geue
,, life? For which causes the fleshe truly of al
,, other mē doth not auaile or profite in dede
,, any thing: but the fleshe of Christ alone is
,, able to quicken and geue life, because the
,, only begotten sonne of god dwelleth in it.
,, But he calleth him selfe the spirite because
,, god is a spirite accordingly as S. Paule

2.Cor. 3. saieth: Our lord is a spirite nor yet doe we
,, speake this as thoughe we thought the ho
,, ly ghost not to subsist in his own proper
,, person: but because as he being made man
,, calleth him selfe the sonne of man, so of his
,, owne proper spirite he nameth him self the
                                    spirite.

spirite. For his owne spirite is not, diuerse
or different from him selfe.

This far S Cyrill. by which exposition
of his, you maie easely iudge how far wide
they are from the truth who expound those
wordes as though it should nothing pro=
fite vs to eate the true real fleshe of Christ.
And as though Christ had signified therby
that the spirituall eating thereof by fayth
should only be sufficient. For S. Ciril tea=
cheth you plainly that by this word spirite
he ment the godhead which was vnited in
one person with that flesh of his, and whi=
che gaue vnto it that power to quicke and
geue life which no other mans fleshe euer
had. And therfore when he saied the fleshe
auaileth nothing he ment not of his owne
flesh but of that flesh which the Capharni=
tes imagined, that is to saie the common
corrupt flesh of man without any such spi=
rite or godhead vnited there vnto. For so
thei imagined, that thei shoulde haue his
flesh (whom they neither beleued nor tho=
ught to be true god, but a mere man only)
cut oute in pieces, and deuided amongst
them as other commen flesh is wont to be
ordered. To cal them from which fleshly,
grosse and sensuall imagination, he saied
vnto thē, that kind of flesh or that his flesh
so vnderstode, could profite them nothing.
But that it was the godhead dwellinge in

D iij   his

his fleshe whiche should cause his fleshe to
quicken them and geue them life. So that
to vnderstand his wordes truely, it was
necessary they should first beleue that he
was true God. For by that meane they
might easely come to vnderstand how his
flesh also, which should neuer be separable
from the Godhead, should being eaten together with the spirite quicken them, and
geue them life. And therefore S. Cyrill
least any man might thinke, because he attributeth this word spirite to the person
of Christ, that he confounded the person of
the holy Ghost with the person of Christ,
sheweth in the later end, that Christ in respect of his Godhead is truely called the
spirite no lesse thē the holy Ghost, without
any confusion at all of persons. For as
Christ is one in substance but separat in
person both from the Father and the holy
Ghost: so he is truly called the spirite also
diuersely in respect of his person, but after
one sort in respect of the nature & substance
of his Godhead. And thus the false exposition which the Protestantes make of
Christes wordes being by so auncient a
Father so plainly refelled, and thereby one
of the chiefe foundations of their Sacramentary doctrine proued weake & saury,
you haue good occasion to mystrust the
rest of al their building, seme it for the time
                                        vtwardly

brwardly neuer so gay and gorgeous, and
to repayre wholy to that one faith of the
Catholike Church, which is buylt vppon
so sure a rocke and perfite foundation that
it can neuer fayle.

❡ Testimonies out of the sermon, whiche S.
Cyprian made of the supper of our Lord.

The ix.
Chapiter.

Whereas you haue heard so ma=
ny plaine places out of those
two auncient Greke Fathers,
I suppose you longe to heare
somewhat out of the Latin Doctors also.
And therefore that you may the better vn=
derstand how throughly this truth is con=
firmed, and howe generally the same hath
bene alwaies allowed throughout al parts
of Christendom euen within the compasse
of those first six hundred yeres, whiche our
new Superintedents do pretend specially
to folow, you shall haue now some of those
places likewise at large sette before your
eyes, where they haue most largely writen
of this matter. And first I wil begin with
that most holy and most auncient Bishop
S. Cyprian, whose antiquitie is such that
he liued not only longe before the Latins,
whose testimonies shalbe hereafter trans=
lated: but also before the Grecians alredy
alleged. Moreouer of what authoritie he
hath bene continually for his holinesse, and

D ij　　　　hath

alwaies ought to be amōgst Christē folke, no man can doubt, seing he died for Christes sake a blessed Martyr, and therefore lyueth nowe without all doubt a glorious Saint with Christ in heauen.

His Martyrdom also was so famous & notable, that euen in S. Ambrose and S. Augustins daies a solemne feast was kept yerely in the Churche in memorie thereof, as it may appere by sermons made by thē both, on that day. And S. Augustine writing against the hereticall Donatistes of his tyme, wisheth expressely to be holpen by S. Cyprians good prayers. Of whiche as we haue in these miserable dayes muche more nede, so God graunt we may be also partakers. And as I doe wishe the same most hartely in translating these testimonies, so I wishe you most hartely in reading them to do the like, to thend you may better vnderstand that whiche is writen, & soner attain that comfort thereby, & stedefastnesse in true religion, which is þ chiefe scope of my writing. And now seing both þ authoritie & antiquitie of S. Cyprian is such as you haue heard, endeuour to pondre more diligently þ which he writeth in this principall matter, being assured þ by mantayning þ faith whiche he taught, you shall mantaine not only the faith of a blessed Martyr, but also such an auncient faith

as is

Ambros.
Serm. 72
Aug. epi.
120. cōt.
Donat.
li. 5. c. 17.

as is witnessed by him, who is more then
thretene hundred yeres olde. These his
testimonies whiche I shall here translate,
are taken out of that sermon, wherein he
preached opēly and of purpose that whiche
was the generall belief of the church in his
time concerning this matter: so that there=
fore also you haue so muche more cause to
weigh and consider ernestly, whether you
may not find in them many plain wordes
witnessing that reall presence, whiche the
Sacramentaries denie.

   If you desire to vnderstand also how
it is proued that S. Cyprian lyuing so
many hundred yeres since, made this ser=
mon: although tradition alone whereby
the same is deliuered vs in his name toge=
ther with the rest of his workes, be so suffi=
cient a profe thereof, that the Sacramen=
taries them selues dare not deny the same,
but rather seke al meanes possible to wrest
some of these his wordes to their purpose:
yet to thentēt you may hereby also be mo=
ued to geue more perfite attention, I will
recite you one sufficient testimonie out of
S. Augustin, whereby it may euidently ap
pere that euen in his dais this sermō was
attributed vnto S. Ciprian. For S. Augu=
stin writing of baptisme against the Dona=
tistes allegeth an authoritie of S. Cyprian
which is not only in sense but also in many
                                    wordes

wordes very agreeable to that whiche is found in this sermon. S.Augustins wordes are these. Baptismi sanè vicem aliquando implere passionem, de latrone illo cui non baptizato dictum est, Hodie mecum eris in Paradiso, non leue documentum idem beatus Cyprianus assumit. That suffering of death standeth somtimes in stede of baptime, the same blessed S. Cyprian (he had spoken much of him before) taketh no smal document and example of that theefe, to whome beinge not baptised it was saied: This daie thou shalt be with me in Paradise. Herken now to the wordes of S Cyprian in this sermon vpon whiche it may easely appeare S . Augustin alleged hys authoritie: S. Cyprians wordes are these. Ipse dominus noster derelictorum personã gerens in cruce se queritur derelictum, et ne desperarent etiam in vltimis constituti, festinans in adiutorium illico adest & re in arcto posita non differt beneficium sed repente indulgentię celeris documentũ eiusdem statuit & exemplum latroni inquiens: Hodie mecum eris in paradiso. Latrocinium damnationem meruerat & supplicium, sed cor contritum pœnam mutauit in martyriũ & sanguinem in baptismum. Our Lord him selfe susteining and representing on the crosse the person of the forsaken, complayneth

Li.4. cõtra Donatist.ca. 22.

Cypria. de cœna Domini.

neth that him selfe was forsake, & to thentent they whiche are in extremitie should not dispayre, he maketh hast out of hand to come and helpe, and when the matter is in great distresse, he differreth not his benefite, but geueth out of hand a document & exaple of his spedy mercy, saing to y thief: This day thou shalt be with me in paradise. Theft had deserued damnation and punishement, but a contrite harte changed punishement into martyrdome, and blood into baptisme. Thus you haue the authoritie both of this holy doctor him selfe, and of this very sermo of his, out of which the testimonies folowing are taken, sufficiëtly auouched by that other holy doctor S. Augustin. Read now that which he shal teach you with good discretion and diligence, & iudge afterward of the Sacramentary doctrine accordingly as you shall find it to be vnto his clean contrarie. The doctrine of S. Cyprian is as here foloweth.

The supper then being prepared, both old and newe ordinances met together at the Sacramentall and mysticall delicates, and the lambe being consumed, which the old tradition did set forth, our Master setteth before his disciples a meate which can not be consumed: neither is the people inuited now to sumpteous, costly and artificiall bankettes, but the foode of immortality

Cypr. de cœna
D
"
"
"
"
"
"

,, tality is geuen, which differeth from com=
,, mon meates, keping the outward forme of
2. ,, the corporall substance, but prouing and
,, declaring that there is present by an inui=
,, sible and secrete working the presence of a
Gen. 14. ,, diuine power. The mysteries which were
,, signified long before euen from the tyme of
,, Melchisedec, doe now come forth, and the
,, high Priest bringeth forth bread and wine
,, to the sonnes of Abraham doing the wor=
,, kes whiche he did.

,, This is (saieth he) my body. They did
,, eate and drinke of one bread accordinge to
3. ,, the visible forme, but before those wordes,
,, that common foode serued only to nourish
,, the body, and ministred the substance of
,, corporall lyfe. But synce it was said of our
,, Lord: Do this for the remembrance of me,
4. ,, this is my flesh, and this is my blood, howe
,, often soeuer that is done with these words
,, and this faith, this substanciall bread and
,, chalice being consecrated with the solemne
,, benediction, is profitable to the lyfe and
,, saluation of the whole man, beinge both a
,, medicine to cure infirmities, and a whole
,, burnt offering or perfite sacrifice to purge
,, iniquities. The difference also betwixt the
5. ,, spirituall and the corporall meate was de=
,, clared, that, that which was first set before
,, them and consumed was one thing, and
,, that whiche was afterwad by our Master
geuen

geuen and distributed was an otherthing.

So long as those meates whiche were prepared for the feast day, were receaued of the Apostles eating together, the memorie of the old passoeuer was kept, neither was Judas who belonged to the old lyfe, constrained as yet by the diuell inuading and possessing his mind to goe out : but so sone as his traiterous mind touched that sacred foode, & the sanctified bread entred into his wicked mouth, his cruel and myschieuous harte, being not able to abide the force of so great a Sacrament, was blowe away like chaffe from the floore, and he ran hedlonge to traison and bargening , to desperation and hanging.

There arose once a question (as we reade in the Ghospel of S. Jhon) vpon ŷ strangenesse of this word, and the hearers were astoined at the doctrine of this mysterie, when our Lord saied : Onlesse ye eate the flesh of the sonne of man & drink his blood ye shall not haue life in you. The which saying certain of them because they did not beleue neither could vnderstand, they wet backe away frome him : because it semed vnto them an horrible and wicked thing to eate mans flesh , imagining this to be spoken in suche sorte that they should be taughte to eate his fleshe sodden or rosted and cut in peeces : whereas the flesh of his

Ioan, 6.

persou

” perſō if it were diuided into peeces , coulo
” not ſuffiſe all mankind : which fleſh being
” once conſumed all religion might ſeeme
” vtterly to periſhe and be deſtroyed , for ſo
” muche as there ſhould remayne no more
” any ſacrifice for it . But in ſuche imagina-
” tions fleſhe and blood profiteth nothing,
” becauſe as our ſ̄ aſter him ſelf expounded,
” theſe words are ſpirit and lyfe, neither can
” the fleſhly ſenſe attain to the vnderſtāding
” of ſo profound a matter, onleſſe faith come
” thereunto.

” The bread is meate, the blood is lyfe,
” the fleſh is ſubſtance, the body is ẏ Church:
” the body, becauſe of the coming together
” of the members in one: bread, becauſe that
” is meet to nouriſhe : blood, becauſe that
” hath power to quicken and geue life: fleſh,
” becauſe of mans proper nature whiche he
” aſſumpted and toke vppon him . Chriſte
” calleth the Sacrament ſometymes his bo-
” dy, ſometymes fleſh and blood, ſometimes
” bread, as being the portion of lyfe euerlaſ-
” ting, which by theſe viſible thinges he hath
” cōmunicated to our corporal nature. This
” common bread being changed into fleſhe
” & blood procureth lyfe and increaſe to our
” bodies, and therfore the weakeneſſe of our
” faith being holpen by the cuſtomable effect
” of thinges, was taught by a ſenſible argu-
” ment that ẏ effect of eternal lyfe is in theſe
viſible

visible Sacraments, & that we are vnited "　9.
vnto Christ not so much by a corporall as "
by a spiritual trāsitiō or chāge. for he being "
both bread, fleshe, and blood, is made him "
self the meat, substance & life of his Church "
which he calleth his body, communicating "
the same vnto it . And we truly whereas "
we were flesh and blood, we could not haue "　10.
bene reformed in the corrupte and weake "
nature of our body and soule , neither re = "
turne vnto the liknesse of God , onlesse a "
conuenient plaister had bene laied to our "
old sore , and onlesse in healing such an in= "
firmitie which was past hope of recouery, "
contrary thinges had bene remoued with "
contrarie , and like thinges had agreed "
with like. "

This bread which our Lord reached forth "
to his disciples , being changed not in the "　11.
outward forme but in nature , was by the "
omnipotency of the word made fleshe: and "
as in the person of Christ his manhood was "
openly seen, and his Godhead laie priuie "　12.
and secret: euē so the diuine essence or sub= "
stance poureth it selfe after an vnspeakable "
maner in this visible Sacrament, to thend "
that the Sacramentes should be deuoutly "
reuerenced, and that men should come sin= "
cerely vnto the truth, the body whereof the "
Sacraments are, and that, euen to be par= "
takers of the spirite . Not that this vnitie "
　　　　　　P　　　　might

83.
,, might come to make vs conſubſtantiall
,, with Chriſt, but to bring vs to a moſt true
,, & perfite ſocietie with him. For the ſonne
,, only is conſubſtanciall with the Father,
,, neither may the ſubſtance of the Trinitie
,, poſſiblye be diuided or parted. But our
,, ioyning with Chriſt neither mēgleth per-
,, ſons nor vniteth ſubſtances, but ioyneth
,, and coopleth together affections & willes.
,, So the Church being made the body of
,, Chriſte obeyeth her head, and the hygher
,, light being ſpread vppon the inferiour
,, partes, reaching by the fulneſſe of his ſhy-
,, ning from one end to the other, abyding
,, whole in it ſelfe communicateth it ſelfe
,, whole vnto al, & the one ſelfe heat there-
,, of ſo aſſiſteth the body, that it departeth
,, not from the head.

,, This vnleuened bread, this true & ſyn-
,, cere foode through the vtwarde forme and
84.
,, Sacramēt ſanctifieth vs by touching, illu-
,, minateth vs by faith, and conformeth vs
,, by veritie and truth vnto Chriſt. And as
,, the common bread which we dayly eat is
,, the life of the body, ſo this ſuperſubſtan-
,, tial bread is the life of the ſoule and health
85.
,, of the minde. we eat the bread of Angels
,, vnder a Sacrament in earth, the ſelfe ſame
,, we ſhall eat more manifeſtly without a
,, Sacrament in heauen. not that we ſhall
,, there returne to the ſame thinges by corporal

porall ministerie, & often iterated actions, "
but our priesthode being consummat and "
ended, there shall be and remaine a perpe= "
tuall and stable fulnes euer fylling and re= "
freshing vs, whereby the presence of the "
hygh priest shal shew foorth it selfe openly "
vnto al me̅ without any kind of couering. "

The Sacraments truely so much as is " 16.
in them can not be without their propre "
vertue, neither dothe the diuine maiestie "
by any meanes absent it self from the my= "
steries. But although the Sacraments "
permit the̅ selues to be receaued and tou= "
ched of vnworthy perso̅s, yet they can not "
be partakers of the spirite, whose infide= "
litie and vnworthines gaynsaith so great "
a holynesse. And therefore these giftes are "
vnto some a sauour of life into life, and " 2. Cor. 3.
vnto other a sauour of death into death, "
because it is most agreeable with iustice y̅ "
y̅ despisers of grace should be depriued of "
so great a benefite & that in vnworthy per "
sons the puritie of so great grace should "
not make for it self any abode or tariance. "

The doctrine of this Sacrame̅t is new " 17.
the scholes of the Ghospell first brought "
foorth this instruction and Christ was the "
teacher by whom this learning was first "
knowen vnto the world, that Christe̅ men "
should drinke blood, the eating whereof "
the authoritie of the olde law doth most "

P ij straitly

" straitly forbid. For the law prohibeteth the
" eating of blood, the Ghospell commaun=
" deth it to be drunke. &

Thus you haue one part of the sermon
of that worthie martyr S. Cyrian, which
he made of purpose to vtter the Catolike
fayth that was beleued in his time concer=
ninge this matter. I wil not take vpon
me here to discusse euery hard sentence, or
to seeke out euery stronge argumēt which
may be made out of his wordes, but onely
I wyl note a few places (as I haue done
before) whereby your selfe may take oc=
casion to weigh them more depely, and by
your owne discretion find out other such
argumēts, as are made out of them. First
therefore you shall note, where he sayeth
euen in the beginninge, that after the Pa=
schal Lambe and vnleauened bread was
consumed : Christ did set before his disci=
ples a meate which can not be consumed.
by the sound & sense of which wordes, the
Sacramentaries figuratiue and weake
walles are euen at the first battered down
to the ground. For if this Sacrament dif=
fereth much in perfectiō from the Paschal
lambe, which was a perfite figure of Chri=
stes flesh torne and tormented on the cros=
se:then it must neades be much more then
a figure.

But if as S, Cyprian sayeth it be so far
disse=

different both from the lambe and the vn=
leauened bzeade: that whereas those two
substances were presently consumed, the
substance hereof can neuer be consumed:
it must folowe consequently, that the sub=
stance hereof is not bzead as it was in the
other: but some immoztall and incozrupti=
ble substance, that is to say, the true sub=
stance of the body & blode of Chzist. Foz so
this wozd incōsumptible argueth plain=
ly a difference in substance, as it may
euidently appeare by the common mea=
ning of that contrarie wozde, wherby it is
sayd that the lambe and the vnleauened
bzeade were consumed. Foz thereof what
other sense can any man make, but that the
substāces and natures of thē were who=
ly consumed, and not any quality oz acci=
dent only? wherfoze the substance like=
wise of that which is cōteyned in this ho=
ly Sacrament must neades be vnderstode
to be inconsumptible, and consequently
not to be the same substance which it was
befoze in the vnleauened bzead: but the
substance of the body of Chzist, which in
dede cannot be consumed.

And if you will haue the third argumēt
also, which may be made foz the reall pze=
sence out of this one sentēce, you may tru=
ly say with S. Cypzian, this inconsumpti=
ble meate was set befoze the disciples after

The sub=
stance of ꝗ
sacrament
is such as
can not be
consumed.

D iij   the

the eating of the Paschal lambe, ergo it was truly and really there on the table before them, and depended not vpon their fayth and beleife, as the Sacramentaries imagin. for otherwise it is not true that it was set before thē all seinge by that meanes it was not at all set before Judas the traytor, who neither thought nor beleued wel. But S. Cyprian telleth vs playn, that this inconsumptible meate was no lesse truly set on the table before the disciples at the latter course, than the lambe and vnleauened bread were set before thē at the former: and therfore as those were really and not by fayth only present, so must this also.

2.

S. Cyprian sayeth farther in the very next sentence, that here in this Sacramēt the foode of immortalitie is geuen which differeth frō other cōmon meates, wherby what other thinge doeth he, but confirme, this to be the inconsumptible and immortall flesh of Christ, which as S. Cyrill taught you before, shall bringe our flesh also vnto immortalitie? For by sayng that it differeth from common meates, he declareth plainly that it is not bread, seing the same is one of the most cōmon meates that man feedeth on. Also by sainge that it differeth, he must nedes meane a difference in the inward substance, as his

owne

owne wordes immediatly folowinge do
witnesse. For sayth he not, that the vtward
forme of the corporall substāce remayneth
still, and yet declareth that there is vnder
the same forme by an inuisible and secret
workinge the presence of a diuine power?
which wordes what other thinge can they
import, but that the inward substance of
bread is without change of the outward
forme miraculously changed into the true
body of Christ? for what other thinge can
the presence of a diuine power there signifie? if you wil say it may signifie the godhed of Christ, or the grace of god which is
present to the hartes of true beleuers: that
was also before consecration, and is alwayes present wythout any such speciall
workinge. But there (sayeth S. Cyprian) there, I say, euē in that sode, which kepeth still the outward forme of the corporall substance of bread, this diuine power
is present, and that after a far other maner then it is in other thinges. For it is
there by a secret workinge of y holy ghost.
which wordes declare a special new thing
there to be wrought.

    But let vs wade a litle farther and we   3.
shall find in most expresse wordes, both
what y is which is wrought, and by what
meanes it is brought to passe . Christ
sayeth he , sayed: This is my body, and by
        P iiij   saiinge

kainge those wordes and vsinge that so=
lemne benediction, he made of that which
was before common bread, and apt onely
to sede the body, a most perfite sacrifice to
purge sinne and iniquitie. Now what
other thing can this be, but that true body
of Christe which those wordes of consecra=
tion doe so playnly expresse vnto vs ? for
that body alone is the propitiatiō for our
sinnes, that bodie alone cureth all our in=
firmities. And therfore besydes that these

**The Sa=
crament
of Christ=
tes body
& blood is
a sacrifice
propitia=
torie.**

wordes doe manifestly proue the reall pre
sence of Christes body:they improue also
that error of the Sacramentaries which
cannot abyde to here this Sacramēt cal=
led a sacrifice propitiatorie. For here S.
Cyprian telleth you in playne termes ẏ
it is such a perfite sacrifice as purgeth all
sinne, and cureth all infirmities. which
thinge no sacrifice euer did nor can doe,
besides that only sacrifice of the body of
Christ, which was once only blodely offe=
red on the crosse, & in remembrance there=
of is dayly offered vnblodely vnder the
forme of bread vpon the altar.

He telleth you moreouer that Christ did
not only performe this him selfe at his last
supper by pronouncinge those solemne
wordes accordinge as Chrysostome hath
before taught you, but also that by saying:
Doe or make this for the remembrance
of me

of me: he gaue authoritie to his Apostles,
and to all priestes vsinge lawfully those
wordes to do the like. So y̸ when soeuer
those wordes are by his lawfull ministers to that end , and in that sayth of the
Catholike church pronounced , there can
be no doubte , but there is forthwith
wrought by the secret and omnipotent
power of god, the reall , and true presence
of Christes owne flesh and blood.

For farther proofe whereof it is much   **4.**
to be noted in this sentence, that S . Cyprian expoundinge in other wordes the
true meaninge of those sower, Hoc est cor
pus meum: this is my body , vseth in stead
of them, these other, Hæc est caro mea
this is my flesh : doinge vs therby to vnderstand y̸ Christ ment not to geue a spiri
tual, figuratiue , or fantasticall body , but
his most true and reall body which consisteth of flesh and blood . And the wordes
in latin beinge well scanned do confirme
the same most strongly. For y̸ article Hæc,
this, which must of necessitybe determined
by the substantine, caro, flesh, declareth y̸
substance which is present after the wordes of consecration to be the substance of
Christes flesh. For otherwise S . Cyprian
should rather haue vsed the article of the
neutre gender and haue sayd, hoc est caro,
or if he had ment the substance of bred to
                    P y   remaine,

remayne, hic est caro. The like argumente
may be made out of the very wordes of
the Gospel, hic est sanguis meus, this is
my blood. For there the article hic, this,
agreeth likewise necessarily with the sub-
stantiue sanguis, blood. But now one
English article This serueth with vs for al
Genders indifferently, and therefore can
not alone expresse the sense, which is expressed in latine. whereby you maie note also
what an absurd thig it is to require al my
steries of religion to be vttered in vulgar
tonges, seinge as this one example of our
English tonge sheweth, they are thereby
made commonly more darke and obscure,
because the phrase of the one is not able to
expresse that Emphasis & strength which
is in the phrase of the other. For that one
common English This is my flesh answereth both to hoc est caro mea and hæc est
caro mea, wheras in the latin ther is great
oddes. Yea so great that if the sense of hæc
est caro mea might be in English truly expressed, you should easely perceue that the
Sacramētaries can by no meanes pretend
any substauce of bread to be present in the
blessed sacrament. For thei can by no meanes truly resolue the article hæc to belong
to any other thinge then flesh, neither can
they by any meanes say therby, this bread
is my fleshe, whiche sense yet accordinge to
their

their doctrine they must needes make. But
in dede therby ý substance of bread is cleane
excluded, and S Cyprians iudgement con
cerninge the real presence of Christes flesh
most playnly declared.

Note also the sentence solowing where
he vseth in maner the same wordes, which
I noted in the beginninge. For here you
sind againe this difference to be made be=
twene bread the corporail sode of the body:
and this heauenly or spirituall sode of the
soule: that the one was consumed together
with the paschail lambe, this other cannot
be consumed, as the which consisteth of an
immortall and inconsumptible substance.
And therfore he sayth also, that this which
Christ set last before his disciples was an
other diuerse thinge from the former. And
wherein I pray you was it diuerse, if the
substance therof was not changed? For con
cerninge the outward forme, we are assu=
red it was al one with ý vnleuened bread.
He sayeth also that this diuerse thing was
geuen and distributed vnto the Disciples,
so that it cã not be sayd it was bread which
Christ gaue, or which he still geueth by
his ministers: But another diuerse thing
differinge wholy in substance from bread,
that is to say, his owne precious body and
blood, wherefore these substances are here
really present to be geuen and distributed
                                        vnder

vnder the formes of bread and wine & not
by fayth only to the minde of ÿ receuer, as
the Sacramentaries teach.

6.

The same is proued also more perfitely
not longe after, where it is sayed that this
sanctified bread & holy sacrament, entered
into the wicked mouth of Judas. for ther=
by it is euidēt, that the holines therof con=
sisteth in the very thinge it selfe whiche is
vnder the forme of bread, & not in ÿ minde
or beliefe of the receuer. For notwithstan=
dinge Judas minde was far from al good
belefe and so full of mischefe and treason,
that he could receaue no profite thereby,
but rather greate dāmage, because of hys
owne vnworthines, yet that sacred foode
and sanctified bread (saieth S Cyprian) en
tered into his wicked mouth, and by the
great force and vertu of the Sacrament his
wickednes was more confounded. But if
the vertu herof did consist in the faith only
of the receaner, then it shoulde neuer haue
wrought any thing with faithlesse Judas,
neither should it haue bene called holy or
sacred that entred into his wicked mouth.
Wherefore it appereth euidently, that the
holines consisteth in the thing it selfe how=
soeuer the receuer be affected : & so conse=
quently that it is not bare bread, but ÿ true
body of Christ.

7.

By the note folowinge you are directed
where

Euil men receue the true body of Christ.

where you haue in most plaine termes the grosse imagination of the Capharnites expounded, to confirme that whiche I haue writen alredy vpon S. Chrysostome and S. Cyrill. wherby it appereth also howe falsely they slaunder the Catholikes which call them Capharnites, as though because we beleue the true flesh of Christ to be present, therfore we imagined so grossely therof as they did, which loked to haue it in the same forme as they sawe it, and that sodde or rosted as they had other flesh. You maie note also that he saith according to ỹ grosse imagination of theirs, Christs flesh should presently and personally haue bene cut in to morsels and diuided emongest them, so ỹ it should haue bene consumed like other meates, & therwith also all religion should haue bene ended, as beinge without a due sacrifice which in al religion is necessarie. For by these wordes it plainly appeareth that the blessed Sacrament is in deede the true sacrifice of Christen religion, and that wheresoeuer this fayleth, all good religion is there foorthwith banished. He telleth you farther how those wordes, The flesh profiteth nothing, are to be expounded, and that carnal sense and reason, such as the Sacramentaries doe vse, can neuer attayne to the vnderstanding of these mysteries.

Note also a litle after that, howsoeuer ỹ Sacra-

Christes flesh in the sacrament is the true sacrifice of Christen religion.

Sacrament be called by ꝑ names of bread, flesh, body, or blood, it is alwayes to be vnderstand, that a porciō of eternall life is by the visible signes thereof communicated to our corporall nature. which wordes doe argue playnly that Christ (which is most truly the portion of euerlastig life) is there vnder those formes most truly present, and truly receaued, not ōly of our soule by faith but euen by the corporal mouthes and lippes of our bodies.

9.   It followeth in the next sentence likwise that the verie effect of eternal life is present in these visible Sacramētes, or vnder these visible formes of bread and wine. And that you may know how it is there, he saith our faith is taught that, by a sensible argumēt. That is, by the daylie experience we haue in the common bread and wine, which by eating and drinking are changed into our flesh and blood. which wordes what other thing can they signifie, but that we ought to beleue the bread and wine in these holie mysteries by the omnipotēt power of god to be no lesse trulie changed into Christes owne true flesh and blood, then the other common bread is changed into our owne flesh? And the end why the same great miracle is wrought, the wordes folowinge do shew. That is to the end we our selues should be changed into Christ and vnited

vnto

vnto him, not only by a corporal, but more
specially by a spiritual change. for so those
wordes of S. Cyprian doe sounde. for in
sainge not so much by ye one as by ye other,
he excludeth not the former but preferreth
ye later, which is in dede the chief, & without which (as I haue often tymes sayd)
ye corporal eating of Christes flesh nothing
at al auaileth. But the later being presup-
posed in such, as deuoutly and worthely
receaue this holy Sacrament, the former
transitiõ which is caused by corporall ioyning of Christes flesh vnto ours is proued by S. Cyprian his owne wordes immediatly folowinge, to be most conuenient
and most necessary.

For there he sayeth that the corrupt flesh   10.
and blood which we receaued from Adam,
could not haue bene reformed, onlesse such
a conuenient plaister had bene prouided
for ye sore, wherby contrarie thinges might
be remoued by contrarie thinges, and like
thinges haue agreed with like. wherfore
seinge by receauing Adams sinfull flesh of
our parentes we were all corrupt and made
bonde vnto death, it was most conuenient
that by receauinge in this holy Sacramẽt
the innocent flesh of Christ, that corruptiõ
should be perfitely remedied, and our bodies should be throughly made apt by
that cõtrarie medicine, to ryse againe from
death

death. And likewise as Adam by eating corporally and really that aple which was forbidden caused our flesh to be corruptible: so euery one of vs (hauing no necessarie or extraordinarie impediment to the contrarie) by eating in like maner corporally and really Christes flesh should be made immortal. For although both yonge infantes and other doe obteine this effect without that corporall eating, yet for the truthe of this doctrine whiche you haue heard before in S. Cyrill, & which is generally taught in ý old Fathers, it is enough to vnderstand that this corporall eating of Christes flesh vnder the forme of bread, is the ordinarie meanes whereby suche as haue no lawfull impediment allowed by the Church, are bound to seeke for this effect, which otherwise is supplied by Baptisme, as the effect of Baptisme is also in cases of necessitie supplied by a good will and feruent desire. And as it was sufficient for the fulfilling of those prophecies which were concerning the apparition of God in flesh, that some men liuing at that tyme and in those costes where he was borne, should with their bodily eyes see him, and so testifie the same vnto ý world: so it is sufficiēt here also, that such as may (by the ordenarie meanes appointed by ý Church) come vnto this holy Sacramēt, doe

doe bodily receaue therein vnder ý forme
of bread Christes most holy flesh into their
mouthes and bodies. And that all such do
actualip also performe the same , it is also
most requisite , seing Christ hath appoin=
ted this Sacrament as a most conuenient
meanes, to recouer perfitly all that which
was lost by Adam , and seing Baptisme &
all other Sacraments take their strength
hereof,as conteining within it Christ him
selfe most really present,so that all ý fruits
of his passion must nedes thereby most
perfitely be deriued vnto vs.

But if you will vnderstand throughly
howe that whiche hath the forme of bread
conteineth in deede within it the true flesh
and blood of Christe, note once for all that
one sentence,where S . Cyprian saieth so
plainely , that the bread whiche our Lorde
reached forth to his disciples,was changed
not in the outwad forme , but in nature or
substance , and was by the omnipotent po=
wer of God the worde made fleshe . What
man can deuise to expresse in wordes more
substantially and plainely that whiche the
catholike Church teacheth both cócerning
ttansubstantiation and the reall presence?
Saith he not the nature of bread was there
at the institution of this holy Sacrament
changed , although the outward forme re=
mained stil? And that by ý word nature he

II.
Transub=
stantiatió
& the reall
presence
most per=
fitely con=
firmed.

D meas

meaneth the inward substāce, the contrary
word effigie outward forme ioyned there=
unto most euidently proueth.

Doth he not tel you moreouer, wherin=
to it was changed? Saieth he not that the
bread was made flesh?and that you should
nothing doubt thereof, doth he not declare
by whō this great miracle was wrought?
Saieth he not that it was brought to passe
by the omnipotente power of that worde
which made all thinges of nothing? what
wordes are plaine , if these doe not moste
playnly witnesse the true Catholike faith?

But notwithstanding they are so plaine
and euident as you see, yet it is wonderful
howe litle they preuaile with those whiche
as it may appeare are of set purpose who=
ly bent to impunge the truth . For what

M. Iuell
in his re=
ply.
Art. 10.
Fol. 425.

shifte thinke you hath he, who would be
counted a chief Champion of the Sacra=
mentaries ,vsed in this place? forsooth
whereas he can picke out not one word in
the whole sentēce to make for him,he hath
endeuored to shift those last words (which
make so sore agaiſt him) with like phrases
picked out of other Doctors. For whereas
S. Cyprian saieth that breade,in this Sa=
crament was made fleshe: he to cast a mist

Aug. in
Ioā.trac.
21.

before the eyes of the simple,allegeth a like
phrase out of S. Augustin, where he saieth
that we by being members of Christe are
not

not only Christians, but are made Chri=
stes, because Christe him selfe saieth, that
whatsoeuer is done to one of those little
ones whiche are his members, the same is
done vnto him. And S. Leo saith that our
body is by baptisme made the flesh of him
that was crucified, because we are thereby
made members of Christe, and conformed
and made like vnto him. Nowe as man is
not changed into the nature of Christ, al=
though he be by those phrases of spech said
to be made Christe, so this worthy Cham=
pion would conclude that breade is not
ment here by S. Cyprian to be changed
into the true nature or substance of fleshe,
although he saieth that it was made flesh.
I may iustly cry out here and say. O most
miserable, wicked and abhominable shift.
For what can be more miserable then in a
matter of such importance to seke a refuge
of phrases, which are so vncertaine, and of
diuers men so diuersly vsed? Againe what
can be more wicked, then thereby to make
this holy Doctor S. Cyprian to be in one
sentence cleane contrary vnto him self? for
if bread is ment by S. Cyprian to be made
fleshe, none otherwise then a man by S.
Leo, and S. Augustin is ment to be made
Christ, howe are those wordes next before
without contradiction, where he saith that
the nature or substance of bread was chan=

Leo ser. 14 do Pass.

Q ij　　　　ged?

ged? or howe can this Phraser conclude at al by those phrases that bread is not ment here to be changed, being this change is by S. Cyprian so plainly expressed? But this kind of shifting is not only miserable and wicked: but of all other shiftes if it be well considered most vyle & abhominable. And therefore whereas the same is vsed of this Aduersary so often, I thought it necessary by this occasion, briefly to shew the absurditie thereof. For if suche shifting may be vsed in matters of diuiniti, what one truth is there in al Christen religion which may stand sure? might not he whiche vseth the same, disproue as wel by those very phrases before mentioned, the truth of Christes incarnation? may he not say likewise that God was made man, no otherwise then man is made Christe, because the phrases are like? You may gesse therefore to what narrow straytes the Sacramentaries are driuen, when they are forced to vse suche foule shiftes, whereby Antichrist may as easely proue his purpose as they theirs.

But let it be tolerable sometyme to argue vppon a like phrase, when the wordes ioyned to the phrases in both places shew no euident disagreing: yet is there no reason why he should haue sought phrases in S. Augustine and S. Leo to expound S. Cyprian. If he would nedes haue had a
like

like phrase, he should haue taken ẏ whiche
it appeareth S. Cyprian did in those wor=
des specially imitate, that is to say that
phrase of the Gospel where it is said: Ver- *Ioan.1.*
bum caro factum est, the worde was made
flesh. For vnto those wordes S. Cyprian
doth here plainly allude saying: Panis om-
nipotentia verbi factus est caro, the breade
by the omnipotēcy of the word was made
fleshe. He might also haue found another *Ioan.2.*
like phrase in the same Ghospell, where it
is saied: that water was made wine. But
none of those made for his purpose, because
they do both proue the true presence of the
thing whiche was made. And yet they doe
both agree far better with S. Cyprians
wordes then that phrase which he alleged.
For vnto the former S. Cyprians wordes
do plainly allude, and the later declareth a
change to haue bene made there of water
into wine, as the like is here expressed in S.
Cyprian of breade into fleshe. But those
other phrases haue smal likenes with S.
Cyprians words, and withal they imploy
a contrary sense by reason of that change
of nature, which is here by S. Cyprian so
plainly mentioned, whiche can not be in
those other phrases truely vnderstode. So
that if the argument of phrases be any
thing worth he hath for his two vnlike &
strang phrases out of S. Leo and S. Au-
　　　　Q iij　　　　　gustin

Iustine two most like and agreable phrases out of holy scripture it selfe , whiche doe most euidently make against him. For although God the worde being by nature immutable was not changed when he was made fleshe, and although the water kept not his former outwarde forme, when it was made wine : yet God was made true fleshe (that is to say , toke true flesh vpon him)and water was made true wine. And therefore in that point they do agree with that whiche S. Cyprian saieth is wrought in this Sacrament, and do confirme the truth of the real presence of Christes flesh which he saith here is made. But as like wordes being applied in a righte sense may somewhat confirme a truthe, so those phrases alleged to disproue here S. Cyprians true meaning doe in dede nothing els but detect the Iuglers falshode, and geue men to vnderstand what they ought to think of those other places where vpon he vseth other like trickes. For those wordes which go before in S. Cyprian making expresse mention of a change wrought in the inwarde substance of breade , and of the remayning still of the outward forme, doe euidently declare after what sorte S. Cyprian ment that bread was made flesh, that is to say, by the change of the nature thereof into the nature of fleshe without

any

any change of the outward forme. And so
likewise the circumstances of Christes incarnation and byrth expressed in the Gospel, doe declare howe God the worde was
made fleshe. And the circumstances of the
feast at the mariage doe expound vnto vs
how water was made wine. And this is ye
right way to finde out the true meaning
of phrases, and not by one phrase vsed in
one sense to draw all other like phrases to
the same sense, especially when as ye words
of those sentences where they are vsed, or
the circumstance of the matter, geue a clene
contrarie. Wherefore I trust you perceaue
now not only by the words of S. Cyprian
in this place: but also by the open shamefull shift, whereunto the Sacramentaries
are driuen by the plainenesse of them, how
strongly they witnesse vnto vs this vndoubted truth of Christes reall presence in
the blessed Sacrament.

To confirme which thing S. Cyprian
hauing vsed those words whereby ye bread
here is proued to be made fleshe, no lesse
truely then God him selfe was made flesh,
commethe immediatly to proue the same
by ye truth of the Godhead, declaring that
if Christes Godhead was truely present
vnder the couer of his flesh and manhood,
his true fleshe is truly also in this Sacrament vnder the couer and forme of bread.

12.

Q iiij So

So that if Christe was either true man or true God, his true fleshe by S. Cyprians verdict must nedes be here truely present, and they whiche deny the same, must consequently denie the true groundes of all Christen religion. For in the later part of this sentence, S. Cyprians words are euident that euen as in the person of Christe his manhod was openly seene, and vnder the same his Godhead lay hid and couered: so the diuine essence (that is to say, the true nature and substance of God) poureth it selfe after an vnspeakeable manner in this visible Sacrament, and lieth priuy vnder the visible formes of bread & wine. Nowe what Christen man (the blasphemouse Arrian and such like excepted) can denie but that the true nature of God was truely, really, and substancially present in the person of Christ vnder the forme and shape of his humanitie? whiche being graunted it foloweth necessarily by this similitude, y the same true nature together with y true flesh and blood of Christ (from which that nature is neuer separable) muste also be truely, reallie, & substantially present in this visible Sacrament. The which last words are likwise of no smal importance to proue the truth of the real presence. For thereby it euidētly appereth that y same diuine nature can not be saied to be present by grace only

only to the faith of the beliuers as the Sa=
cramentaries teache , but that it is present
in this visible Sacrament , that is to saie,
vnder the verie visible formes of bread &
wine . For fayth you wote well is not a
thing visible but an inuisible vertue which
consisteth in the minde and vnderstanding.
Wherefore by sayinge this visible Sacra=
ment , he meaneth those outwarde formes
which are seene and felt with our senses: &
so by affirming that the true nature of god
is miraculously vnder them, euen as the
Godhead of Christ laie couered vnder his
humanitie , he confirmeth moste strongly
that Christes true body and blood whiche
are not separable frome his Godhead, are
vnder the formes of bread and wine most
really and truly present.

But truly it is to be thought y if those
men which deny the real presence of Christ
in the blessed Sacrament had seene him
when he liued here in the world present in
fleshe , they would as sone then haue bene
perswaded with the Arrians to denie his
Godhead , as they are perswaded now to
denie here both his manhod and godhead.
For theyr carnall and grosse argumentes
do serue as wel for y one as for the other.
And if they discredite the truthe of his
body in the Sacrament , because they see
not flesh and blood in theyr own outward

formes, but vnder the formes of bread and
wine: how can it be but they would likewise haue discredited ý Godhead of Christ,
whiche appeared not in his owne proper
forme, but tooke vpon him, as S. Paule
witnesseth, the forme and shape of a seruãt
which was a great deale more vnlike and
vnequal to the true forme of God, then ý
formes of bread and wine are vnto the true
formes of flesh and blood. And therefore
it is muche to be feared least nowe also the
discrediting of this matter hath broughte
manie into a mase concerninge that other
of the Godhead, as I shal perchaunce haue
occasion to speake more hereafter by reasõ
of the Arrians heresie whiche agreeth so
well with the Sacramentarie doctrine. for
suerly they that beleue vnfaynedly that
Christe our Sauiour is true God, muste
needes be easely persuaded, that those his
words spoken at his last supper were fulfilled truly, and are to this day of sufficiẽt
power through his omnipotency to worke
all that which he then saied.

You may note againe in this sentence
wherefore Christ left vs in the Sacramẽt
so singular a treasure. For S. Cypriã saith,
the same was done to thentent we (knowing Christ him selfe to be there so truely
present) should come both vnto this and
other Sacramentes which depẽd al hereof more

of moze deuoutly . & so be instructed moste perfitely in all truth concerning good religion: foz so muche as the Sacramentes in whiche our religon chiefely consisteth are ỹ substance & bond of truth.The which to be in dede the true end and effect of this hygh treasure we maie learne also now by experience of the contrarie . Foz who seeth not that they whiche deny the presence of Chzist in this holy Sacrament haue lost therewith al good deuotion, and doe dayly wander moze and moze from that truth which is tought by the Church in ỹ other Sacramentes, and almost in al other matters of religion?

S. Cyprian saith also that the true receauing of this holy Sacrament causeth a most perfite society and vnity betwene Chzist and vs. which could not be onlesse Chzist were wholy and perfitely as well in his humanitie as Godhead, thereby cõmunicated vnto vs.& therefoze to preuent an obiection which might be made he excepteth one vnity which consisteth in that consubstantialitie oz vnity of substance which is betwixte Chzist and the other two persons of the blessed Trinity. Foz they are so vnited together in one substance, that they are equally one God and differ not in equality of substãce oz nature any one iote.But man although he receiue

The perfite vnitie whiche is by this sacrament caused betwene Chzist and vs.

in the Sacrament the true substance and nature of Christe, yet he is not thereby made one person with him no more then the childe is one perso with his mother of whose flesh and substance he is neuerthelesse truely partaker. For we in like sorte are made most truly partakers of Christes flesh receauing incorruption and immortality thereby, euen as it was sayd before that we receaued our corruptiõ of the flesh of Adam, the substãce whereof we receaue truly of our parẽtes, although we are not ioyned personally, nor made altogether one with them. And not only this effect of immortality, in the world to come ensueth of this vniting of Christes flesh vnto ours, but also we receaue presently meruelous comforte both of body & soule : so that the mind of ye worthy receauer is wholy ruled by god dwelling in it, & ye affectiõs & lustes of his flesh are wholy tamed and made to obey the mind, by the vertue of Christes flesh ioyned therevnto, euen as by the touche of Christes flesh the Leyre in the Ghospell was healed. But all tendeth chiefly to the vniting of our minds and willes vnto God as by whom the whole man ought chiefly to be ruled : and therefore S. Cyprian maketh chiefly mention of this societie which being wrought by so perfit an instrument as the flesh of Christ

ioy=

ioyned to our fleſh, is of all ſocieties (thoſe of Chriſt and the bleſſed Trinitie excepted) moſt perſite.

Neither can any heretike take iuſt occaſion hereof to maintaine the Sacramentarie doctrine, although ſome perchaunce will ſeme to take hold of thoſe wordes, where S. Cyprian ſaith, this vnitie is in ſpirit, and cauſeth our affections and willes to be ioyned together. For the ſame diſproueth nothing at all the reall preſence of Chriſtes fleſh and blood, but ſheweth that to be the chief end of ỹ other: it may proue alſo that as well his glorious fleſh is preſent to tame ỹ euell affections of our fleſhly nature, as the holy Godhead to rule ẽ direct our ſpirit and vnderſtanding. And that S. Cyprian meant not at all as they would haue him, to exclude thereby ỹ real preſence and reall knitting or (as S. Chryſoſtome ſayth before) mengling of his fleſh with ours, not only his euident wordes both before and after, but this whole ſentence, and this very obiection or exception of the conſubſtantialitie of the bleſſed Trinitie moſt euidently ſheweth. For why ſhould he miſtruſt leaſt any man might be deceaued in his wordes, and thinke thereby that man was alſo conſubſtantial with Chriſt, onleſſe he ment in thoſe wordes, ỹ man receaued in dede and really the true
ſubſtan-

ſubſtance of Chriſt? For otherwiſe if he
had ment all of faith and ſpirituall receauing only , there had bene no occaſion at
all why he needed to feare this obiection
more in this place,the in any other,where
any matter of faith is talked of. But wher
as he knew right wel that by this Sacrament the true ſubſtance of Chriſt is by a
ſpeciall and vnſpeakable meanes ioyned
and knit vnto our bodies & ſoules, therefore he thought it neceſſarie to ſignifie that
the ſame was yet after a far more vnſpeak
able maner ioyned in one with God the
Father and God the holy Ghoſt: declaring that with them it is ſo vnited ý they
three perſons are one equall God , but in
vs it vniteth not ſubſtáces ſo, that our ſub
ſtance ſhould be all one and equall with
his, but ý it conformeth our willes & affections to his will , and cauſeth vs to continew the children of God , by powring
moſt abundantly through his moſt reall &
royall preſence, his heauenly grace vpon
vs. And thus you ſee how thoſe wordes
which at ý firſt bluſh might ſeme to make
ſomewhat for the heretikes, being rightly
and truly vnderſtode and being conferred
altogether doe make moſt againſt them.

14.
    Now let vs ſee farther in S. Cyprian
what more places there be chiefly to be no
ted. He ſayth not lóg after that this vnleauened

nened bread this true and syncere foode il-
luminateth by faith, sanctifieth by touching
by meanes of the outward forme and Sacrament. where you may gather another
sufficient argument for the reall presence:
For so much as this holy Sacrament, as
it doth in faith and by faith geue a marue-
louse light & grace to our mind : so it doth
also in touchinge or by touchinge sanctifie
vs, through the visible forme and Sacrament. For thereby it appeareth that the
thing which is to our great comfort both
touched with our mouth, & beleued with
our hart, is present vnder that outward
forme, which we do there openly see: accordingly as he sayd before once or twise
that by these and in these visible thinges
eternall life is geuen vs.

It is worthie to be noted also in this
place, that the word Sacramēt is here taken for the outward forme. wherby it doth
euidently appeare whie the Eucharist is
called a Sacramēt, that is to say, because
the outwarde formes doe represent and
signifie vnto vs, these holy thinges which
are there cōtained vnder them. For where
as breade and wine are the common and
cheife thinges, wherby naturall sustenāce
is geuē to our bodies, therfore the formes
of bread and wine doe represent that liuely body & blood there truly present, wherby,

How the Eucharist is called truly a Sacrament & a signe.

by we are supernaturally nourished both in soule and body, vnto euerlastinge life. And as the true meaninge of this word Sacrament, is generally to signifie, after this sorte by some outward signe, an inward holy thinge: so hereby it appeareth manifestly also, after what sort the Eucharist is called a signe. ÿ is to say, in respect of the outward forme euen as it is called a Sacrament. And so their fondnesse is withall detected, who because it is a true Sacrament, would thereupon conclude that a signe or figure only of Christes body is present. for you see here that S. Cyprian calleth it a signe or Sacrament, not in respect of any truth absent, as they imagin, but in respect of ÿ outward forme which representeth and signifieth vnto vs that inward holy thinge, there most really present.

Neither yet doe the Catholikes denye, but there are many other good senses also wherby it may be called a signe or Sacrament, and that in respect of the body of Christ it selfe: but without any preiudice at all to the reall presence thereof. for so by reason of ÿ inuisible and mysticall beinge, which the body of Christ hath here, it is sometime called a signe and Sacrament or (as you haue before in S. Chrysostome) a pledge and toké of his visible death and
pas

passion, oz any other visible beinge of the
same body vpon the earth , and as it is
now in heauen. Neither doe any of these
true senses derogate any iote frō the reall
presence , moze then the settinge foozth of
plate vpon the Goldsmithes cubbozd , to
signifie that gold and siluer are there to be
solde, pzoneth the same plate to be no true
gold oz siluer. but as one cuppe of golde is
there a signe and token both of it selfe and
such like to be solde there, and yet is it selfe
true and reall gold also : so the body of
Chzist in the blessed Sacrament is a signe
and token of al maner beinge and sufferinge of the same body vpon the earth , it
is also a token of Chzistes speciall loue
toward vs, it is a tokē of his mystical bodie the Church: and all this nothwithstan-
dinge, it is most really his owne true and
natural bodie. But to answer that fond
argument of the Sacramētaries (whereof
they may seeme to haue obteined this no
lesse fond & foolish name) let it be enough
foz you to note specially in this place how
S. Cypzian applieth this wozd Sacramēt
to the holy Eucharist , in which sense both
he and other vse the same so often , that it
may wozthely appeare to be one of ẙ most
true and pzoper significations thereof.

For he sayeth euen within two oz thzee
lynes after, that we eate here on earth the
K   selfe,

selfe same bread of Angells vnder a Sacrament, which we shall eate more manifestly without a Sacrament in heauen: which place it is most euident that he taketh the word Sacrament as before , for the outward formes of bread and wine, vnder whiche we eate ỹ same Christ here, which we shal hereafter without any such strange formes or coueringes enioy together with the Angels to our endles comfort in heauē. And what can be sayed more playne then this, to witnesse also the reall presence: for in these wordes this only difference is made betwixt the enioying of Christ in the Sacrament and in heauen, that here we haue him present as it were vnder certayne courteins or coueringes by often iterated actions and dayly consecrations: there we shal see him openly face to face, without any cease or intermission. So that the differēce is only in the mance and circumstance of beinge, and not in the reall beinge it selfe. And therfore we may iustly conclude by S. Cyprian , that if Christ shalbe truly and really enioyed in heauē, then he is also truly and really present in the blessed Sacrament.

16.

The next sentence proueth manifestly ỹ which hath bene already sayd of Iudas and all euil men which receaue this holy Sacrament vnworthely, For the mysteries,
saith

(saith he)are all one and lacke not the pre=
sence of the maiestie of God how so euer
they be affected that receaue them. where=
vpon it foloweth lykewise necessarily that
the body of Christ is really present not to
the faith only of him that receneth worth=
ly, but euen in the Sacrament it selfe and
vnder that forme which is receaued.

   There foloweth in S. Cyprian a short   17.
discourse whereby another inuincible ar=
gument may be made to confirme this
truth. for he saith that the doctrine of this
Sacrament is new. and his reason is, be=
cause Christen men are taught thereby to
drinke blood which was straightly prohi=
bited in the old lawe. and after a few ly=
nes hauing declared vpon what occasion
blood was before time forbidden, he repe=
teth ẏ same sese agayn more plainly sayng
that here in this Sacrament of the new
testament Christ him selfe commaundeth
vs to drinke blood. Now I would gladly
learne how the most subtile Sacramenta=
rie of them all can auoyd the force of these
two arguments, which may be made out
of those wordes of S. Cyprian after this
sort. Christen men are commaunded by   An inuin=
the Gospell to drinke in this Sacrament   cible argu=
blood, which was forbidden the Iewes   ment for
in the olde law:but true, reall and mate=   the reall
riall blood only was forbidden in the old   presence.
             R ij   lawe,

lawe, & not spirituall or figuratiue blood:
ergo Christen men receaue in this Sacrament, true, reall and materiall blood, and
not figuratiue only & spirituall. The first
proposition is S. Cyprians, the seconde
is euident by the whole course of the old
testament, wherfore the conclusion must
neades be true. But the proterue Protestant will not so yeld, for then be should be
nomore a Protestant, & therfore although
he can not in dede possibly answer thervnto truly, yet if he be pressed therwith,
rather the say nothinge he will perchance
vse that comon distinction of theirs and
graunt, that we receue true blood, but by
fayth only and not really by our mouth &
lippes. where vnto, I replie againe out of
S. Cyprian on this wise. we receue blood
in the Sacrament after a new sort, and as
the same was forbidden to be receaned in
the old law, but that is no new maner to
receaue it spiritually by faith only, neither
was that forbidden in the old law but rather commanded, for al the Patriarches &
Prophetes dranke after y sort of the blood
of Christ, as both S. Paule and S. Augustine doe most manifestly withnesse.
wherefore we receaue it not here spiritually and by faith only, but truly, really, &
substantially, so y the same passeth through
our mouthes and lippes, euen as it was
forbid

1. Cor. 10
Aug. de
vtilit. pæ
nitentiæ
cap. 1.

forbidden to be eaten or dronke of the Iewes. Much more might be sayd if a man
would dilate this argumēt, but this much
suffiseth for him that hath any cōmon sense
or iudgement, to vnderstand what S. Cy
prian taught and beleued in this matter.
Now you shall heare a few moe of S. Cy
prians wordes in the same sermon. they
are as here foloweth.

This sacrifice is continuall, this
whole burnt offeringe enduereth for euer,
no multitude consumeth this bread, no
tyme can make it wax old. The howse of
the Church is one wherein the Lamb is
eaten, no man communicateth thereof
whom the nobilitie of the name of Israel
doth not commende. Manna which ray-
ned in ý desert was a figure of this bread,
so when men came to the true bread in the
land of promisse, that meate fayled. The
loues of the shew bread were wont to be
changed euery Sabboth, because they became colde and hard: and as many hote
ones were set on the table in their place.
Now there is no chāginge of bread, there
is one bread continually hote, and of one
perfite state, which beinge once offerred
vnto God, continueth alwayes in a most
sweete tast & a most pure withnesse. Neither are the presses only of the dignitie of
Leui by special priuilige admitted to these

R iij   loues

1.
Cypria.
de cœnæ
Domini.

2.

3.

" loues or this bread, the vniuersall Church
" is inuited to these delicates. Equall por=
" tion is geuē to al men. He is geuē whole,
" He being distributed is not dismembred,
" He is incorporated (vnto vs) & not miu=
" ried, he is receaued & not included, dwel=
" linge with the weake, he is not weakned,
" nor doth he disdayne the seruice and mini=
" stri of pore folke : A pure faith & syncere
" minde delyteth this dweller, neither dooth
" the straitnesse of our pore and simple co=
" tage, any whit offend or pinch the great=
" nesse of God who is infinite and all=
" mighty.

4.

2. S. Cyprian teacheth vs in these fewe
wordes, first that this sacrifice of the body
and blood of Christ is euerlastinge, & that
this perfect burnt offering endureth for
euer, that no multitude is able to consume
this bread, that no time can make it waxe
olde. By which wordes as you haue the
word sacrifice cōfirmed to belonge to this
Sacrament, whereby the reall presence is
alwaye proued : so you may vnderstand,
what both he and other holy wryters doe
meane when they call it by the name of
bread, and how folish their argument is,
which herof would cōclude that it is no=
thing but bare bread. for in that he saith, it
can not be consumed nor waxe old, he she=
weth that it is no materiall bread at all.

He

He saith moreouer that Manna was a figure of this bread. & shall we then think that the truth it selfe is no better or not so good as the figure? shall we imagin that the truth it selfe is but materiall bread, whereas the figure and shadowe thereof, far passed any bread that can be deuised by man? For doth not the scripture witnesse vnto vs that manna came from heauen, & had in it al kinde of pleasante tast & sweetnesse? doth not the same scripture tell vs also, that it was kept longe after with great reuerence in the Arke of God, for a speciall monument and relique? How can it be auoyded therefore, but that this holy Sacrament prefigured by that miraculous foode must nedes haue in it a more diuine and heauenly substance, then any materiall bread euer had? which beinge graunted, the reall presence of the diuine flesh of Christ is consequently cofirmed.

And that it is in dede no bread, although for the outward formes sake and for the generall signification of that worde it be often so called, many sentences folowinge together a litle after, doe proue most euidently. for many wordes therein are vsed which can neuer be verified but on Christ him selfe only. Haue you not there ÿ this bread once offered to God contineweth still a most pure and sweete sacrifice? and

B iiij　what

(margin: ꝛ.)

(margin: Sap. 16.)

(margin: Heb. 9.)

(margin: 3.)

what other thinge is that besides the true
body of our only sauiour Jesus Christ?
saith he not that equall portion is geuen
vnto all, and that euery man receaneth the
whol? signifeth he not in effect that Christ
is therein distributed, & yet one member,
is not diuided from the other? for how
can that worde dismembred be ment of ma
teriall bread? or how can it signifie any
other thing then Christ him self who hath
in dede al the members and partes of a na
turall body, and can not be dismembred?
Saith he not also that this heauely foode
is incorporate vnto vs, that is to say ioy
ned and vnited vnto our flesh and bodies?
and what truth then is in their assertion
which say we receaue the same by faith
only?

Sayeth he not also that the same is rece=
ned, but not included? & what other thinge
is that to say but that god himselfe is rece=
ned in this Sacrament, who is not subiect
to the boundes of any time or place. And
as those wordes are in that sense most tru
ly verified of Christes godhed:so they con
firme no lesse truly the real presence also of
his humane nature, which although it be
receaned vnder the forme of bread into our
bodies:yet it is not so included or shut vp,
either in our bodis or within the compasse
of that forme of bread : but that it is stil vi
sibly

sibly and in his proper forme in heauen.

But wil you heare what sense certayne M. Iuel
shamcles Sacramentaries make of them? in his re-
It is proued hereby (say they) that the Sa plie. ar. 3
crament ought not to be closed or shut vp tol. 413.
in any pixe. And so they allege them moste
impudently, against the reseruation of the
blessed Sacrament , which the church hath
alwaies vsed for the comfort of the sicke:
as though S. Cyprian who of all the doc- Serm. 5.
tors sheweth most playnely ÿ reseruation de lapsis
was in his time lawfully vsed , had ment
by those wordes non includitur , he is not
included, that the Sacrament ought not to
be kept. which fond interpretation , howe
far it is from this holy Doctors meaninge
your selfe I doubt not (hauinge the whole
place now lyinge before your eyes) do wel
perceue. For bothe the wordes before and
after. doe shew that S Cyprian speketh no
thing at all of reseruation, but that he de=
scribeth onely the maiestie of him who is
conteyned in this holy Sacrament . And
the very last wordes of this sentence wher
he saieth that god beinge infinite and almightie, is not pinched with the straytnes of
our pore cotage , do proue manifestly that
sense to be most true . But by what wrest=
inge can these wordes possibly make a-
gainst reseruation? He is receued (sayeth S
Cyprian) not included. If the latter part be

R v   longe

longe to kepinge in a pixe, then must the former belonge to the same also. For in such lyke sainges which are callid antitheta, the one parte must affirme that which ẙ other denieth. If then the sense of the latter part be, that the sacrament ought not to be shut vp in a pixe: the former must lykewise signifie, that it ought to be receued in a pix. And what good sense can any man then make hereof? is the sacramēt to be receued or put in a pixe, but not to be shut or closed fast vp? what man that hathe his common sense, wil make S. Cypzian to speke so foolishly? or how is reservation thereby then disproued? For if it may be put in a pixe, it may be reserued also althoug it be not shut vp. But let ẙ word Recipitur is receued, haue ẙ sense which the Sacramētarie hym selfe wil make. How will he wring out of non includitur, is not included, that the Sacrament ought not to be reserued? Fyrst if he construe the whole sentence rightly, he shall finde that Sacramentum is not the right nominatiue case to includitur, neither yet panis, as it signifieth bread: But rather Christus or Deus. For so bothe the sense and the words folowing doe plainly geue. But let that goe also: doth nō includitur signifie here, that, that which S. Cypzian speketh of ought not to be included? or rather doth it not signifie, that the sam
                                    is not

is not o2 can not be included? ffo2 so the wo2des both befo2e and after seeme rather to impo2t. As fo2 example the right sense of those wo2des is this, Ch2ist is distributed and geuen vnto sund2ie persons by means of this holy Sacrament, but he neither is no2 can be mangled o2 cut in pieces: he is also inco2po2ate vnto vs and receiued into our bodies, but he neither is no2 can be iniuried o2 w2ōged thereby: he dwelleth al so with the weake, and yet neither is no2 can be weakned. and after a like maner we must intep2et those other wo2des, $\tilde{y}$ Ch2ist is receiued, but neither is no2 can be included. in which sense they make nothing at all against reseruation, o2 els they must p2oue that the Sacrament is not o2 can not be reserued, both which experience teacheth to be most false.

But let vs consid2e well the wo2de in - cluditur it seife: doth includi signifie to be reserued? O2 is euery thing that is included therefo2e reserued there, where it is in cluded? O2 that which is not included is it therefo2e not reserued? the Sacrament it selfe being receaued into our bodies, is in= cluded within vs, but I suppose no man will say that it is therefo2e reserued as in a pixe. Again Ch2ist was reserued nine mo= netbes in the Uirgins wombe. He was also th2ee dayes and th2ee nights in the se= pulch2e

pulchre, yet it is true to say he was not in=
cluded in any of those places, because his
Godhead was neuerthelesse in heaue, and
in the whole world besydes. whereby it
appeareth that not to be included, & not to
be reserued, are not al one but two diuerse
things. The Church sayeth most truly of
the blessed Virgin, that Christ was recea=
ned within her wombe, whom the whole
world could not comprehend : and in like
sort S. Cyprian meaneth here, that he by
this holy Sacrament is receaued within
our bodies & soules who is in dede incom
prehensible, and can not be so included or
shut vp in any one place, but ẙ he is eue=
ry where besydes. Yea not only his God=
head is euery where, but his body is also
both visibly in heaue & inuisibly as in one
host, so in many thousands at the same
moment. So ẙ the being of Christes body
in many places at once after that sort as it
is in the Sacrament, or the being therof
visibly in heaven notwithstanding it is
here inuisibly, might wel haue bene gathe=
red of S. Cyprian his wordes. But
that the Sacrament ought not to be kept,
there is not one worde which soundeth
to that sēse. wherfore you may see to what
shifts they are driuen which vse such wre=
stinge, & what litle shame they haue which
so shamefully abuse the holy Doctors. and
so much

so much more lacke of shame and grace or rather abundaunce of malice appereth in him, who daring not to auouch this mat= ter in his owne name, hath yet of late al= leaged the same sentence to this purpose, euen since the falsehode of his fellowes vsed therin, hath bene by other catholikes detected.

M. Iuel as before.

But to returne againe to our principall matter, as emongst these sewe words of S. Cyprian a great many do plainely de= clare, that which is in the blessed Sacra= ment not to be materiall bread, but y true body of Christ: so I might translate a nu= ber of other like, both out of this sermon and other parts of his works, if I feared not least I should seme ouer long and te= deous. For in this very sermon besydes al that you haue already heard, he calleth this holy sacrament in one place, the singu= lar sacrifice which surmounting all sacrifi= ces recōcileth vs vnto God. which words cā not possibly be ment of any other thing then of the true body of Christ. And in an other place he sayth, that these mysteries conteine within them the summe of all my= steries. whereof what other sense can be made but that Christ him selfe who per= siceth all, is most persitely conteined euen within the compasse of y outward formes which we see and taste in these mysteries?

Thirdly

Thirdly he sayth ẏ our Lord euen to this day maketh, sanctifieth, blesseth, & diuideth to such as receaue deuoutly, hoc veracissimũ & sanctissimũ corpus suũ, this his most true & most holy body. whereby as it is cõfirmed ẏ Christ his real & true body is here made present : so they are also confounded which blaphemously report, that ẏ priests take vpon them to make God. for ẏ priest is but an instrument by whom God worketh this great miracle. And therefore as neither the husbãd man maketh the corne, nor he that setteth or graffeth trees, maketh the aples, although they are Gods instrument in that behalfe: so (if I may compare heauenly and earthely things together) the priest maketh not by his own power, this reall presence of Christs body, but it is our Lorde him selfe who is the principall and cheefe worker therein.

One thig more there is omitted of me in this sermõ, & that in the verie place before trãslated, which I should haue noted vnto you in the beginning of these laste notes: but now ẏ you may beare it better away, it shall not skill if you be warned thereof somewhat out of order toward the end. S. Cyprian saith there, that the house of the Churche is one wherein the lambe is eaten, and that no man ought to communicate thereof, whome the nobilitie of the name

name of Israell doth not commend. war=
ning vs thereby that none can receue this
holy Lamb of God in the blessed Sacramēt
to his comfort, onlesse he receue the same
in the vnity of the Catholike Church, that
is to say, after that sort and at those priests
handes, whiche this one Church hath ap=
poynted. also him selfe must be one of this
noble familie or houshold of Israell, and
muste truly beleue al that, which this one
Catholike Church teacheth as wel in this
matter it selfe as in al other. wherefore I
trust you also wil take your self hereby suf
ficiently warned, earnestly to seeke out, or
rather neuer to forsake that one Catholike
Church, which is euen by this one questiō
of the reall presence so euidently shewen
and set foorth before your eyes: I trust (I
say) you will wholy abstaine frome med=
ling with any cōmuniō rather thē receaue
at their hādes or after their maner, which
either by heresy or schime haue forsaken
this one house; & are departed out of this
noble familie.

For whether that which they deliuer be
truly consecrated, or whether it be bare
bread only, you must nedes be thereby in
great daunger of manie mischifes. If it be
the true communiō of the body and blood
of Christ, for that verie cause it is most hai=
nous in the sighte of God, to receaue so

How dan
gerous it
is to be
partaker
of any he=
reticall or
schismati=
cal com=
munion.

preciouse

precionse a treasure so rashely and vnad=
uisedly of them , who are out of all god
communion & societie. For the more wor=
thie the thinge is , the more is the offence
when the same is vnworthely and disor=
derly handled. but if for want of a lawfull
priest or some other like necessarie circum=
stance, no consecration at al is made, what
thing may be more greuouse, then so to de=
lude and mocke God:and to be in so high=e
a matter partaker of their doinges,who
are not only by heresie and schisme exclu=
ded from the companie of all faithfull, but
also do most vnlawfully presume, to coun=
terfeyte and falsifie the chefest misteries of
our redemption ? None are more straitlie
punished in al dominions where iustice or
policy taketh place , then such as counter=
feite the princes coine,and all such as wit=
tingely take part with the: whether those
coyners geue the true valew of the money
and offend only in doing it after some pri=
uate maner out of the vniforme coyninge
house, or whether they corrupe the valew
also geuing choper in steade of golde, and
lead or tinne in stead of siluer. And y same
reason taketh place vndoutedly before the
iust iudgement of God, in these holy mys=
teries , which being the true coine where=
by we muste purchase grace necessarie to
bring vs to that heauenly citie , can not be
                                    minis

ministred o2 receaued out of the vnitie of
y Catholike Church, without the perill of
euerlastinge death both vnto the mynister
and the receuer. Wherefore let S. Cyppiãs
woldes sticke wel in your memozie, and be
not partaker of this holy Sacrament out
of that one house, least otherwise of a most
wholsome medicine you make it by youre
owne defaulte a most perilous and deadly
poysone.

¶ Testimonies fo2 the reall p2esence out of
   S. Hilarie.

THus you haue heard somewhat out **The 10.**
of S. Cyp2ian, whereby you may **Chapiter.**
boldly say, that as by his death he
was a holy Marty2 and perfite wit
nesse against those Tyrantes which did
not acknowledge Ch2ist fo2 God: so by
his bookes and w2itings he is to this day
a perfite witnesse to the confusion of all
such as denie Ch2ist in the blessed Sacra=
ment. I will now ioyne vnto him that
other aunctient Bishop and holy Confes=
so2 S. Hilarie, who although he suffered
not Marty2dome actually, yet he endured
much troble fo2 Ch2istes sake, and had
many so2e conflictes with the heretikes of
his tyme, by whose p2ocurement he was
banished also out of his countrie y space of
foure yeres and mo2e whilest he was Bis=
        S   shop

shop of Poitiers in Fraunce. He flozished about the yeare of our Lord 37° at what tyme the Arrians heresie (which denyed Christ the sonne of God to be equall with God the Father) ouerflowed al Christendome a great deale moze, then the Lutherans oz Zuinglians secte hath yet done in our dayes, oz (I trust in God) euer shall. This holy Bishop fighting continuaily with all his might and learning against those pestilent Arrians , wrote in his banishment twelue bookes, which he intituled De Trinitate, that is to say, of the Trinitie. And in the eight booke a litle after the beginning, whereas the Arrians affirmed God the Sonne was not one to God the Father in substance but only in will, to dispzoue that their assertion he allegeth a text of Scripture where Christ prayeth y

Ioan. 17.
we all may be one with him, as he and his Father are one. But we (sayth S. Hilarie) by receauing Christes true body & blood in the blessed Sacrament , are not vnited to him in will only , but also to his flesh & substance: wherefoze it must nedes solow that Christ is vnited to his Father also by the nature and substance of his Godhead, and not by will only. which argument of his as it pzoueth euidently how the truth of the reall presence of Christ in the blessed Sacrament was then appzoued and receaued

ued of al men (for otherwise he would neuer haue vsed that reason against them,
which were so ready to catch hold of euery
litle aduantage:) so whereas in these our
miserable dayes the same truth is called in
question, and that heresie of the Arrians
generally condemned, we may iustly turne
the same with no lesse force vpon the Protestantes to the great shame of them al, &
say: we are one with Christ by receauing
him in the Sacrament as he is one with
his Father: but he is one with his Father
by nature and substance, wherefore we are
one likewise with him by receauing there
his nature and substance, and not by faith
only as they bable. But you shall heare
now S. Hilarie him selfe, who writeth on
this wise.

   I aske this question nowe of those
which bring in that vnity of will betwene
the father and the sonne, whether Christ be
in vs at this day by truth of nature, or by
concord & agreement of wil? For if ye word
was truly made flesh, and if we truely receaue that word (being made) fleshe, in the
meate of our lord: how shal he be thought
not to abide naturally in vs, who both be
ing borne man toke vnto him the nature of
our flesh, which can not be be separated, &
also mēgled or adioyned the nature of hys
fleshe to the nature of eternity vnder the

Hilar. li.
8. de tri-
nitat.
"
"
"
"
"
"
"
"
1.
"
"
"
"

S ij   Sa

>> Sacrament of flesh which is to be commu=
>> nicated of vs? For so we al are one, because
>> both the father is in Christ, and Christ is in
>> vs, whosoeuer therfore will deny ý father
>> to be naturally in Christ, let him first denie
>> either ý himselfe is not naturally in Christ,
>> or that Christ is not in him, forsomuch as
>> the father in Christ, & Christ in vs, causeth
>> vs to be one in the. If therfore Christ toke
>> vpon him truely the flesh of our body, and
>> ý man which was borne of Mary, be truly

2. >> Christ, if we also receue truli vnder a my=
>> stery the fleshe of his body, and shal by that
>> meanes be one with the father and him, be=
>> cause the father is in him, & he in vs: how
>> affirme they the vnity to be only in wyll,

3. >> wheras the naturall proprietie by the Sa=
>> crament, is the Sacramēt of perfite vnity.

>> We must not speak according to the sense
>> of men or of the worlde, in matters be=
>> longing to god, neither may we by a vio=
>> lent and shamlesse exposition of heauenly
>> thinges, wrest out peruersly a wicked mea
>> ning clean contrary to the trueth. Let vs
>> reade the thinges which are writen and lee
>> vs vnderstād aright that which we reade,
>> and so we shall accomplishe the duty of per
>> fite faith. For that which we now say con=
>> cerning the naturalle veritie and true be=
>> ing of Christ in vs, onlesse we learne it of
>> hym, we speake folishly and wickedly. For
>> he

he him selfe saith: My flesh is verely meat "

and my blood is verely drinke. he that ea= "

teth my flesh and drinketh my blood abi= "

deth in me, and I in him. Of the trueth and "   4.

veritie of his fleshe and blood, there is no "

place left for any man to doubt: For nowe "

both oure lorde himself openly declareth, "

and we perfitely doe belieue, that it is tru= "

ly his flesh and truely his blood, and these "

being receiued and dronke bring that to "

passe, both that we be in Christ, & he in vs. "

Is not this the truth? It may happen tru= "   5.

ly that to them it is not true, which denye "

Iesus Christ to be true god. He is the him "

selfe in vs by flesh, and we are in him, whi "

lest that which we are, is with him in god. "

But that we are in him by the Sacrament "

of fleshe and blood communicated of vs, "

he hym self witnesseth, sayinge : And thys Ioan. 6.

worlde now seeth me not, but you shal see "

me: because I lyue, you also shall lyue : be- "

cause I am in my father & you in me, & I in "

you. If he would haue an vnity of wyl on "

ly to be vnderstode, why declared he a cer= "

tain degree and order of makinge perfite "

that vnity: but only, that whereas he is in "

the father by the nature of his diuinitie and "

godhed, it should be belieued, that we are "

on the other side in him, by his corporall "

natiuity, and he likewise in vs by the my= "   6.

stery of Sacramentes? And that after thys "

S iij   sort

,, sorte a perfite vnity should be taught by a
,, mediator, whereas we abiding in him he
,, should abide in his father, and abiding in
,, his father should abide also in vs: and so
,, we should goe forward to the vnity of the
,, father, for so muche as we are naturally in
,, him, and he naturally dwelleth in vs, who
,, is accordinge to his byrth naturally in his
,, father.

7. But that this naturall vnity is in vs, he
,, himself hath testified by these wordes. who
,, so eateth my flesh and drinketh my blood,
,, abideth in me and I in him. For no man
,, shalbe in him, but he in whom himself aby
,, deth, hauig assumpted in himselfe y flesh of
,, him only who shal take & receaue his flesh,
,, Now he taught before, the Sacrament or
,, mysterie of this perfite vnity, saying: As
Ioan.6. the lyuing father sent me and I lyue for the
,, father, so he that shall eate my flesh he him
,, self shal lyue also by me. He therefore liueth
,, by his father, and looke in what maner he
,, lyueth by his father, after the same maner
,, we shal liue by his flesh. For euery compa=
,, rison or similitude is taken and put foorth
,, to informe our vnderstanding, & to make
,, vs conceaue the matter which is treated,
,, according to the example that is propoun=
,, ded. Now this is the cause of our life, that
,, we which doe consist of flesh haue Christe
,, by fleshe abyding in vs : who shall lyue
by

by him in the same sorte , as he lyueth by "
his Father . If therefore we lyue by him " **8.**
naturally according to flesh , that is to sai, "
hauing receaued the nature of his fleshe, "
how can it be chosen but he must haue his "
Father in him selfe naturally according to "
the spirite or Godhead , whereas him selfe "
liueth by his Father. But he lyueth by his "
Father, whiles that, his natiuitie brought "
not vnto him anie strange or diuerse na- "
ture, whiles that, concerning his being, he "
both is of him , neither is separed by anie "
accidental vnlikenes of nature from him, "
whiles that , he hath his Father in him "
selfe by natiuitie in vertue of nature. "

And this muche hath bene saied of vs "
for that ye lying heretikes falsly affirming "
an vnity of will only betwene the Father "
and the sonne, vsed for proufe thereof the "
example of that vnitie whiche is betwixte "
God and vs : as though we were vnited "
to God the sonne , & by the sonne to God " **9.**
the Father by obedience only and will of "
deuotion , and no natural propriety of cō- "
munion were graunted vnto vs by the "
Sacrament of flesh and blood: whereas in "
dede the mysterie of true and natural vni- "
ty is to be declared and preached by the "
honour geuen vs of God the sonne , and "
by that the Sonne dwelleth and abideth "
in vs carnally, we being corporally & vnse "

,, perably vnited & made one in him.

    This far S. Hilarie: who if he seem vnto you somwhat darke and obscure, merueile not, for somuch as he talketh of that hygh and incomprehensible mysterie of the blessed Trinity, which neither wit ca worthely conceaue, nor words by anie means plainly expresse. neuerthelesse as I doubt not but you perceaue, y his whole drifte is to proue those two persons, God the Father, & God the Sonne, to be one in nature and substance, and not in wil only, as the Arrians blasphemousl y taught: so you vnderstand wel enough also, how plainlie he both teacheth and proueth that we are made one likewise in Christ, by receauing in the blessed Sacrament the true naturail fleshe, and substance of his body: and not by receauing the same by consent of minde and faith only, as the Protestätes wickedly affirme. And as we muste not discredite that former part with the Arrians, because we can not possibely by naturail reason comprehend it, so neither should we doubt of this later parte with y Sacramētaries, repugne it neuer so muche to our sense and reason: specially whereas that other truth dependeth here in S. Hilarie after a sorte of this. Truly there is matter inough ministred here by S. Hilarie to make a large volume, not only for the authoritie of the man

man, whiche is great amongesse all men
that make any account at all of auncient
writers: but much more for the stronge ar=
gument whiche he groundeth so substan=
tially vpon holy scripture, that no heretike
can possibly auoide the force therof, onlesse
he will vtterly denie both partes, as wel
that of the Godhead of Christe, as of his
true flesh in the Sacrament: which thinge
neither the Arrian did, nor the Sacramen=
tarie doth yet opely professe. For he grau=
ted that of the Sacrament, although he de=
nied the other, and these men of our dayes
graunt that other, and denie only as yet
the truth of the Sacrament. but I feare me
they are in hart shrewdly bent to the Arri=
ans side also, as it maie somwhat appeare
by that manie of the Sacramentaries in
our owne contrie, of late yeres haue bene
openly conuinced of that abominable here
sy. And therfore it maie be supposed y they
lacke only some desperate capitaine which
should geue the onset, and cause the same
openly to be blasted abrode. For if this on=
ly argument of S. Hilarie were throughly
vrged, the same alone would manifestly
proue, that in effect they be alredie of that
mynde.

And therfore first of al note I pray you
diligently, whether by the whole discourse
and argument of this place they whiche

　　　　　　S v　　　　deny

deny Christes natural and true presence in
the blessed Sacrament, are not proued
by a consequent with Arrians to deny the
true & natural vnitie of godhead, which is
betwen Christ & his Father. For where as
Christ said: as I liue for my Father, so he
that eateth me shall liue for me: and at an
other tyme praieth, y we may be one with
him as he & his father are one, S. Hilarie
maketh his argument vppon those places
after this sort. we liue by Christ and are
made one with him in substance by eating
in the Sacrament the true substance of his
flesh, wherefore Christ liueth by his Father, and is one with him likewise in true
substance of that nature which is common
betwene them, that is to say, of the Godhead. And so he conuinceth euidently by
Scripture the Arrians heresie, which denying this conclusion, affirmed Christ to
be one with his Father in will only & not
in substance. Now whereas our Sacramentaries deny the former part of this argument and say that we are not made one
with Christ in substance by reeeauing the
true substance of his flesh and blood, but
are ioyned to him by faith only & spirite,
how can it be auoided, but that they denie
in effect the conclusion also? Especially
whereas both partes are grounded a like
vpon those textes of Scripture before re-
here

Ioan. 6,

Ioan. 17.

The Sa-
cramenta-
ries mo-
ued by S.
Hilary to
be in effect
Arrians.

hersed, and seing they do serue as well to
conclude the former part by the last, as the
later parte by the formest? And again that
of Scripture being most true, that we are
one ẃ Christ by eating his flesh, as Christ
is one with his Father, if the Sacramentaries say we are not one with Christ by eating the substance of his flesh the other ne-
gatiue semeth then likewise to folow, that
Christ is not one in substance with his Father, which is the blasphemous heresie of
the Arrians. From the shame whereof as
I hartely wishe all Sacramentarie Protestantes to be preserued, because the farther they runne in blindnes the lesse hope
remaineth of their returne & greater heap
of Gods wrath is procured: so to th'end
you may more diligently auoyed the Sacramentarie doctrine, I cã do no lesse here
but declare such other great presumptions
as doe euidently proue, that the same tendeth vnto that or to greater absurditie.
For as I proued vnto you before out of
S. Chrysostom vpõ the sixth of S. Ihons
Gospell, that the Sacramentaries agree
merueilously with the incredulitie of the
Iewes by vsing that their incredulous
How: although in an other maner, & extremitie cleane contrarie to the Iewes: so
here it may appeare also manifestly ỳ they
agree with the Arrians in falshod and
here-

wherein
the Sacra
n̄ entaries
doe mani-
festly a-
gree with
the Ar-
rians.

heresie although in an other kind & after a
contrary sorte. For as the Arrians confes=
sed the trueth of Christes presence in the
blessed Sacrament, or at the least would
not seeme openly to denie the same, as
being a thinge then generally acknowle=
ged of all men, but denied only the trueth
of his Godhead: so these men contrariwise
allowe the truth of Christes Godhead, or
at least are ashamed openly to impugne
the same, as being throughout Christen=
dome so constantly beleued, but endeuour
tothe and nayle to discredit the true pre=
sence of his bodie in the blessed Sacramēt.
So that whereas the Catholike faith ke=
ping alwayes the golden mean in ỹ midst
betwen ỹ extremities of falshode teacheth
as you haue now heard in S. Hilarie,
both that Christ is equally true God with
his father, and that we eate his true fleshe
in the Sacrament: thereby it is declared
how both those extremities are extreme
false, how lyke alwayes will to like, and
how our Sacramentaries agree with the
Arrians in extreme madnesse and falshod,
as they agreed before with ỹ Capharnai=
tes in incredulitie and lacke of fayth. And
therfore they cannot iustly be offended if
any man seing them so many wayes al=
lyed to the Arrians suspect and feare least
in continuance of tyme they will openly
defend

defend that heresie also . For it is more cōmonly sene ,that one which is maliciously
disposed, falleth frō one extreme mischief
to an other, rather then to ye mean it selfe,
although the same be in his owne nature
easie inough to be found out.

There want not examples(as I sayed
before) of Sacramentaries which in our
tyme haue ben found perfite Arrians,and
such as haue suffered death in that quarell
also . But to proue that they may easely
fail both into that and far greater errours
before they beware , onlesse they take hede
in tyme , there is chaunced of late a most
notable example in the countrie of Pole
comōly called in latin Polonia . For there
a numbre of this Sacramentarie sect hauing for their Grand Capitain one Ber-
nardin Ochine an Apostat fryer of Italie,
and sometime alse a spranke Italian prea-
cher in London , haue waded so far in
theyr Sacramentarie religion, that they
be not only come to pluralitie of wynes &
to be like the Arrians in varying from the
Catholike fayth cōcerning the blessed Trinitie,but are in dede a great many of thē
ouer head and eares in Judaicall doctrine and Ceremonies .　Yea they are so far
drowned therein, that diuerse haue of late
circumcided them selues and openly professed a great parte of the Iewes religion.

　　　　　　　　　　　　　And

Certain
Sacramē
taries in
Polonia
first be-
came Tri
nitaries &
of late
Iewes.

And least they should lacke authoritie of the world to beare them out also in this wonderfull extreme madnesse , the diuell who neuer fayleth to help furnishe such feastes, hath prouided certaine rych men of those costes to be herein both folowers of their foolyshe fact , and protectors of theyr impious doctrine.

The duke of Vilna one of theyr singular Patrons , died this last sommer not without y̑ iust and manifest plage of God. For to ease as he thought y̑ extreme payne which he felt in his entrailes by reason of the french Juell which of long tyme had incresed vpon hym he vsed the aduise of a Jew , and contrarie to the counsell of all Physicions would nedes haue his whole bodie to be anoynted ouer with quicke siluer. whereby it came to passe through Gods iust iudgement, that after he had suffered three dayes together, exceding intolerable tormēts , his syde burst open and his head clone a sonder , & so he dyed most miserably. And this to be most true two worshipfull mens letters sent from thence, which I my selfe haue seen & read doe testifie . And therefore vnderstande you that God by this terrible example as well of his death , as of the others continuall blyndnesse hath mercifully warned all of that Sect, to looke spedely to them
selues

selues and repent betyme , least otherwise
besides those endles tormentes which certainly remayne for thē in an other world,
they be lykewise tormēted in this lyfe also,
& suffered to fall yet farther into far greater shame and blyndnesse . And he hath
thereby also most louingly warned all
good Catholikes to kepe them selues warely from consenting to any one point of
their heretical doctrine,least by yelding
an inch, the diuell get an ell, and so cause
one absurditie once graunted to be occasiō
of many horrible heresies.And thus some
reason is shewed why a man may iustly
feare least our Sacramentaries wyl lykewise become such in the end openly, as S.
Hilaries argument proueth them to be alredie in effect.

But because they will denie (I trust)
that they are in conscience gilty of the Ar-
tians heresie, I am content not to burden
them there with any farther . Only let
it be sufficient to note , that the absurditie
of their opinion concerning the blessed Sa
crament is such , that therevpon the Arrians heresie may easely be inferred, which
the most part of them are ashamed for the
absurdnesse thereof openly to defend.And
now whereas we suppose them not to be
Arrians but to confesse Christ to be of one
substāce with God the Father: let vs trye
                                                      whe-

whether S. Hilaries argument may not be so turned vpon them, that they ought to be ashamed of their Sacramentarie heresie also. For if we are one with Christe by eating his fleshe in the Sacrament, as he is one with his Father, then must we be one with him by eating the true substance of his fleshe, as he is one with his Father, by the true substance of his deitie and Godhead. and so consequently that true substance of his fleshe must be really cōteined vnder those visible formes which we receaue. But now some Sacramentarie will perchaunce kycke thereat and say, by the same argument it semeth to folow also, that we are consubstantial and equall in nature with Christ, as he is equal with God the Father: to say which thing is most absurd, and cruelly reproued before in S. Cyprian.

Wherefore to answer briefly therevnto, as it is not necessarie that a similitude or comparison agree in all pointes, but only in some one respect for which specially it is made: so S. Hilarie vseth not here this comparison made by Christ himself in the Ghospell, to shew that we are altogether one with Christ, or that Christ is all maner of wayes one with his Father: but only to proue that Christ is one in substance with God the Father, which point the
Arrians

Arrians denyed. And therefore he proueth
that most substantially, saying Christ is
one with his Father by the substance of
his Deitie no lesse then we are one with
him by receauing the substance of his flesh
in the blessed Sacrament. But we receaue
the true substance of his flesh, wherefore
Christ hath likewise the true substance and
nature of his Father. So that the force of
this argument consisteth in the truth of
substance, which is on both sides: but not
in the maner of vnion, which folowing
thereupon diuersely causeth a great diuersitie betwene God & vs. For Christ hath
that substance of the Godhead by nature,
we haue the substance of his fleshe in
the Sacramente and so consequently in
our bodies, by speciall dispensation and
priuilege. And therefore although vpon
that vnitie of nature betwene Christ and
his Father there foloweth necessarily equa-
litie also of power, and consubstantialitie
of nature: yet the same foloweth not betwene Christ and vs, because the maner of
the vnion is not like. But the truth of the
substance on both sydes, which is the point
wherein S. Hilarie maketh this comparison to agree, is most perfitely thereby proued: and so the true presence of Christes
substance in the blessed Sacrament is also
T most

most strongly confirmed. And this much generally concerning the chief argument of S. Hilarie in this place. Now let vs note some particular words which make specially for this purpose. And what playner wordes can any man wishe then those are, where he saith, that Christ to make vs one with him, ioyned together the nature of his fleshe with the nature of his deitie vnder the Sacrament of flesh, to be communicated of vs. For by those wordes it is declared plainly, that whole Christ as wel his Godhead as his humane nature, is truly present and communicated vnto vs vnder the formes of bread & wine, which are the Sacrament and outward signes of his true flesh and blood there miraculously conteined vnderneth them.

And in ye beginnig of this sentece he ioyneth together these two propositiōs, God the worde was made flesh, and the same word made flesh is truly receaued of vs in this diuine foode, declaring thereby most euidently that he toke the one for no lesse sure ground against the Arrians than the other. And if the same had not bene in his time also generally so taken, the Arrians would no doubt haue laughed to scorne his whole argument which he buylded therevpon, Neither any mean wyse man

I suppose

I suppose can thinke, that such a learned
and holy Father would at all haue vsed
that later proposition to proue so true and
weyghtie a conclusion, against such cap-
tious and suttle heretikes, if it had bene in
dede either not true, or not generally in
his time approued.

would it not seeme very ridiculous if a
mā of our Age should goe about to proue
vnto the Protestants this truth, that Par-
dōs are good, by this false reason, because
they saue men from hell: or that Pilgrima-
ges are to be vsed, because there is no o-
ther way to heauen? would not the world
laugh at such kind of proses, and would
not the Protestantes them selues take
vantage thereof & cry out thereby a great
deale more both against Pardons and Pil-
grimages? In like sorte doubtlesse the Arrians would haue cryed out both against
S. Hilarie & his conclusion, if to disproue
their heresy, he had vsed that which either
they them selues or any part of Christendom besides had then thought to be false:
as the Sacramentaries would now beare
vs in hād he did. Or if they goe not about
to perswade that, how auoid they the auctority of this auncient Bishoppe witnessing the faith of his tyme to be against thē?
or why doe they not willingly embrace
T ij the

the truth of Christes true presence in the
blessed Sacramente, whiche S. Hilarie
in this his discourse againste the Arrians
so plainlie confirmeth? But they lacke
not shiftes I warrante you to shifte a-
way bothe this and manie other as plane
testimonies of auncient fathers, although
they vse not that false shifte whiche I now
last mentioned.

And here to refreshe you somwhat in
these my tedious notes, I cannot forget to
copt vnto you one preti but yet very homly shift, which an Archeprelate of that sect
vsed on a time to deface vtterly all that the
Catholikes might alleage for the reall presence, out of this discourse of S. Hilarie.
For he set foorth in print a sentence out of
this place, to proue y there was in y Sacramēt a bare figure & mystery only of Christ
his bodie, and not the truth thereof. But
to make you wonder thereat a great deale
more, before you learne of me anie farther
therin, I would you did first reade y whole
place twise or thrise ouer, to see whether
you can espie anie word woich might seme
to haue bene written in that sense. For after
you shal vnderstand the homly shift which
was vsed, you wil I am sure rather laugh
at his foly, and detest his impudenci, than
wonder at his diligence, Yf you loke a litle

after

after the beginning to my second note, you
shall find in S Hilarye these wordes, and
if we also receiue truely vnder a mystery the
flesh of his body. the latin whereof is. Nosque verè sub mysterio carnem corporis sui
suminus. which conditional proposition S.
Hilary ioyneth with these that goe before,
if Christ toke true flesh of the virgin, and if
that man borne of Mary be truly Christ, to
declare that al be of one like truth, and therby to conclude the true vnitie of those two
personnes god the father, & god the sonne.
So y we ought no more to doubt by these
plain words of S. Hilary, that we eate truely the fleshe of Christ his bodie vnder a Sacrament, then that Christ toke true flesh of
the blessed virgin.

And considre a litle J pray you, what
weight euery word bereth. For he was not
content to saie that we eate his flesh or eate
his bodie, but putting both together he saieth, we eate the flesh of his bodie, and that
truly also and verely, as muche to saie as
without trope or figure concerning the vertie of the flesh. neuerthelesse to expresse the
maner how the same is eaten, he addeth farther, Sub mysterio, vnder a Sacrament or
mysteriewhich is no more to saie (accordiglie as you haue heard before out of S. Cyprian) but vnder the outwarde formes of
bread and wine.

T iij   Now

Now considre another while whether it be possible to make these wordes to serue for the Sacramentaries opinion, and not only not to proue that which I haue saide but vtterlie to destroy the same. I beleue verelie that as I wished before you did often reade ouer the whole, to proue whether by your self you could find out anie words for that purpose:so now I haue tolde you the wordes them selues, I maie yet geue you half an hour yea ahole daies leisure to deuise how possible anie such sense may be wrong out of them. But I will not holde you so long in suspense of ye which was so slightly done. The letter, e, you know wel is quicklie chaunged into a rounde, o. He therefore whom we talke of, did nomore but chaunge the latin aduerbe verè into the adiectiue vero, and then alleaged the place first in latin thus Notque vero sub mysterio carnē corporis sui sumimus. and then made this sense in Englishe, that we receaue the flesh of his body vnder a true mystery, which is cleane contrary both to the saing and meaning of the holy doctor. for S. Hilaries wordes are, truely vnder a mystery, which declare that the fleshe of Christ is truly & really receaued of vs vnder the forme of bread. But a true myste-rye importeth a bare & naked figure with-out

A homly shift mac-tised by an Arche-protestant

out any farther trueth. so that you perceue how by changing one letter in the latin & diminishing one syllable in the English, that which maketh in dede for the Catholike religion, is not without great impudency wrested to serue the Sacramétaries heresie.

If you desyre to know what prelate he was that vsed this gyleful shift, it was no lesse mã thẽ Thomas Cranmer sometime Archebyshop of Canturbery: Of whose pseudomartyrdom his disciples and folowers haue euẽ as much cause to vaunt, as he had to bragge of this his false & shamlesse dealing. And which is most worthy to be noted when the falsyfiing of this place was in ỹ open disputatiõ at Oxford layed to his charge, he had no excuse to lay for him selfe, as that it was done by any negligence or errour: but stode a great while stiffly in this defense, that it was so in S. Hilary. And when by conference of all the chief printes that were extant, the contrary was shewed to his face, his last shift was, that the changinge of one letter could not make any great diuersity in the matter: wherbnto reply was made again merely, that Pistor and Pastor, differed but in one letter, and yet the signification was so diuerse, that the one might signifie a Byshop, and the other a

T iij   Baker.

Baker . I would not haue rehersed this matter so boldly , had I not my selfe ben present at the open detecting therof : but in very dede I heard euery thing my self euen as I haue told you, neither was that great Prelate able by any other meanes to discharge him self of this abominable prac tise with which he was there so worthely charged . The great shame therof redonn deth not only to hym, but to all his adhe rent es, and those especially which are not ashmed to counte hym ether for a constät martyr or good confessor , whereas he so shamfully belyed this holy mä S. Hilary, who was in his whole life a perfite Con fessor & in wyl at the least a true Martyr. The same falshode also must nedes be so much the more detestable , for that it was vsed of such a personage, so openly and in so hyghe a matter and that of purpose (as it may seeme) to entrappe the sely pore sou les and driue thë hedlong in to heli fyre.

3.   But to confirme more perfitly the truth of the reall presence, note in S. Hilarie the later end of y former sentence. for he conclu deth y Christ can not be one with God the Father by wil onlie, seing the natural pro prietie or proper nature of Christe is vnto vs by y blessed Sacrament a holy signe of perfite vnity. which wordes do euidentlie proue y by this Sacrament we are ioyned ynto Christ, not by wil only (for they y same

could neuer proue ꝑ God ꝑ son were vnited to his Father moꝛe thē by vnity of wil)
but they proue ꝑ we are vnited vnto Chꝛist
by his proper & true nature receued in this
sacramēt, which doth most liuely repꝛesent
and signifie vnto vs that perfite vnitie,
which is betwen Chꝛiste and his mysticall
bodie the Church. Note farthermoꝛe in S.
Hilarie those woꝛds where he saith, there
is no place left now foꝛ anie man to doubt
of the true pꝛesence of Chꝛistes flesh in the
Sacrament, seing the same is both taught
so plainly by Chꝛiste, where he saith: My
flesh is verily meate, &c. and cōfirmed by ꝑ
beliefe of the whole woꝛld. Foꝛ here you
haue it resolued in plaine termes, howe
constantly this matter was then beleued
and taken as grounded most substantiallie
vpon scripture. and ꝑ as I saied befoꝛe S.
Hilary would neuer otherwise haue vsed
it foꝛ a pꝛinciple to cōfound the Arrians.

Note also a litle after foꝛ this purpose
where he saith: They only maie happen to
denie this truth, which denie Chꝛiste to be
true God. As who should say, this is such
a confessed truth amongest all Chꝛistians,
that there is no feare leaste anie man will
denie the same besides the Arrians onlie.
Foꝛ they perceauinge so stronge an argument built vppon scripture to be made a-
gainst them, must of foꝛce shifte away the

former part thereof, onlesse they wil recante theyr heresie and graunt the conclusion. For if they mighte freely haue vsed that interpretation of Christes words which ye Sacramentaries do now a dayes, making men beleue that all was spoken by figures, tropes, and signes: they would easelie haue auoided S. Hilaries argument without any farther denial. For Christes wordes of geuing vs his fleshe to eate, beinge ment figuratiuely: ye coclusion which was made of Christes being one with his Father, muste nedes haue bene ment figuratinely also. and so the same should haue made more for the Arrians heresie, then againste it. For they them selues defended that he was one with his Father by a figure and similitude: so that hereby the faith of ye time which would not suffer the Arrians to vse anie suche false glose is merueilously well proued. That also is not a litle confirmed which I spake before concerning the greate affinitie whiche is betwene those Arrians & our Sacramétaries. For now you heare S. Hilarie him selfe saie, he feareth they onlie will denie the truth of the Sacrament, which denie Christe to be true God. And thus you see also howe a large volume mighte be easely written, if a man would stande in amplifieng this only argument to proue them Arrians. For there

nci=

neither larketh good ground, sufficient authoritie, nor abūdance of examples. There
are manie other sentences in this place of
H. Hilarie muche worth the noting, but
because I haue bene perchaunce alredie
ouer long, I wil leaue the ample confide-
ration of them to your own discretion and
iudgement, and will touche only a fewe,
more briefly.

Therefore you maie note farther howe   **6.**
he ioynethe together our dwellinge in
Christ by his natiuitie, with his dwelling
in vs by these mysteries of his bodie and
blood. To geue vs (no dout) to vnderstand, that as mans true fleshe was taken
of him at his birth: so the same mans true
fleshe is taken againe of vs in the Sacrament. Note also that he proueth this natu-   **7.**
rall vnitie berwen Christ and vs, by Christes owne wordes which he spake concerning the eating of his fleshe and drinking
of blood. For hereby it appereth he so vnderstode Christes wordes, that he should
meane to geue vs the nature and substāce
of his fleshe and blood, and not a signe or
figure whiche can neuer make anie suche
naturall vnitie. But he easeth me of the
labor to proue this by manie wordes, for
him selfe expoundeth his owne meaning
a few lynes after, sayinge: we lyue in this   **8.**
naturall vnitie with Christe according to
the

fleſh in ẙ we receaue the nature of his fleſh and haue Chꝛiſt by fleſh abiding in vs. And toward the end he reiecteth vtterly and condemneth the Sacramentaries opinion, whiche would haue vs to be ioyned vnto God by liftinge vp only our hart deuoutly and obedientlie into heauen : and not by comminicatinge naturally and pꝛoperlie the true fleſhe and blood of Chꝛiſt. Foꝛ S. Hylarie maugre theyꝛ teeth concludeth Chꝛiſte to abide in vs by meanes of the bleſſed Sacrament, carnally and coꝛpoꝛally. And now to cōclude likewiſe theſe few notes, take laſt of all this aduertiſement, that if (as I ſayed in the beginninge) many ſentences ſeeme vnto you here verie harde to be thꝛoughlic vnderſtanded, notwithſtanding I haue vſed ſuche diligence in tranſlating them as I could, meruelle not thereat, but learne thereby that matters of Diuinitie are not foꝛ euerie capacitie. And meruelle rather at the raſhnes of thoſe fonde craftesmen, and vnlerned miſtreſſes, whiche take vppon them to diſcuſſe the hygheſte pointes in religion : whereas if they were well examined they ſcaſe vnderſtand thoſe termes, which holy wꝛiters doe vſe in expoundinge and teachinge them.

S. Di-

C S. Hilaries authoritie and good name defended against M. Iuels slaunderous report in his replie to D. Harding. art. 6. pag. 349.

WHE I beganne first to translate these testimones of the auncient Fathers, I thought it should be sufficient to set forth at large their wordes only which are of the eldeste sort, and whiche haue bene alwaies in the Churche of greateste name both for theyr lerning and vertue : specially whereas the Protestantes haue so braggingly craked, that no one father within the first sir hundred yeres hath either clause or sentence to confirme that, which the Catholikes teach in this matter. But now it is most manifestly perceaued by their writinges of late published, that they (seeing those Fathers to make so manifestly against thē) beginne to fleere by litle and litle frome that proud bragge: not that they wil yet yeld one iote to confesse their error, but as heretikes are wont to doe, they fleere so from one absurditie, that rather thē confesse the same, they wil be sure to fall in a greater. And so they being not able to maintayne ý theyr proud Chāpiōs challenge, both he himself ý ý rest haue attēpted not only to discredit some of those doctors works frō whēre most plain

The xi. Chapiter.

testi-

testimonies may be brought against them, but also to bring the holy Doctors them selues into contempt. whiche assault if it take good successe in the peoples eares, thē think they the field is wonne, and that thē selues shalbe in stead of the auncient Doctors, to interprete scripturs according vnto their own fansy without controllmēt.

This attempt of theirs is euident to be sene in their writings, and namely in that huge Reply of late set forth, where besides those 255 vntruthes (whiche being falsely imputed to another aré truly to be retourned backe vpō his head that gathered thē) there are moe lies, I say not (as the prouerbe is)thē lynes, but there are (I speake as I thinke without any figure or Hyperbole) moe lyes by a great many then leaues, counting six lyes to euery syde of a leaf : as it doth partly already, and shall shortly (by Gods grace) more perfitely appeare, to the authors eternal shame and confusion. In this worthy Reply (I say) that new attempt is diuerse tymes aduentured. I haue already refuted one place, where S. Chrysostomes Liturgie was by certaine false surmises there disproued. Now I haue fortuned vppon an other, wherein not only the worke of a Doctor, but euen that holy Doctor himselfe S. Hilarie now last alleged, is most shamefully slaun-

slaundered. For the author of those lyes burdeneth him there with shamefull and abhominable errors, yea and rekoneth him emongest impiouse and wicked heretikes. Which was done no doubt of purpose to bring his authoritie in discredit: for that he writeth so strongly & substantially, for the truth of the reall presence, that the Sacramentarie doctrine, and his authoritie can not possibly stand together.

And therefore although at the first I thought it nedlesse to write any thing in the commendatiō or defense of this or any other doctor, yet seing I haue before defended S. Chrisostomes worke, I thinke it much more necessarie, here to say some what also in defense of S. Hilaries good name: especially wheras therby not only ŷ testimonies before alleaged out of him, shall stand in their full authoritie: but also mē may be the better warned to espie this wicked attempt, of discreditinge the holy doctors, and withall to consider the falshod which is vsed therein. And let this also be sufficient for my excuse, ŷ although this whole chapter must nedes make some digression from my principal purpose, yet it tēdeth wholy to cōfirme ŷ authoritie of those testimonies which I haue last alleaged, & therfore in ŷ respect swarueth not so much, but it may be well borne with all.

T 8

To come now to the matter, there are in
that sardel of ives before mentioned, two
most abhominable errors layd to S. Hilaries charge. The one, that he held Christ
receved no flesh of the blessed virgin, but
brought the same from heauen. The other,
that he helde Christes bodie was impassible, and felte no more griefe when it was
strycken, then water, fyre, or aier when it
is diuided with a knyfe. And these great
errors are alleaged as though they were
vttered by him in his tenth boke de Trinitate. wherfore for the true tryall thereof,
it behoueth to declare somewhat at large
the contents of that booke, and then to see
what words are there which may sound
to any such sense. Also vppon what occasion he vseth them, and what was his
true meaning therein. For many thinges
are spoken often tymes in disputing with
heretikes (as S. Hilarie doth in all those
twelue bookes) which otherwise should
not haue bene spoken. And many strange
words are often tymes vttered, which although they be not foorthwith of some
well vnderstanded, yet haue a most true &
Godly meaning. As for example S. Paul
sayeth: Deus Christum pro nobis peccatū
fecit, God made Christ synne for vs. And
againe: Deus misit filium suum in similitudinem carnis peccati, God sent his sonne
in the

M. Iuell
pag. 349.

1.

2.

2. Cor. 5.

Ro. 8.

in the similitude of the flesh of synne. Both
which sayinges if they be not rightly vn=
derstanded, may not only seeme strange,
but very erronious & wicked, who know
eth not also how many words and senten
ces there are in the booke of Iob, which re
quire an humble and very discreet rea=
der? And therefore we must consider like=
wise in S. Hilarie both what he sayeth,
and vppon what occasion.

First therefore it is to be vnderstanded
that those twelue bookes of S. Hilarie
De Trinitate were writen as the title de=
clareth to defend the Catholike faith of y
blessed Trinitie against the most impious
blasphemies of the wicked Arrians. who
as you haue heard before, denyed Christ
to be equall God with God the Father,
impugning with all their might the con=
substantialitie and vnitie of nature in the
blessed Trinitie. which Trinitie the Ca=
tholike Church teacheth vs to consist of
three persons, God the Father, God the
Sonne, and God the holy Ghost, and of
one nature or substãce whereby they three
are all one God. Now those Arrians to
improne that sacred vnitie and equallitie
of nature betwene God the Father & God
the Sonne, found out a number of places
in holy Scripture, which as they thought
made much for their purpose, euen as our

The argu
ment of
S. Hila=
ries twel=
ue bokes
de Trin.

U   Sacra=

Sacramentaries do find certaine for them selues now a dayes also. And although in dede no falshod can haue any true ground in holy Scripture, which is all infallibly true, yet it is euident that the Arrians pretended a far greater number of places for their syde: and those such also as (to one that regardeth the bare words, and not that sense which the Catholike Church and auncient Fathers geue) doe far more euidently proue their heresie, then the Sacramentaries of our tyme doe or can allege any for their sect. For what plainer words could an Arrian wishe for to proue that Christ was inferior and not equall to his Father, then those spoken by Christes owne mouth : Pater maior me est, my Father is greater then I am? Thinke you that if our Sacramentaries had but halfe so plaine words to proue that Christes body were not in the blessed Sacrament, they would not iolyly triumphe vpon the Catholikes more then they doe? would they not beare the world in hand, ꝟ Scripture were on their syde, and set far greater bragges on the matter? what they would then do we may collect by that we heare the vauntes and vaine crakes they make now, whereas they haue nothinge like shew or appearance of any one worde to make for them, as the Arrians had of many. But had they twise so many as the

Ioan. 14.

Arrians, and the same also twise so plaine
yet the truth should in the end neuerthelesse ouercome. And as in those wordes before recited, the true sense of the Catholike
Church preuailed: which was that they
are to be vnderstanded of the humanitie of
Christ and not of his Deitie (for concerning his humane nature, he is in dede inferior to God the Father, but concerning
his diuine nature equall God with him)
euen so what sense so euer the Sacramentaries could haue brought, that sense neuerthelesse should haue had the victorie,
which the côsent of the Catholike Church,
and of auncient Fathers gyueth: and not
ý which their frantike braynes imagine.

But to returne to our purpose, as the
Arrians alleged that one place falsly vnderstanded, so they alleged many other besydes: all which S. Hilarie in his forsayed
bookes proueth to make nothing for their
opinion. And to all he côfuteth those arguments which they ground vpô those places. The tenth booke (whereof I haue specially to write) maketh answer chiefly to ý
Arrians obiections made out of those sentences which Christ spake about his pas-
siô, wherby he declared ý infirmitie of mãs
nature, & ý he toke truly & really ý nature
vpon him. For there you shall find much
spoken in ý sense, as for example where he

The argu ment of S. Hila-ries tenth boke.

U ij sayd:

Math. 26

Math. 27

Luc. 23.

sayd : My soule is sorowfull euen vnto
death . and againe: Father if it be possible
let this cup passe from me. also when he
was vpon the Crosse he cried out: O God
my God why hast thou forsaken me? and
last of all, he comended his soule to God y
Father saying : Father into thy handes J
commend my spirite. All which sayinges
do, as you see, declare the naturall affections of a man beinge in that case as Christ
was. & therfore the Arrians would thereby haue concluded , that he was not at all
true God. for they reasoned after this like
sort. He was sorowfull before his passion
and desyred to haue it remoued from him,
whereby it appeareth he feared death as
other men doe: and therefore he was not
God, who hath no cause to feare any such
thing. Moreouer he complained that God
had forsaken him, and last of all commended his soule into the handes of God,
wherefore it is to be thought that himself
was not true God : for then what neaded
he to haue sought farther helpe.

All which and many other like obiections made by the Arrians to disproue the
deitie of Christ S. Hilarie in his tenth
boke answereth most perfitely, both by al-
leaging other words spoken by Christ a-
bout the same tyme, which doe euidently
proue his Godhead: and also by declaring
how

how those places alleaged by the Arrians
are to be vnderstāded. And first cōcerning
y textes of scripture which he apposeth to
these brought by the Arrians he sheweth,
that as Christ sayed his soule was sorow=
full euen vnto death:so he sayd also that it
was in his power, to deliuer vp his soule   Ioan. 10.
and to take it again , & he sayed moreouer
that they shoulo see the sonne of man sit=
tinge on the right hand of the power of
god. which wordes do euidētly proue that
diuine nature which the Arrians would
by the other places haue disproued. Also as
he sayd:Father if it be possible let this cup
passe from me,so he sayed againe: The cup
which my father hath geuē me shall I not   Ioan. 18.
drinke it? And as he sayed, O god my god
why hast thou forsaken me:so he sayed al=
so to the theef,this day thou shalt be with   Luc. 23.
me in Paradise . And as he commended
his soule into the handes of his father , so
him self also with a great voyce gaue vp y   Mar. 15.
ghost,declaring thereby most manifestly y
y power of his diuine nature. And for the
true vnderstādīg of those places which y
Arriās alleaged , he declareth throughout
his whole boke , y Christ suffered all those
infirmities and sorrowes which are men=
tioned in the Gospell specially about the
tyme of hispassion,not of any cōpulsion or
necessitie of nature,as the Arrians would
                    U ij   haue

haue it, but of his owne mere mercy and good will toward vs both to witnesse vnto vs the truth of his humane nature, and to cause vs the more to loue him, consideringe how much & how voluntarily he suffered only for our sakes. For if he would but haue vsed y̆ almightie power which was naturally in his humane body euē from the first moinēt of his incarnatiō by reason of y̆ vnitie, which was betwixt the godhed and his flesh: he neaded not to haue suffered at all any one infirmitie. but as Adam lyuing in the state of grace, was voyd of all kind of sorowe & heauinesse: so the humanitie of Christ was by that his speciall and gracious nature through that singular vnion, much more perfitely voyd of al those sorowes, which by Adās transgression were generally dew vnto mankind. For they were not dew at all vnto Christ, because he could not possibly be partaker of that trāsgression, whereas he was not conceiued by the seede of man.

Now to confirme this point S. Hilarie bringeth in the supernaturall incarnation of Christ, & so cometh to talke of y̆ matter which is now first layd to his charge for an error. where it is sayd that he held, Christ receaued no flesh of the blessed virgin but brought the same frō heauē, whether

ther he held so in dede oz no, now you shal
heare. He reasoneth to his purpose on this
wise. The nature of Christes passions and
sozowes was such, as the nature of his bo
dy & soule was. But he had not his body
and soule accozding to the common course
of other men: foz his soule him selfe made
as beinge god, and flesh he toke of the vir=
gin. yea he bzought both body & soule af=
ter a sozt out of heauen, in that he was con
ceued by the holy Ghost who is one God
with hiinselfe, and in that the same per=
son wherewith that body was one, came
from heauen: whereuppon it foloweth
that the passions also of his body and
soule were not like other mens passions
cominge of the infirmitie of nature, but of
his owne choice and election. This is
the whole summe and true sense of all
that which he wziteth in this matter. and
thereby it may appeare euidently, after
what sozte he saith, that Christ bzought
this body from heauen. not that he ment
(as this false repozter saith) that Christ
toke no flesh of the blessed Uirgin, but
that the same flesh was conceaued by the
holy Ghost and not by the seed of man.

But now let S. Hilarie speake foz him
selfe, and in one sentence he shall declare
his true meaning in this whole matter:
U iiij   his

his wordes are these: Virgo nõ nisi ex san
cto spiritu genuit quod genuit. Et quámuis
tantum ad natiuitatem carnis ex se daret,
quantum ex se feminę edendorum corpo-
rũ susceptis originibus impenderét, nõ ta-
mẽ Iesus Christus per humanę cõceptionis
coaluit naturam. The virgin did not beget
that which she begot, but of ŷ holy Ghost,
and although she gaue of her selfe somuch
vnto the natiuitie of flesh as womẽ should
geue vnto the conceued beginninges of bo
dies to be brought forth, yet Iesus Christ
grew not together by ŷ nature of humane
conception. what wordes can be plainer
then these, to shewe that S. Hilarie held,
Christ toke true flesh of ŷ virgin? For what
is true flesh, if not that whiche euery man
taketh of his mother? and S Hilarie saieth
here, that our Lady gaue altogether vnto
Christ as much concerning his fleshe as o-
ther women do to their childrẽ, which they
conceaue and bring forth. But herein cõsi-
steth ŷ difference, that other men take their
beginninge of the seede of men, Christ toke
his beginninge and was conceued by the
holie Ghost: and after such sort S .Hilarye
meaneth, that Christe brought his bodie
from heauen. For so the wordes folowinge
do more plainly witnesse, where he apply-
eth to this purpose ŷ sentence of holy scripture

ture. No man ascendeth into heauen but he which descended from heauen, the sonne of man which is in heauen wherevpon he addeth imediatcly: Quod descendit de cœlo conceptę de spiritu originis causa est. Non enim ex se corpori Maria originem dedit: licet ad incrementum partumque corporis omne quod sexus sui naturale est cōtulerit. That whiche descended oute of heauen is cause of the beginninge which is conceued by the holy Ghost. For Marie gaue not of her selfe beginning to that bodie, although she conferred to the increase and bringinge forth of that bodie, all that is due by nature to her sexe and kinde.

By the first part of those wordes it appeareth, how he ment that Christes bodie came from heauen that is to say, in respect of the deitie which gaue beginning to that bodie: for the person of Christe beinge one, causeth the workes of bothe natures to be attributed to eche nature indifferently. So that nothing is attributed to hys Deity, but the same may also after that sort in respect of his person be ascribed to his humanity. For as it is true to say that man died: so it is true to say, that god died. And as god descended out of heauē, so the scripture saith, the sonne of man descended oute of Heauen, not that hys humane nature was

Ioan. 3.

Hilar. de Trinitat. lib. 10.

D v   in hea=

in heauen before it was here on earth, but
because ý Godhead wherunto it was vni=
ted came from heauen, & so likewise S. Hi
larie meaneth ý Christes body came from
heauen, not ý it was first formed in hearē
& so brought into the virgins wombe (as
this reporter would haue S. Hilarie to
meane) but that god who gaue beginning
therunto came frō heauen. And the words
folowing declare expressely his mind con=
cerning that wherevpon the other part of
this slaunder dependeth, although they
seeme in dede to be those whervpō it was
chiefly grounded . for meeter wordes to
ground that slaunder vpon, are not in all
the tenth booke. But euery man that wil,
may see how euidently these make in dede
against it. S. Hilarie saith not here that
Christ toke not his body of the virgin, but
he saith she gaue not the beginning to his
body. which is in dede most true , for in
that respect it came from heauen as being
conceaued by the holy Ghost. And again
he saieth (which is cleane contrarie to the
reporters words) that our Lady gaue so
much to his body , as naturally any wo=
man doth geue . If then naturally wo=
men geue true fleshe to their children, how
slaunderously is it reported, that by S. Hi
laries doctrine Christ toke no fleshe of his
mother : But what nede I vrge this,
                                        seinge

seing he hath so ofte tymes in ẏ boke these wordes assumpta ex virgine carne flesh taken of the virgin. Et corpus ex virgine assumpsit, and he toke his body of the virgin. Both woich sayings are cleane contrarietorie to the reporters wordes, and doe euidently declare, that S. Dilarie neuer ment as he reporteth.

And if any man be not as yet satisfied herein, what plainer wordes to shew how S. Dilarie ment that Christes body came from heauen can any man aske, then these are? Vt non ex humana conceptione origo Hilar de esse corporis existimaretur, dum coeleste Tri. li. 10 esse corpus ostenditur. That whilest it is shewed to be a heauēly body, it should not be thought that the beginning of that body was of humane conception. So that therefore he meaneth it came from heauen, because it was not begotten by the seede of man. But whereas in the common course of mans generation and conceptiō there concurre both a father and mother, Christ was miraculously conceaued and borne here in the earth without a father, but had of his mother all ẏ which women naturally doe geue. So that now it may throughly appeare ẏ all which S. Dilarie speaketh of this matter, is to be referred chiefly to that diuine conception, which was by the holy Ghost. For in that respect

only

only he sayeth before, our ladie gaue not beginning to Christes bodie, because the same was caused by the holy ghost. & now he sayeth also the bodie of Christ is heauenly for the same respect. And therefore hereby that first lyenge slaunder is sufficiently by S. Hilarie him selfe detected. And by the same meanes a ready way is made to the detection of the second. for as S. Hilarie vseth this argument of the incarnation incidently, to shew what kynd of bodie & what kynd of flesshe Christ had, that is to say, such as was not conceiued of mans seed, but of the holy Ghost, thereby to declare that he suffered not at al by ye necessitie of a corrupt and synful nature as we doe: so if ye miraculous incarnation be well considered, all that he speaketh cōcerning the second matter, ye is cōcerning Christes passion, is easie to be vnderstanded.

Now therefore he hymselfe shall likewise declare at the fyrst euen in one worde the effect aswell of his whole aunswere to those obiections of the Arrians before recited, as the true vnderstanding of all those wordes concerning the suffering of Christe, wherevpon the seconde slaunder is grounded. For in that place where he describeth briefely the whole argument of the tenth booke, he speaketh of the Arrians and the scriptures by the alleaged

The second slaunder confuted.

leged on this wise. Diuinę professionis naturæque immemores ad argumentū impietatis suæ, dispensationis gesta & dicta tenuerunt, They being vnmindful of the diuine profession and nature, held for an argument of their impietie the doinges and sayings of dispēsation, that is to say, those things whiche Christ saied and did, by the way of dispensation. whereby S.Hilarie meaneth those places before recited cōcerning the sorowes and infirmities whiche Christ suffered. For those the Arrians alleged, & would not heare of the other, which gaue so euident testimonies of his diuine nature. And so by that one word dispensatiō, he declareth that those sorowes which Christ suffered at his passion, dyd not naturally concerning his nature vnited to ẏ Godhead and conceiued by the holyGhost put him to any payne or torment, but only by the way of dispensation , that is to say , by yelding for our sakes that right of glorie and of impassibility, which of duetie his body should haue had actually euen as his soule had from the first moment of his incarnation. In which respect also some call the whole life & specially the passion of Christ miraculous, because it was in dede a miracle that a nature so supernaturally vnited and conceued as that was should by any meanes suffer any infirmitie.

　　　　　　　　　　　　But

Hilar. de Trinitat. lib. 1.

But now, although in dede that one sentence before alleged taken out of the argument of the tenth booke, might by reason of that one word dispensatio suffice for all: yet hearken farther what he sayeth in the tenth booke it self. First where he bringeth in those obiections of the Arrians before mentioned he writeth thus: Volunt enim plerique eorum ex passionis metu & ex infirmitate patiendi, non in natura eum impassibilis Dei fuisse: vt qui timuit & doluit, nō tuerit vel in ea potestatis securitate quæ non timet, vel in ea spiritus incorruptione quæ non dolet: sed inferioris a Deo Patre naturæ, & humanę passionis trepidauerit metu, & ad corporalis pænę congemuerit atrocitatem. For the most part of them wil haue that Christ by reason of the feare of his passion and the infirmitie of suffering had not the nature of God impassible: so that he, which feared, and sorowed, was not in that securitie of power which feareth not, or in that incorruption of spirite which soroweth not: but that he feared by the feare of a nature inferior vnto God, and by such a feare as man is commonly subiect vnto, & that he sorowed at the greuousnesse of y bodily paine.

Which words shew euidently y the scope of y Arrians was to proue by those places of Scripture before mentioned, y Christ had

Hilar. de Tri. li. 10

had such a naturall feare and grief of the
paynes which he suffered, that he had no
naturall power by the helpe of his Godhead to auoyd those paines, although he
would neuer so fayne haue escaped them:
and thereby they would haue concluded, ȳ
he had no impassible or immortall nature,
that is to say, no Godhead at all, but only
such a corrupt and bodily nature, which
was subiect to all maner of infirmities,
euen after that sort as our nature is.

Now as this was their wicked assertion, so it appeareth hereby also whereunto the dzyst of S. Hilaries answer vnto
them tendeth, and after what sort all that
he writeth in this booke against them, is
to be vnderstanded. For to goe directly a-
gainst their assertion he must shew ȳ Christ
neither feared death nor suffered any grief
after such sort as we doe which haue but
one nature, & that, naturally subiect without choyse, to all such mysteries. But that
he had always a diuine nature vnited to
his humanitie by the meanes whereof his
humanitie was not at al by course of ȳ his
nature wrought by ȳ holy Ghost, necessarily subiect to any humane passion, & ȳ, ȳ
paine which his body actually suffred was
by dispensatiō only of ȳ Godhed, by which
Godhed he had power to haue kept his bo
dy impassible if it had so pleased him, euen
as his

his Deitie was impassible. This much it
was S. Hilaries part to proue against the
Arrians, and the same he proueth in dede
throughout his whole tenth booke most
perfitely.

But as it is commonly seene, that he
which will make a croked rodde straight,
boweth it very much the contrarie way,
so it happeneth in disputing with peruerse
and croked heretikes : that to bring them
vnto the truth men leane often tymes very much to the contrarie syde : not that
they speak therefore any vntruth, but vpő
such occasion speake often tymes far more
vehemently on that syde, then they would
otherwise do. So we find that S. Paul dis
puting with those which did put such confidence in the ceremonies of the law, spake
much more vehemently against those ceremonies, then euer he would haue done if
no such occasion had bene geuen. And likewise S. Augustine in writing against the
Manichees seemeth to one which is ignorant, or which of malice will not see the
ground of his talke, to draw neare to the
Pelagians: and likewise writing against
the Pelagians to leane somewhat to the
Manichees, whereas in dede he confuteth
them both most perfitely. If then it happen ẙ S. Hilarie going about to reproue
the falshod of the Arrians assertion in that
sort

Epist. ad
Rom. &
Galat.

fort as J haue alredy declared write some=
what vehemently on ý syde which he de=
fendeth , is he to be blamed therefore ? Jf
whereas they saied Christ suffered altoge=
ther like an other man , meaning thereby
to disproue his Godhead , he in defense of
the Godhead saith that he suffered not al=
together like an other man: maie he not be
borne withal ? what if vpon such occasion
he saieth that Christ suffered no paine at al
vppon the Crosse ? what if he speake the
same also not only in respect of his diui=
nitie, but of his bodily nature? what if he
saie that his verie senses felte no payne at
al? Maie not that be defended without re=
proche of error? may it not be gently inter=
preted ? Yea maie it not be saied that the
same is most true in a right good sense? for
by necessitie of that his nature , his senses
felt no paine in deede , although by the dis=
pensation and permission of his Godhead
they felte for our sakes far more greuouse
paines then euer any man felt . And thus
it is euident how clerely S . Hilarie maie
be defended concerning this point where=
in his cheif conflicte is with the Arrians,
although him selfe had not saied one word
more for his owne defense.

But nowe together with those wordes
wherupon this slaunderouse reporte is
made, the interpretation which himself ge=
                    F   ueth

neth of them shall euidently appere. First
those wordds out of which that foule spi‐
der gathered this venim which he hath so
spitefully spit out agaist this blessed Saint
are these; Homo Iesus Christus vnigenitus
deus per carné & verbúvt hominis filius, ita
& dei filius, hominem verum secundunm
similitudinem nostri hominis non deficiens
a se deo sumpsit: in quem quamuis aut ictus
incideret, aut uulnus descenderet, aut nodi
cócurrerent, aut suspensio eleuaret, afferrét
quidem hæc impetum passionis, non tamen
dolorem passionis inferrent: vt telú aliquod
aut aquam perforans, aut ignem cópun‐
gens, aut aera vulneans. The man Iesus
Christ only begotten God, as by fleshe the
sonne of man so also by the word the sonne
of God, not defecing or fayling from him
selfe God, toke vpon him true man accor‐
ding to the similitude of our man: In whó
although either a stroke shoulde fall, or a
wound shoulde lighte, or knottes should
meete together, or whó hanging shold lift
vp, wel might these things bring vnto him
a sway of passion, but a payne of passion
thei should not bring: euen as a dart either
perciug the water, or pricking the fyre, or
wounding the ayer. These are of al likely‐
hod those wordes, vpon which it is gathe‐
red that S. Hilarie thought Christes bodie
was

was impassible, and felte no moꝛe greife
when it was stricken, then water, fier, oꝛ
aer, whē it is diuided with a knife, foꝛ moꝛe
plaine woꝛdes to that purpose S. Hilarie
hath not in al his tenth booke. And yet if
one marke wel, these pꝛoue not necessarily
that which is laied to his charge. Foꝛ in al
this sentence the woꝛde bodie is not men=
tioned: nether are those later woꝛds necessarily to be referred vnto Chꝛists humani=
ty, but they may be right wel vnderstāded
also as spokē in respect of his deitie, which
was neither by nature, noꝛ yet actually
passible. But let vs graunt that all these
woꝛdes are ment by S. Hilarie euen of
Chꝛistes humane bodie. Foꝛ he hath
some woꝛdes in other places which sound
after that soꝛt, as where he saieth a litle af=
ter : Virtus corporis sine sensu pænæ vim
pænæ in se desæuientis accepit: ẏ power of
his bodie without sense of paine, receaued
the foꝛce of payne exercisinge his crueltie
vpon him. And yet he sayeth not here neither symplie, his bodie, but the power of
his bodie. But let it be sayed playnly that
his verie body suffered no moꝛe paine thē
fyre, aier, oꝛ water. will it folow straygbt=
waie that it is an erroꝛ, and that he foꝛ so
wꝛiting is to be rekoned emongst heretí-
kes? Befoꝛe we geue such rash iudgmēt of
so āciēt a father, it is wisdō to cōsider after

X ij　　what

what sort he ment the same. For if he ment
it after this sorte only, that Christes bodie
was by nature no more bound to be sub=
iect to woūds & whippes, thē the ayer, fier,
or water, are by nature subiect thereunto:
both his wordes and meaning are in that
sense most true. Now let his wordes folo=
wing in the next sentence shew, whether
he vsed this similitude in that respecte, or
no. they are these: In natura non est vel a-

Ibidem.

quam forari, vel pungi ignem, vel aera vul-
nerari, quamuis natura teli sit vulnerare,
compungere & forari. It is not in the nature either of water fire or ayer, to be per
ced, pricked, or woūded, although it be the
nature of a dart to wound, prick or perce.

By whiche wordes it is euident, that
he made that former comparison in re=
spect of the nature of those elementes on=
ly, to declare, that as by nature they could
not feele anie suche violence done vnto
them: so Christes bodye by nature was
not bound to be subiecte to anie torment,
although actually it suffered. And to con=
firme this to be the right meaninge of S.
Hilarie, what wordes can be plainer then
those allite after, where he saieth: Et homo

Hilar.
Ibidem.

ille de deo est habens ad patiendum quidé
corpus, & passus est, sed naturam non habens ad dolendum. Naturæ enim propriæ

25

ac suæ corpus illud est, quod in cœlesté glo-
riam trásformatur in monte, quod tactu suo
fugat febres, quod de sputo oculos format.
And that man is of God hauing a body to
suffer, & he suffered: but not hauing a nature to feele sorow or greife. For that body
is of his owne and proper nature, whiche
in the mont is transformed into heauenlie
glorie, whiche with his touching driueth
away feuers, which of his spettel formeth
eyes.

In these words that distinction of actu=
all suffering or feeling of paines, and suffering by necessitie of nature is plainly expressed. And here S. Hilarie quitteth him
selfe moste perfitely of that second error,
and sheweth howe all his other wordes
concerning that matter are to be cōstrued.
For he graunteth that Christ had a bodie
to suffer, and that he was in dede actually
passible, for he saieth: Passus est, he suffered,
that is to say he sustayned actually a l those
cruel tormentes. But howe was the same
bodie then impassible? Read forth and you
shall find: Sed naturam non habens ad dolendum, but not hauing a nature to feele
sorowe: so that therefore and in that respect onlie it is saied impassible, for that by
nature, it was not subiect to anie passion.
And howe proueth he, that by nature it
was suche? The wordes folowing declare

X iij   that

that also. for then the body of Christ did shew it selfe in his right nature, when at his transfiguration it was shewen glorious & heauenly. & as it was then through the abundant grace of the godhed so singularly vnited therevnto altogether impassible: so it might allwayes naturally haue continewed, if that vertu of the godhead had not (as it was sayed before) by speciall dispensation restrained it self. This nature of his body was shewed also , as S. Hilarie sayeth , when by touchinge it healed feuers, and with his spettle made the blynd to see , and finally when so euer he wrought any lyke miracle. for then the power of the godhead shewed it selfe in Christs humane nature which through y power was able allwayes naturally to worke lyke miracles . not that they were not therfore true miracles (for they were allwayes aboue the course of our comon nature) but because they were wrought by the natural power of that humane nature, which was it self altogether miraculous , as beinge conceued without the seede of man, brought foorth into y world without violatinge the virgins wombe, and ioyned in one person with the sonne of god.

I suppose by this tyme it is not only suffi=

sufficiently proued after what sort S. Hilarie ment that Christ suffered no payne
at his passion : but also how he beleiued
as al Catholikes doe that Christ suffe=
red in dede most greuous and excedinge
great paynes . But for the more suertie
set vs heare one or two places moe. for
that verye same distinction of nature and
dispensation, is so often repeted in that
boke , that vnlesse a man will of set pur=
pose (as it seemeth this Slaunderer hath
done) he neade not construe him amisse.
He sayeth in one place speakinge of Christ
as he suffered , that he had doloris corpus, sed non doloris naturam , that is to
saye, a body of sorow or a body subiect to
sorow: but not a nature of sorow or bound
to sorow. And againe he saieth in the same
place, Christ felt sorow sed nō doloris nostri sensu , but not by the sense of our so=
rowe , that is to saye, not naturally and
by necessitie as we feele sorow. And in the
same syde he hath twise together the word
dispensation declaringe, that all Christes
passion was a worke of dispensation, for
so he calleth it dispensatione passionis, the
dispensation of his passion.

Moreouer what words may be playner
to expresse his true meaning thē these? Col **I bidem.**
latis ergo dictorū atque gestorū virtutibus

demonstrari non ambiguum est, in natura
eius corporis infirmitatem naturæ corpo=
reæ non fuisse: cui in virtute naturæ fuerit
omnem infirmitaté corporum depellere,
& passionem illam illata licet corporilit,
non tamen naturam dolendi corpori intu-
lisse. The vertues then and powers of
his sayinges and doinges beinge compa=
red together, it is out all doubt declared,
that y̑ infirmitie of corporall nature was
not in the nature of his body, vnto whom
it was in the power of nature to driue a=
way all infirmitie of bodies. & although
that sufferinge was put to his body, yet
it did not bringe vnto his body a nature
of feelinge greif or sorow. who seeth not
how often he repeteth here the word, na=
ture? He sayeth not y̑ no infirmitie was
at all in Christes bodie, but that in the na=
ture of his bodie our naturall & necessarie
infirmitie was not. & why? marie because
it had power by nature to put away all in
firmitie as beinge conceiued by the holy
Ghost. and therefor also although it suffe=
red: yet it had not the nature and necessitie
of suffering.

    I will allege one sentence more, and so
end this matter. Therfore last of all note
well these wordes where he sayeth. Si ibi
necessitas est, & natura: si ibi vis est, & diffi
dentia, & dedecus, Sin autem hæc è con-
trario

Hilar. de
Trin.l.10

trario in sacramento passionis prædicátur:
quis rogo furor est, repudiata doctrinæ A=
postolicæ fide , mutare sensum religionis,
& totum hoc ad imbecillitatem & contu-
meliam rapere naturæ, quod & volútas est
& sacramentum : quod & potestas est, &
fiducia, & triumphus? If (in the passion
of Christ) there be necessitie, then there is
nature . if there be violence, then there is
mistrust and shame . but if in the mysterie
of the passion these thinges be sayed contrariewise: what madnes is it I pray you
refusing the fayth of þ Apostels doctrine,
to change the sense of religion , and vio=
lently to wrest all this to the weakenes &
contumely of nature , which consisteth in
will, & is a mysterie: which is both power
confidence and triumph or glory? Thus
far S . Hilarie in which few wordes he
concludeth the effect of all that hath bene
sayed before of this matter. he concludeth
the effect of his answer to the Arrians , &
sheweth the absurditie of their obiectiōs.
In the first sentence he playnly expoun=
deth, what he hath ment by sayinge that
Christes body suffered not payne by na=
ture. for if by necessitie(sayeth he) then by
nature: geuing vs to vnderstand therby,
that therfore he suffered not by nature, be=
cause necessitie of nature did not force him
to feele þ paine. Neither was he violently
                                    and

and againste his will driuen thereunto as
the Arrians imagined, wresting al to ꝑ con-
tumelie & reproch of his diuine nature whiche they belieued not to haue bene such in
him, ꝑ it had ben able to kepehis body from
feeling anie paine, whereas in dede by the
almightines thereof al cõsisted in his own
freewil & power. And therefore in the end
more glorie and renoune, redouned therby
vnto him, & vnto vs also much more cause
was geuen of greater loue and deuotion.

This doctrine S Hilarie confirmeth to
be not only most true, but also to haue bene
receaued from the Apostles, and to be the
true meaning of ꝑ wholeCatholike church.
wherfor wonder not that I haue bestowed
so many words in declaringe S. Hilaries
mind throughly herevpõ, for seing he writeth it as aApostolical doctrin, I thought
it most requisite ꝑ he shoulde be throughly
purged of all suspition of error in ꝑ behalfe:
but you may iustly wonder at his extreme
impudêce, who notwstanding S. Hilaries
meaning is bi his own words so easiero be
found out, would yet so impudently slan-
der him. But before we rippe vpthis fault
ani farther: take now the whole true meaning both of S Hilarie and of ꝑ Catholike
church cõcernig this mater breifly collected
into these few wordes. Christ had it in his
power & nature not to feie pain, but in dede
and

& actually he felt paine . Also Christ by ne=
cessitie & constraint felt no paine , but by
free choise & election he felt paine . Finally
bi course of ẙ nature which was cōceiued by
ẙ holy Ghost & vnited in one person w̄ god
he felt no pain : But by that dispensation
and Iconomie , whiche God vsed in fleshe
submitting his fleshe for our sakes to al hu=
mane infirmities, sinne only excepted, after
this sort he felt naturally accordinge to his
naturall complexion, a most greueous and
cruell paine. And so it is most true bothe ẙ
he felt paine naturally, taking nature for ẙ
ordinarie course of our infirmites wherun
to he submitted himselfe : and also that na=
turally he felt at all no paine more then fire
ayer or water, taking nature for that course
whiche ordinarily was due to his bodie
being cōceued of the holy Ghost , & whiche
he might alwaies haue vsed ordinarily, as
he shewed the same once most euidently at
his transfiguration.

Now then what falshod is there in these
assertiōs ? what error is ther in S Hilaries
writings being thus as he mēt thē, right=
ly vnderstode ? But I should rather aske
what impudēcie he lackethe ẙ could so fals=
ly report thē ? & what a shamlesse forehead
he hath ẙ could find in his hart so shame=
fully to belie such an auncient doctor ? men
say it is shame to belye the Diuell, & what
name shal we thē geue him ẙ belieth such an
holy

holy and sacred Saint? Truly as his own
name differeth not one iote from Iuel and
lacketh but one letter of Diuel, so this fact
of his resembleth wel the Diuels nature, &
is in dede to extreme abhominable and diuelish. For what is more proper to the diuel then slaundering, vpon whiche respect
he hath that very proper name geuen him?
And therfore hereafter vntil this slaunderer repent of his mscheiuous fact, this one
name may serue them both moste iustlye.
Whereunto that agreeth very wel whiche
S. Augustin writeth of al heretiks, saying:
Hæreticus si non frater diaboli, certè adiu-
tor & filius . An heretik isif not a brother,
certeinly a helper and sonne of the diuell.
And therefore we must so much lesse wonder at the slaunders made by this pelting
heretike, for he doth therein but folowe his
kinde, & put in practise the definition and
true nature of his and his fathers name.

Neither doth he herein any whit dissent
from his welbeloued brethrē the Arrians,
who burdened S. Hilarie in his life time
with ȳ same, or one very like error to that,
vpon whiche he maketh his first slaunder.
for S. Hilarie himself thus reporteth of thē
in the beginning of his tenth boke: Solent
ita de nobis implere aures ignorantium, vt
nos asserant negare natiuitatem, cum vni-
tatem diuinitatis prædicamus . They are
wont

Aug. lib.
de past.
ca.12.

wont by suche reportes made of vs to fill
the eares of the ignozant, that they say we
denie the natiuitie (of Chzifte) when we
preache the vnitie of the Godhead. And
therefoz to auoyde the occasion of all such
flaunders we find in the same place, that he
did wzite these bookes against them with
such diligence, and did so exactly set foozth a
demonstration of his whole faith : vt ne
mentiri saltem aduersum nos aliquid crimi-
nis possint. That they shoulde not be able
(saith he) so much as falsely to burthen vs
with any crime. wherefoze seing this slaū-
derer hath notwithstanding burdened him
in maner with the same, and likewise with
worse, and those gathered out of the same
boke where he wziteth this , howe can he
auoide but that he is bzother to those heretikes, & sonne to ẏ Father whose name,
manners, and nature, he so liueth repzesen
teth? I speake nothing (God is my iudge)
vpon hatred of the person, oz malice to the
man . But if vppon this occasion I wzite
somwhat roundly against those his slaunderous repoztes, let me be boane withall.
His owne fault is cause thereof, t he holy-
nes of this Sainct hath stirred me therevnto, and the truth it selfe compelleth me.
Also his repoztes are nowe pzoued open
slaunders , and therefoze I may the moze
boldlie chalenge him thereof.

But

But what if those slaunders could not haue bene so openly detected? what if so many plaine places could not haue bene found in S. Hilaries own workes, wherby he might haue bene made to saye so much in his owne defense? what if those wordes only had bene writen which seeme most to make for those errors? Should they therefor haue bene ascribed straightway vnto him as his errors? Should he therefore haue bene thought to haue defended such great and abhominable falshods because some fewe wordes seemed to sound that way? Or should he which in such case had so reported of him, thereby haue escaped blame? I suppose verily it might haue bene sufficient to euery meane honest nature, that the authoritie of this holy Father hath continued so great and famouse so many hundred yeares together without any such haynouse error layed to his charge. It might haue suffised to vnderstand how and vppon what occasion he wrote those twelue bookes, that is to say, how he wrote them against the Arrians, how he wrote them in defense of the Catholike faith, and that (as him selfe doth note) with greate diligence and circumspection. These circumstances should of right haue perswaded, that although he might by reason of ý Arriãs speake somewhat

Lib. 8.

what vehemently on the contrary part,
yet he would neuer haue defended in dede
such foule absurdities as were as bad o2
rather wo2se then those of the Arrians, ⅋
whiche were also befo2e his tyme openly
condemned fo2 heresies. O2 if he had held
them, a man might thinke oflikelyhode
some anncict w2iter befo2e this tyme wold
haue warned the posteritie thereof.

  S. Hierom who was so studiosly con=
uersant in his wo2kes that (as him selfe In Epist.
witnesseth) bringe in Gallia Belgica at adFloren
Tieuers w2ote ont with his owne hand tium.
one good bigge boke of his cntituled de
Sinodis: who also in the life of S. Hilarie
maketh hono2able mention of these very
twelue bokes de Trinitate, he I say would
not by all likelihode haue left such grosse
erro2s vncontrolled. Neither is it to be
thought but that S. Augustine, who in
disputing against heretikes alleageth this
holy fathers autho2itie so often, would
at some tyme o2 other both haue espied
and noted this greate faulte, if it had
bene true: especially whereas him selfe
w2ote so vehemently against the Ma=
nichees, vnto whose heresies S. Hilarie
must neades somewhat haue acco2ded, if
he held that Ch2ist toke not true flesh of ꝑ
virgin, o2 ꝑ he suffered not truely. And if ꝑ
                          had bene

had bene so S. Augustine would much
lesse haue geuen him that greate commē=
datiō which now he geueth in these wor=
des: Ecclesiæ Catholicæ aduersus hæreti-
cos acer rimum defensorem venerandum
quisi gnorat Hilarium Episcopū Gallum?
Who knoweth not Hilarie, that reuerend
Bishope in Fraunce, a most stout defen=
dour of the Catholike Church against he=
retikes? He would neuer haue called him a
stout defendor of y Catholike church agaiſt
heretikes, if he had found in his workes
part of the Manichees heresie so openly
maintayned. And that he beinge so pro=
found a clearke should, if it had bene ther,
not haue found it, y is a great deale more
then almost incredible.

   Any man also that were any whit well
affectioned to the auntient fathers autho=
ritie, would easely haue contēted him selfe
with that lerned man S. Thomas of A=
quine his verdicte in this matter. And
the maintayner of this slaunder might, if
it had liked his Superintendentship (es=
pecially where as he is, as it apeareth by
the margēt of his great Biblebable so wel
sene in such Scholemē) haue easely found
that which he maketh an error, put out
there in S. Thomas for an obiectiō, toge=
ther with y answer alitle after folowinge
in this wise, Hilarius à carne Christi non
                      veri=

Contra
Iul, Pel.
lib. 1.

Tom. 3.
quæst. 15
Art. 5.

veritatem doloris, sed necessitatem exclu-
dere intendit. S. Hilarie intendeth not to
exclude from the fleshe of Christe the truth
of grief, but ý necessitie. which necessitie as
S. Thomas there sheweth more at large
came vnto vs by ý corrupt nature whiche
we receue through synne from Adam, and
therfore Christes fleshe was most worthely free frome it, as the which neither was
conceued in synne, nor could possibly by
nature commit anie sinne. Al these reasons
besids many moe which might be reherced
shoulde haue staied anie reasonable man in
a good opinion of S. Hilarie, althoughe
none of his owne wordes could haue bene
alleaged for his defense. what shall wee
therefore saie nowe, seing besides all this,
his owne defense is by his owne wordes
before so amply witnessed? Truely I my
selfe at this tyme will say nothinge, but
S. Augustine shall in this case say that to
this shamelesse and misreporting Sacramentarie, which he writeth of the same S.
Hilarie to Iulianus the Pelagian, de origi-
nali peccato, concerning originall synne.
S. Augustines wordes are these: Hunc vi-
rum tanta in Episcopis Catholicis laude
preclarum, tanta notitia famaq; cóspicuum,
aude siquid tibi frontis est criminari. Accuse
if for shame thou darest this man (S. Hilarie) being so much praysed amongest Ca-

Cont.
Iulian.
pelag. l. i

　　　ý　　　tholike

tholike Byshoppes, and by so great fame
and brute renoumed . But what if this
worthie Superintendent (who for his lying
is worthely to be attended) hath alredi done
beyond all that whiche S. Augustine bid
the Pelagian there doe, if for shame he dared? what if all those defenses before re-
herfed notwithstanding , he hath alreadie
not only dared, but hathe in deede accused
this most holy father , and that not of one
but of two such crimes as (although vpon
some ferefull respect and a litle shamefull
ciuilitie, he termeth them the errors of a
holy doctor) were in dede if they were true
most vile and detestable heresies? For as I
saied before S. Hilarie if he had held them,
might hardly haue bene excused by ignorance, seing the defendours of them were
bothe in his tyme and before his tyme so
openly taken and generally condemned
for heretikes.

what wordes therefore shall we vse to
him that hathe alredie so fouly slaundered
such a reuerend Byshop and auncient Catholike doctor ? Shall we bidde him saye
somewhat against so holy a man if he dare
for shame? Nay seing he hath alredie vpon
his owne head most impudently dared it,
let him for verie shame (if he haue anie
shame in his forehead, either any feare of
God, or loue of his neighbor & of his own
soule,

soule, in his harte) recant the same openly,
and so make at the leaste some parte of
a mendes.

He can not pretend ignorance for his
excuse who preteðeth to be so wel acquain=
ted with the doctors phrases and wri=
tings. neither cā he wel pretend ouersight
or lacke of warning, whereas in those ve=
ry places wherehēce he gathered his poy=
son he might haue taken warninge not to
mistake the holy doctors meaning by these
words twise writen in the margent, Cautè
legas, reade warely : but he of mere malice
as it appereth, turned Caute legas into cal=
lide & calumniose intelligas . He turned
wary reading into guylefull & wrong vn=
derstanding.

But he wil perchāce endeuour somwhat
to cloke the rage of this his malice which
the auctoritie of Erasmus, who may seme
to haue set this matter first abroch emōge
those his ouer free & sometime moste false
censurs vpon the auncient doctors. which
if he alleage for him self, yet then he shonld
haue done no worse then Erasmus did.
The scholer shonld haue kepte his penne
within that compasse which his maysſter
vsed . He shonld haue suspended his de=
finitiue sentēce with videtur, it seemeth, as
Erasmus dothe . He shonld haue conten=
ted him selfe withe that sobre Councell

Y ij   which

whiche this his mayster geueth him in his epistle before Saint Hilaries workes, were speakinge of those verie matters of whiche we haue before talked so muche, saieth, there are many places in S Hilary quæ ciuilem & commodum requirunt interpretem, which require a ciuil and gentill interpretor. he should I say haue folowed this counsel, & not with suche cruelcie haue pronounced of these matters so absolutely, that they are in S. Dilarie like as those other in theManiches & Eutychians plaine errors.

But seing it is nowe clene otherwise, what other thing doth he but heape those coles of shame and dishonestie vppon his own head, which Erasmus kendled? And whereas Erasmus began wrongfullie (as it may appeare by y authoritie of S. Thomas, S. Dirom, S. Augustin, &by, S. Hilaries own wordes before so plainly alledged) to dishonor this holy father, casting him as it were, into y frying panne of false suspition: what other thing doth this Super erasmian endeuour, but to the vttermost of his power vtterly to discredit and disfame him, and so to take him out of Erasmus his frying panne, that he casteth him hedlong (so muche as in his power lieth) into the fier it selfe, together with the impiouse Manichees and wicked Eutychians:

for

For together with them he rekoneth vp
this holy Saint, as a writer of most false
doctrine, and defendor of most horrible errors. Then which rekoning of his, specially whereas it is alreadie proued to be so
slaunderous and so malicious: what could
haue bene inuented more barbarous, more
Turkish, or more Tyrannicall? For enuie it
selfe being of y greatest vices not the least,
is saied yet to ceasse towardes suche as are
departed this life, and therefore to byte,
snatch at, or misreport the dead, is counted
a thing most barbarous. we haue wondered of late yeres at cruel factes practised by
the Huguenots of France, both vppon the
lyue and deade : and they were in deede so
impious and wicked, that a man would
thinke there could be no degree of mischefe
added therevnto. I wil for example recite
one or two only, touching y crueltie which
they exercised on y dead: for thereby a most
deadly & inuincible hatred must nedes appeare. They practised the same not only
vpon such dead stockes and stones as had
the image of any goodthing: but euen vpõ
the dead bodies of Christen men, and not
content therewith, extended it also to the
holy bodyes of most blessed Sayntes.

One Loys de Perusiis writinge of those
tumultes which were stirred by the Hu-
guenotes in Prouince about Auignon, reporteth

(margin) In his booke intiteled. discours des guer res, &c.

Y iij

porteth that in one place they toke an Image of the Crucifix, bound it vpon an Asses backe, and so went leading the Asse, whippinge and scourginge the Crucifix through the toune. Also he telleth of another crueltie far passinge this, which they practised vpon dead mens bodies. They hauinge first by force gayned the toune called Mornas, and afterwardes by agreement the Castell it selfe, which is one of the cheife fortresses of the Counte of Auinion, contrarie to their faith and promisse, murthered out of hand most cruelly both the Capitain and his company. And not content therewith, toke the Capitains dead bodie, together with diuerse other of his souldiars, stripped them starke naked, knocked hornes violently into their heades, and so sent them in a bote without sterne or guyde, downe the Riuer of Rone towardes Auinion, with white staues in their handes, and this writinge teyed about them. O ceulx d'Auignon, laisses passer ces porteurs, car ilz ont payé le peage a Mornas. You of Auinion suffer these bearers to passe, for they haue payed for their passage at Mornas. And so the next daye they were taken vp in dede about Auinion and buried.

what

what Turke o2 Pagan could haue v=
sed mo2e crueltie then this? and yet this
is not all by a great deale. fo2 it was not
sufficient fo2 that extreme hatred which
they bare against the Catholike religion,
to rest with crueltie practised vpon the cō=
mon so2t of Catholikes of this age, that
far passinge malice of theirs required far=
ther degrees of mischefe. what did they
then? could they inuent yet mo2e impietie?
Those holy bodies of most auntient and
Catholike fathers, those which the Arri=
ans, the Gothes, the Hunni, the Uan=
dals, which the Saracins them selues, of
reuerence spared: those I say they toke
out of their tombes and spoyled, & which
is yet mo2e impious they burnt those bo=
dies into ashes, and afterwardes threw
down their ashes into the riuers. what
did Iulian the Apostata mo2e? o2 what cā
any ty2an inuent to do mo2e ty2annically?
After this so2t they handled the body of y
most aunciēt & Apostolike Bishop S. Ire=
næus at Lyons. Thus they handled ho=
ly S. Martins body at Tours. Yea they
restained not to shew this impious cruel=
tie to the sacred bodie of this our holy Ca
tholike docto2, and their owne contrie
man S. Hilarie.

Y iiij But

But to what purpose haue I rekoned vp all these examples? Forsooth for no other but to signifie, that as these are such as cannot sufficiently be wondered at: so that detestable fact of slaundringe and defaminge S. Hilarie, is yet much more wicked and horrible. For those other cruelties were practised by desperat and rash harebraynes in the furie of tumultes and battell, wherein especially when they are moued for religion, there is wont to be no meane of vnmercyfullnesse. but this crueltie is vsed by one that would seeme lerned, wyse, and sobre, and it is done of him premeditatly, and not without great deliberation. Againe those cruell actes, although they witnessed a great inward malice, yet they extended actually no farther then to those dead bodies remaining here vpon earth: but this wicked infamie blasteth abrode the great dishonor of that blessed soule of S. Hilarie, whiche liueth immortally with Christ in heauen. Yea the author thereof doth what in him lyeth to proue that holy and blessed soule of his, to be tormented amonge the wicked Manichees and hereticall Eutychians in hell fyre, for if he held as great errors as they, and such as were no lesse openly condemned then theirs, how should he auoyde lyke punishment? or if he recanted them

bee

before his death, thē how chance that doth not appeare in some historie of his life, either in his workes? or whie is he then at all blamed? But in dede S. Hilarie neuer thought, nor dreamed to defende any such wicked error. And therfore I may well conclude, that this Slaunderer far passeth by this impious fact of his, all those impieties before mentioned. and that he would litle haue spared S. Hilaries holy reliques if he had bene present at that spoyle at Poitiers, who dealeth now so vnmercyfully with his good name. He would not haue feared to burne his dead bodie, who endeauoreth so shamefully to deface those vertues of his minde, for which he hath bene alwayes throughout Christendome so much honored and estemed.

But it is now tyme to make an end of this extraordinary matter, and therfore I will saye no more, but god graunt that man grace in tyme, to acknowlege and confesse this his most horrible & haynous impietie. For let him neuer thinke to come where the blessed Saintes are, so long as he conspireth after this sort so trayterously against them. And in the meane season let other men trust his dealing in other matters, as they haue tried him trustie in this. Let them learne that, by this one example,

Y v　　which

which they may find confirmed by many moe. ⁊ is to saie, how that sect dispairing otherwise of their cause, goe now about to discredit those holy auntient Fathers, of whome they them selues haue heretofore so muche bragged.

Fynally let the authoritie of this holie Doctor Saynte Hylarie remaine sonnde and inuiolate, let that Catholike fayeth whiche he hath taught before concerninge the blessed Sacramente, be thereby more perfytely credited, and more hartely beleued.

¶ Testimonies out of those two most famous and holy Doctors, S. Augustine, and S. Ambrose.

The xij. Chapiter.

Although no man cā speake or write more plainly in the matter of ⁊ blessed Sacrament, then those whiche I haue before alleged, so that thereby iust occasion is geuen me to thinke you therein fully satisfied, and this matter sufficiently confirmed, yet I can not leaue out the testimonies of those famous and great learned Doctors S. Augustin and S. Ambrose, whose names are so well knowen euen to the vnlearned, and authoritie so great

great amongst all men w iche any whitte
esteme learning , that one worde of their
mouthes alone might seeme sufficient to
ende all strife and controuersy. And as for
S. Augustine, had he written neuer a wor=
de at all of this matter, yet there could ha=
ue ben no dout of his belefe therin , seing
he was christened and receaued his fayth
of that holy byshope of Milan S. Ambro=
se, whose most playne wordes shal here=
after appeare . for it is not likely that he
would dissent in so weyghty a matter of
faith, from him who taught him his who=
le fayth . and if he had mislyked any such
matter, he would no doubt among so ma=
ny workes which he wrote haue reproued
S. Ambrose therefore. The like myght be
sayed of S. Ambrose in case he had written
nothing. for then Saint Augustine should
likewise haue ben a sufficient witnesse of
his belief.

But thankes be to god as they then ly=
uing both about one ryme on earth stode
alwayes with the Catholike church and
fought day and nighte with theyr pennes
and preaching against the heretikes of
their tyme: so lyuing now in heauen, and
leauing theyr workes here behind thē, they
are not only two most strong pillers of ẏ
　　　　　　　　　　　　church.

Church, but also by their words and writinges doe fighte most valiantly against those enemies, by which the same Church is so pityfully in these our days assaulted. First you shall heare that perfite leasson, which S. Augustine learned of S. Ambrose, and afterward you shall heare the same truth more plainly expounded by S. Ambrose himselfe. wherefore to begin to Augustine hearken I pray you diligently and you shall finde him so contrary to the Sacramētaries humor, that whereas they say the Catholikes offend God highly in Idolatry by worshipping Christes body in the blessed Sacrament, whiche by their opinion is nothing but bread, S. Augustine will teach you that they offend God highly which doe not worshippe y̆ same, being in dede the true flesh of him who is both God and man. But you shall heare him selfe speake, and so iudge of the contrarietie of their humors afterward.

His words here translated are writen vppon that Psalme, wherein the holy Prophete Dauid extolling and magnifying y̆ glorie of Christ the Sonne of God, who should come into the world to confound al Idolatrie and superstition, biddeth vs among other things to worshippe his footestole, whereby S. Augustine vnderstandeth the Sacrament of the altar, for that
                                                    therein

therein is cõteyned the true flesh of Christ, which was no lesse inferior vnto his God= head, then is a footestole to a man or wo= mã resting their feete thereon. The words of Dauid are, Adorate scabellum pedum eius quoniam sanctum est. Adore ye and worship his footestole, because it is holy. Now folow the words of S. Augustine.

Consydre brethern what that is which (Dauid) biddeth vs adore. In an other place the Scripture sayeth : The heauen is my seate, and the earth is my footestole. Doth the Scripture then biude vs adore the earth , because in an other place it sayeth , the earth is Gods foote= stole? And how shall we adore the earth whereas the same scripture plainly saith, ẙ shalt adore thy Lord God? & here it saith adore his footestole, and to expound vnto me which is that footestole it saith the earth is his footestole . Thus I am in great dout and perplexity. I am afrayed to adore the earth , least he condemne me who made both heauen & earth. Again I am afrayed not to adore the footestole of our lord, seing the psalme saith vnto me: Adore his foote= stole . I search what is this footestole. and the scripture telleth me ẙ earth is his foote= stole. Being in this doubt I turne my self to Christ: for him I here seeck . & I find how that both the earth without impiety

Aug. in Psal 98.

Esa. 66.
Matt. 5.
"
"
"
"
Deut. 6.
"
"
"
"
"
"
"
"
"
"
"
"

may

" may be adored and worshipped, and also
" howe his footestole without impietie may
" be adored and worshipped.

" For he toke earth of earth because flesh
" is of earth, and he toke fleshe of the fleshe
" of the virgin Mary.

" Et quia in ipsa carne hîc ambulauit, & ipsã
" carnem nobis manducandam ad salutem
" dedit:nemo autem illam carnem manducat
" nisi prius adorauerit, inuentum est quem-
" admodum adoretur scabellum pedum Do-
" mini, & non solum non peccemus adoran-
" do, sed peccemus non adorando.

" And because he walked here on earth in
" that verie same flesh, and gaue vs the ve-
1. " ry same flesh to eate for our saluation, and
" no man eateth that fleshe onlesse firste he
2. " adore and worshippe it : it is founde out
" howe suche a footestole of our Lorde should
" be adored and worshipped, and that we do
" not only not synne in adoringe and wor-
3. " shippinge it, but that we sinne in not ado-
" ring and not worshipping.

" But doth fleshe geue life? Our Lorde
" him selfe when he spake in the commen=
" dation of that earth, saied : It is the spi=
" rite that geueth life, the flesh auaileth no-
" thing. Therefore when thou doest bowe
" downe and prostrate thy selfe vnto anie
" (suche) earth, doe not beholde it as earth,
4. " but behold that holy one whose footestole
that

that is, whiche thou doest adoze and woz= "
ship, because foz his sake thou doest adoze "
and wozshippe it. And therefoze Dauid ad= "
ded farther therevnto : Adorate scabellum "
pedum eius, quoniam sanctum est. Adoze "
and wozship his fotestoll, because it is ho= "
ly. who is holie? He, foz whose loue thou "
doest adoze and wozshippe his fotestoll. "

　And when thou adozest and wozshippest "
him, be not altogether in carnall cogita= "
tion, and nothinge quickened with that "
whiche is spirituall. Foz it is the spirite "
that geueth life (saieth Chziste) the fleshe "
auaileth nothing'. But when our Lozde "
commended this matter, he spake of his "
fleshe, saying: Onlesse a man eate my fleshe "
he shall not haue in him life euerlastinge. "
Certaine of his Disciples were offended "
thereat euen almost the seuentie, saying : "
This is an hard talke. who is able to vn= "
derstand it? and they went theyz way and "
walked no moze with him. "

　It seemed harde to them that he saied, "
onlesse a man eate mie fleshe he shall not "
haue lyfe euerlastinge. They vnderstode "
it folishlie and thought of it carnally, ima= "
gining ŷ our Lozd would haue cut of some "
peeces of hys bodie, and haue geuen them, "
& therfoze they saied, this is an hard talke. "

　They them selues were harde and stif= "
necked not the talke. Foz had they not bene "
hozd "

,, hard but gentle and meeke , they woulke
,, haue sayed. he speaketh not this causelesse
,, but for some secret mystery that lyeth hid=
,, de therin. they would haue taryed with
,, him humbly,& not haue bene so stubborn:
,, they would haue learned of him y̆ which
,, after theyr departing other which taryed
,, did learn. For whereas his twelue disci=
,, ples remayned with him the other being
,, departed , they began as it were soro̅w=
,, fully to tell him of the losse of those which
,, were offended with his wordes , and de=
,, parted backe from thym. but he instructed
,, them saying : it is the spirite that geueth
,, lyfe the flesh auayleth nothing. the wor=
,, des which I haue spoken are spirite and
5. ,, life, vnderstand ye spiritually that I haue
,, spoken . you shall not eate this body
,, which ye see , neither drinke that blood
,, which they that crucifye me shal shed. I
,, haue commended vnto you a certain Sa=
,, crament or mystery, which being spiritu=
,, ally vnderstode shall geue you lyfe. And
,, although that must nedes be visibly cele=
,, brated , yet muste it be inuisibely vnder=
6. ,, stode. Extolle & magnify our lord god,and
,, adore his fote stole for it is holy. ⋇

    Hitherto S. Augustines learned dis=
course vppon that verse of the Psalme.
Nowe consider I pray you howe wel the
same agreeth with the Sacramentaries doc=
trin

trine. They say, we eate in the blessed Sacrament a figure only of Christes fleshe. S.Augustin saith, Christ gaue vs the same flesh to eate for our saluation, wherein he walked on the earth, and which he toke of the blessed virgin. Thei say, no man ought to adore or worship in this Sacrament, Christes flesh and blood. S.Augustin saith no man ought to eate that flesh, onlesse he firste adore it. They say, we can not chose but synne greuously, and commit idolatrie by geuing any godly honour vnto it. S. Augustin saith, we can not chose but synne if we refuse to adore it. The whiche only saying proueth sufficientlie, that he beleued God to be there vnder the forme of breade truely and really present. For he was not so simple to thinke ȳ a bare peece of breade could be honoured as God without idolatry.

And that he ment suche an honour to be due vnto this blessed Sacrament, not only those wordes of adoration which he vseth so often in this place doe plainly declare, but also that obiection whiche he bringeth out of Scripture against him selfe, saying: Howe can this be true that we must adore his fotestole, seing the Scripture teacheth that God only is to be adored? For onlesse he ment by that adoringe of Gods fote-

Deut. 6.

                        S   stole

stole such an adoratiõ as is due vnto God only, this place of Deuteronomie maketh nothing to his purpose. And therefore to reconcile all, he proueth that we adore in the blessed Sacrament which is that fore= stole, no other thing but God him selfe: for so much as therein is conteyned the true flesh of Christ which being vnited in one person with his Godhead, and being ther truly present together with the God= head, hath worthely the same honor done vnto it, which belongeth to God himselfe. And so by adoring this his forestole we do according to that text of Scripture, adore

4. stil God only and no other. And therefore he repeteth again this adoration and bid= deth vs wheresoeuer we find this kind of earth, that is to say the flesh of Christ in this Sacrament, not to behold it as other cõmon flesh which came of earth, but adore God therevnto vnited whose flesh it is.

5. But the Sacramentaries will counsell you in this place to looke only toward the end, and marke diligently those sentences folowing where he writeth that Christ bad the Iewes vnderstande his wordes spiritually, and moreouer that Christ ment not by his talke had at Capharnaum, to promisse that he would geue that body to be eaten which his Disciples then saw,

neither

neither that blood to be dronken of them,
which they ẙ crucified him should shedde.
Of which places as the sayed Sacramentaries make great vaunt, so I besech you
also for your more perfite instruction in
the truth hereof and in the falshod of their
doctrine, weigh them indifferently, and remembre withall how truly and syncerly I
deale with you in this matter, whereas I
leaue out no part of the Doctors wordes,
although they seeme to make most for our
aduersaries. But whether that be so in
dede let vs now examine diligently, and
you shall see I warrant you, that their
great boste will make in the end but a very small rost.

First I suppose no man will denye but
that it is most necessarie, these later wordes
of S. Augustine be so vnderstanded, ẙ they
be not cleane contrarie to that which he
sayed a litle before. For how is it possible that so great a clearke and good a man
could in one syde of the leaf, and in so
hyghe a mysterie of our religion, write
contrarie to him selfe? The which one
truthe takinge place, what holde can
they take of his other wordes in these
places, seemed they neuer so playne for
their syde? For a litle before (as you
haue alredy hearde) his owne wordes

J ij   are

are founde to make most directly againste them. One sentence must expoūd, and not destroy and confound the other. If therefore by these later wordes, he ment as the Sacramentaries fondly imagin, that there is in the blessed Sacrament no reall presence of Christes body, but the presence of bread only, whereby we should be warned to feede spiritually by faith on him absent: what meaning shal those wordes before haue, where he saieth, Christ gaue vs the same flesh to eate, which he toke of the virgin, and that we muste adore it also before we presume to eate thereof?

Verily if a man examine them with a simple and sincere iudgment, and wil not to shamefully wrest them, he must neades confesse that they proue S. Augustine to haue beleued the true presence pf Christes fleshe in the blessed Sacrament. For what thinge can be more truely present vnto vs then that which we receaue into our mouthes and which we doe eate? But he saieth in most plaine termes that we doe eate the true flesh of Christ. For we eate that same flesh (saith he) which was taken of the virgin, and whiche we ought first to adore. Now what thinge is there to be adored besides God almighty, and the true fleshe or humane nature of Iesus Christe, which

S. Aug. wordes, doe plainly proue ÿ reall presence.

is

(sioyned in one person with his Godhead?
wherefor if we eate that flesh which was
taken of the blessed virgin, and if we adore
that flesh which we eate, it must nedes folowe that we eate the true flesh of Christe,
and that the same is by S . Augustines
verdit there truely present in the blessed
Sacrament, where only we doe properly
eate it. Then also ther can be no substance
of bread neither present nor eaten, onlesse
you will saie that S. Augustine willed vs
to commit idolatry and doe that honor of
adoration to a peece of bread, which is due
vnto God only . But I suppose no Christen harte neither yet the heretike him selfe
beareth so litle reuerence to that reuerend
Father . that he will suffre any such sonde
cogitatiõ entre into his brest. And yet this
must the Sacramentaries doe, if they wyll
nedes wring those later wordes of his to
proue their false opiniõ, For they bring all
to such a spiritual sese, ý they leaue vs nothing to eate besides naked bread, and ifS.
Augustine meant so, then he did in effecte
will vs to commit idolatry . For he signifieth that it is our ducty to adore that
which we eate. wherefore we must of force
conclude that spirituall vnderstanding of
Christs wordes, whichS. Augustine afterward talketh of, to haue bene far otherwise
meat of him thẽ ý Sacrmentaries do ima-

Z iÿ   gin.

Men say commonly that it is an yll glose, which destroyeth the text, & againe that it is an yll byrd which berayeth her own nest, both which absurdities are committed by them in this place. For they destroy the truth of the former text, by their false glose made vpon the later, and by alleging those wordes for their opinion, they shamefully beray this their owne nest, buylt with stickes and strawes of fayre wordes falsely vnderstanded. For they make this holy Doctor whom they would so fayne haue on their syde, not only to write contrarie to him seife, but also to be a starke lyer and a plaine teacher of Idolatrie. Let vs see therefore whether it be not more conuenient so to vnderstand his wordes that he may agree both with him selfe, and the whole Catholike Church, whereof he hath bene rekoned aboue these thousand yeares a sure piller, rather then by vaine & false gloses to make him cōtrarie both vnto him selfe & also vnto God.

You must here call to mind that which I haue in one or two places before signified, which is that the Catholike Church so teacheth, and always hath taught the true flesh & blood of Christ to be really present & eatē of vs in the blessed Sacrament, ŷ it meaneth not thereby to disalow & exclude al maner of spiritual meaning which may

may be made of Christes wordes, oz al ma=
ner of spirituall eating. But rather alow=
eth both together. And therefore first of all
we are warned by all Catholike preachers
and teachers not only to thinke on recea=
uing his pretious body & blood there real
ly present into our mouthes, but princi=
pally to regard y̆ we may spiritually ther=
withall receaue him into our hartes and
mindes, by remembring his great bene=
fites & specially his bitter passion, and by
making our soules cleane & pure that they
may worthely both receaue & kepe such a
treasoz. And y̆ Catholike Church admoni=
sheth vs so ernestly of this spirituall recea
uing, y̆ we are assured y̆ other Sacramen=
tal & external kind of receanig y̆ true body
into our mouthes vnder y̆ forme of bzead,
without this, is not only litle to our pzo=
fite, but also to our great discomfozt & con=
demnation. So it happened to the traytoz
Judas who receaued doubtlesse into his
mouth y̆ same true body of Christ which y̆
other did, but to his own cōfusion, because
he was not in spirite well disposed as the
other Apostles were, but altogethe r set to
muchief and wickednes.

Which truthe as you haue heard befoze
euidently witnessed by S. Chrysostome
& S. Cypzian: so therevnto those wozdes
of S. Augustine him selfe do serue mer=

I iiij   neilous

How this
wozde
spirituall
is diuers
wayes
truly vsed
cōcerning
the blessed
Sacra=
ment.

Aug. in
Ioan.6.

neylous well which he writeth vppõ the
vi. of S. Ihon on this wise. He that a-
bydeth not in Christ, and in whom Christ
abydeth not, without dout he nether eateth spiritually his flesh, nor drinketh his
blood, although he doe carnaly and visibly presse with his teath the Sacrament of
the body and blood of Christ: but rather
he eateth and drinketh the Sacrament of
so worthy a thyng vnto his own condem-
natiõ, because he being vnclean presumed
to come vnto the Sacraments of Christ,
which no man receaueth worthely but he
which is cleã, of whõ it is writē. blessed are
the cleane of hart, for they shal see god.

In these wordes you see euidently that
cõfirmed which I sayd before the church
generally teacheth. ỹ is to say, how there
is a spirituall receauing of Christ with
a pure and cleane cõscience into our hartes, & a corporall or reall receauing of his
fleshe vnder the forme of bread into our
mouthes, & also how this later receauing
rather hurteth then profiteth, onlesse the
former be ioyned therewith. I might vpon these playn wordes of S. Augustin cõ-
clude also, that he neuer talketh so spiritually of this blessed Sacrament, that he
meaneth therby to take away ỹ reall presence, as the Sacramētaries imagin. For
here he cõfesseth that euē the wicked man
preseth

presseth & toucheth with his teeth y Sacrament of the body of Christ, & eateth the Sacrament of that worthy thing to his damnation , which the goodman eateth to his saluation. So that one thing is eaten of both. whereby the reall presence is euidently proued.

But let vs goe forward and see whether there may be found any other good sense, wherin y Catholike churche alloweth this worde spirituall, to be vsed in speaking or writing of the blessed Sacrament. for somtimes it may be vsed in respect of that meanes by which we doe conceaue and apprehend the being of Christes body there. As that is truely sayed to be knowen spiritually, which is not visible nether perceaued by our senses, but apprehended by fayth, which consisteth only in the spirite and vnderstanding. And according to this meaning the church singeth openly in the feast of this holy sacrament, which is on Corpus Christi day in this wise. Et si sensus deficit ad firmandū cor syncerum sola fides sufficit, that is to say: Although al sense fayle, yet to strengthen a pure hart in this matter, fayth alone suffiseth. and so the Church cōfesseth that the truth of this Sacrament is spiritually apprehended by fayth only . nether doth the same spirituall apprehension diminishe

minishe any whit the reall presence of
Christ his body. No more then the beleuing of God the Sonne to be made true
man, doth derogat from the truth of his
being true man in dede. But both may
stand together very wel, that he was truly
& really made man, & borne of the blessed
virgin, and that we doe spiritually & by
faith only apprehed y⁰ same. For our sense,
and naturall reason can neuer perceaue,
either that God could be made man, or
that a man could be borne of a virgin.
And so likewise the wordes reall and spirituall are vsed in the blessed Sacrament without any inconuenience. for the
true body of Christ is there really present,
and apprehêded of vs spiritually by faith.

There is a third true sense also wherin
the Church vseth this word spirituall, and
that neither in respect of the beleuing neither yet of the receauing, but euen in respect of the reall presence, and being. for although the being of Christes body fleshe
and blood in the blessed Sacrament is con
cerning the substance thereof most true &
perfite, yet may it right well be called also
spirituall, for so much as it hath not that
maner of being here, as it had when he
walked on the earth, or when it was
straetched on the crosse. But hath here
such a miraculous and mysticall being,
that

that whereas it is the very same true body, yet it is conteined vnder the litle compasse of those formes of bread and wine,
and vnder euery part and portion thereof. And so the true and real body of Christ
is sayd to be here spiritually, for so much
as it hath here those proprieties which do
belong vnto a spirite. neither is it mer-
uetle (as S. Damascen writeth) if Christ
his holy body had all proprieties of a spi- De fide
rite when he would, seing the same was Orth. li.
conceiued by the holy spirite in the vir- 4. ca. 14.
gins wombe, and therefore he practised
the same by and by at his first entring in
to the world. for he came forth without
violating or breaking any of those bandes Ioan. 20.
of her virginity. Also after this sort he entred in amonge his disciples the dores
being fast shut. for to doe that thing it belongeth naturally vnto a spirite and not
vnto a body, ʒ only body of Christ excepted which was so supernaturally cōceued.

And therefore his disciples were not a
litle amased there at, thinking it had bene
some ghost. but Christ hauing thus declared ʒ his body now glorified had actually
those properties of a spirite, which were
before also alwayes in his power, to shew
that this notwithstanding the same cea-
sed not to be a true bodi, proued strait way
that he was no spirite, saying: Spiritus car Luc. 24.
né & ossa nō habet sicut me videtis habere.

A spirite hath no fleshe and bones as you see me haue. So that you may hereby euidently perceaue how Christes true fleshe and blood may be truly and really present although the maner of his presence be called spirituall, as the maner of his entring in among his disciples was spiritual whē as he entred notwithstanding truely and really . And thus you haue many good senses, in which the spirituall vnderstanding of Christes wordes nothing derogateth from the reall presence of his flesh.

The true vnderstanding of S. August. wordes.

Now let vs returne again to S. Augustine and considre, whether as his former wordes where he speaketh so plainly of adoration due vnto the blessed Sacramēt, doe confirme the reall presence of Christ his body which the Catholikes beleue: so his later wordes also haue not that last spirituall meaning which the Catholikes doe truly teach, rather then ye other which the Sacramētaries doe falsly and wrongfully attribute vnto thē. To proue which thing, that argument before mentioned might alone suffice. For by this meanes both those sentences be true, which otherwise are so contrary, that the one quite destroyth the other. But read once more I pray you S. Augustins wordes, & marke vppon what occasion those later of which the Sacramentaries take hold, doe folow.

doth

Doth he not speake a litle before of ý stub=
born Capharnites, and of that grosse ima=
gination which they conceiued vppon
Christes talke? Doth not he say that they
imagined his flesh should be cut in pieces
and so eaten of them like other flesh of the
shambles?

As Christ therefore sayd vnto them, the
spirite geueth lyfe, meaning not thereby
to deny that which he spake before, promi=
sing to geue his flesh to be eaten, and sayd
moreouer that the flesh auayleth nothing,
meaning their fleshly and grosse interpre=
ting of his wordes, & not ý his precious
fleshe auayled nothing, whiche was the
price of our redemption, which (as you
haue heard before in S. Cyril) quickneth &
geueth lyfe to the world: So S. Augustin
to reprone likewise that their grosse and
bucherly imagination, maketh Christ ex=
pound his own wordes vnto al such Ca=
pharnites more plainly, saying: Under=
stand ye spiritually that I haue spoken.
You shall not eate this body which ye see,
nether drinke that blood which they that
crucifie me shall shed. as who should say,
be ye not offended o ye stubborn Caphar=
nites, for that I promise you my flesh to
eate, and my blood to drinke. ye shall not
haue it as you haue other meat to feed
your belies withall, but for a spirituall
                                        foode

foode to comfort both your soules and bo=
dies vnto euerlasting life. Neither shall
you haue it visibly in the likenesse of flesh
as this now is which you see, and as it
shalbe streatched on the crosse, but after
a more diuine and spirituall maner, vn=
der another forme, in a Sacrament, and
mystery, which your sense shall nothing
abhorre. And the eating of my flesh being
aiter this sort spiritually vnderstanded,
shall not only not offend, but quicken,
make liuely, and strenghthen, all such
as spiritually and deuoutly receaue the
same.

This is the true report of S. Augustins
meaning, as your selfe may easely per=
ceaue if you confer all his wordes toge=
ther, the former with those that folow. for
a great parte of his talke is wholy dire=
cted against the Capharnites, which ne=
ther had any cogitation of a spirituall re=
ceuing of so precious a foode with a pure
and cleane conscience, neither of any my=
sticall way how a mans fleshe might be
geuen in such sorte, that it should not of=
fend the senses, nether would tary with
Christ to learn the same of him as the o=
ther disciples did, but minding only their
besy cheare and grosse imagination, strait=
way gaue him ouer.

And therefore to confound those and all
other

other their like S. Augustin declareth
right well how neither Christ himself nor
the Catholike Church taught by the holy
Ghost ener ment so grossely, y̆ we should
eati hes flesshe vnder the same forme in
which he walked on the earth, or drinke
his blood in that visible forme as it was
shed on the crosse, but inuisibly vnder the
formes of bread & wine. so that by saying:
you shal not eate this body which you see,
he denieth not the eating of the same body
in substance, but sheweth that we shall
not eate it in the same forme as it was
then being vysible flesh. For he sayd before that Christ gaue vs the same flesshe to
eate in which he walked on the earth. by
which wordes he must nedes mean the
same flesshe in substance, for the same in
outward and visible forme we are sure
he gaue not. and therefore consequently
these later wordes were he denieth that
body to be geuen, must of force be ment
of the visible forme only. And the wordes
them selues doe plainly imploy the same,
for by saying: This which you see he saith
in effect), this visible body, or this body
after this visible forme and maner. And in
speaking likewise of the blood he vsed
those termes which haue some respect to y̆
vtward forme.

    And therefore whereas he denyeth
                                    that

that blood to be dronken which they did shed, who crucified him. He meaneth that it is not dronken in that visible forme of blood as it was there shed.

This sense then of S. Augustins words being most true, and so well agreable both to y which you haue heard before of himselfe in the same place , and to that which the Catholike faith teacheth , I doubt not but you vnderstand how litle vantage the Sacramentaries can haue thereby toward the maintenace of their false opinion. And by this you may learne to iudge of all other like places of the auncient Doctors which they wrongfully endeuour to wrest vnto there syde, whensoeuer they find any mention made of spirituall receauing , or spirituall presence of Christes body in the blessed Sacrament. As though the Catholikes denyed any of them , or as though that being graunted the reall presence, and true receauing of the same into the mouth were taken away. For so S. Augustine himselfe in an other place speaketh ,saying that the body of our Lord entreth into our mouth. If you desire to heare his own words they are these: It hath pleased the holy Ghost, that in the honor of so great a Sacrament, the body of our Lord should entre into the mouth of a Christian man before outward meates. By which wordes

Epist. 118 ad Ianua rium.

he

he geueth a reason also why this blessed
Sacrament hath ben vsed in the church to
be receued allwayes fasting, although the
same was not obserued of Christe at the
first institution thereof.

And so there is no doctor which talketh
of the spirituall receauing, but in the same
or some other place or both (as you haue
heard now out of S . Augustine) he wit=
nesseth playnely the reall presence which
they impudētly deny. but they cānot bring
one place out of any doctor wherin he so
affirmeth the spirituall presence or spiri=
tuall feading on Christ his flesshe, that he
denyeth or dessyeth the other as they doe.
wherfore let vs, in despite of theyr false
doctrin concluding with S.Augustin, ex=
tolle and magnifie our lord god, and adore
his footestole which is the blessed Sacra=
ment of the altar . For it is holy, for it is
y͂ holy body of our sauiour Jesus Christ,
it is the same body in substance, although
inuisible and vnder the forme of bread,
which was borne of the blessed virgin,
which walked here on the earth , & was
at thelast with great tormētes crucified for
our sakes, which rose the third day, ascen=
ded into heauen, sitteth on the right hand
in equall power with god the father , and
which shall appeare visibly vnto vs at y͂
dreadfull day of iudgmēt, whē as he shall

6,

to our greate discomfort and confusion be ashamed of vs, if we be ashamed or dout to confesse him here in the blessed Sacramēt: as cōtrariwise if we acknowledge and confesse him here before men, according to the true Catholike faith, he shall appeare to our endlesse comfort and blysse.

Now to close vp your stomake, and throughly to establishe your faith concerning the truth of this heauenly banket, and consequently, concerninge all other matters of religion, I will set before you those plaine wordes of that other moste holie Bishoppe S. Ambrose, whiche alone (as I saied before) doe sufficiently declare what S. Augustine belieued, for so muche as he learned his beliefe of S. Ambrose. For by that meanes he reuerenced alwayes both him and his doctrine verie muche, as him selfe witnesseth where he writeth of S. Ambrose these wordes: Veneror vt patrem, in Christo enim Iesu per Euangelium ipse me genuit. I reuerence him as a father, for he through the Ghospel in Christ Iesu begotte me. And therefore to the end you should be more persitely assured of S. Augustins meaning in the place before alleged and in this whole matter, I haue put S. Ambrose behinde him, whereas otherwise he should of right haue bene firste. Marke diligently I beseche you, whether

he

Contr.
Iul. pela.
lib.1.

he doth not throughly agree with ẏ, which you haue hearde before in other, & namelie whether he doth not euidently witnesse what saith that was, which S. Augustine learned of him. That which is here translated is writen in the last Chapter of his boke intiteled, de ijs qui mysterijs initiantur. The summe also or title of the chapter is this.

　　❡ Of the vertue of the Sacrament of the body & blood of Christ, & the excellency thereof being cōpared with Manna & the waters of the rocke. It is proued also by many examples that the body of Christ whiche we receaue, it not bread, but that flesshe whiche was borne of the virgin, which was crucified, which was buried.

Consider now (saith S. Ambrose) whether is better the bread of Angels, or ẏ flesh of Christ which is truely the body of life. That Manna came from heauen, this is aboue heauen: that of heauen, this of the Lorde of the heauens. That if it had bene kept vntil the next day was subiect to corruption, this is altogether incorruptible. And whosoeuer tasteth it deuoutlye, he shall not possibly feale corruption. water flowed to the Iewes out of a rocke, blood floweth to thee out of Christe. water satisfied them for an houre, blood washeth thee for euer. The Iewe dranke, and yet

Amb. de ijs qui mysterijs initiatur. ca. vlt.
"
" 1.
"
"
"
"
"
"
"
"

Aa ij　　thirs

,, thirsteth, thou hauing once dronke canste

,, thirst no more.

,, Furthermore that was in a shadowe,

2. this is in truth. If that whiche thou won-

,, drest at is a shadowe, howe greate a thing

,, is this at the shadowe whereof thou doest

,, wondre? and that the same is a shadowe

,, which was done in the tyme of those fore-

,, fathers hearken to S. Paule who saieth:

1. Cor, 10 They dranke of the rocke folowing them,

and that rocke was Christe. And againe,

,, But God was not pleased in many of thē,

,, for they were ouerthrowen in the wilder-

,, nes, and these thinges were done in figure

,, of vs. Thou haste knowen thinges of

,, greater price and excellency. For the light

,, is better then a shadowe, The truth bet-

,, ter then a figure, and the body of our crea-

3. tor and maker muche better then Manna

,, from heauen.

,, But perchaunce you wil say, I see ano-

4. ther thing with my eyes, howe then doe

,, you tel me that I receaue ybody of Christ?

,, This then remayneth yet by vs to be pro-

,, ued. How manie examples therefore doe

,, we vse, to shew that this is not that which

5. nature formed, but that whiche benedic-

,, tion consecrated, and that the power of be-

,, nediction is greater then the power of

,, nature, for so muche as through benedic-

tion

tion nature it selfe is changed?

Moyses held in his hand a rodde, he cast the same foorth and it was made a serpent. Againe he tooke vp the Serpente by the taile, and the same returned to the nature of a rodde. You see then by the grace geuen to that Prophete, that nature both in the rodde and serpent was twise changed. The riuers of Egipte ranne of cleane and pure water. Blood sodenly brake out from the springes and fontaines. There was no drinke to be had out of the riuers, and at the Prophetes prayers the blood of the riuers ceassed, the nature of water returned.

The Hebrues were compassed in round about, closed on one side by the Egyptiās, & shut vp on the other sideby reason of the sea. Moyses lifted vp his rodde, the water diuided it selfe, and congeled together on eche side like walles, and a fotepath appered through the middest of the waters. Iordan turned backe, and contrary to nature retired thither where his first spring is. Is it not then manifest that the nature both of the sea waues, and course of the riuers hath bene changed?

The people of our Forefathers thirsted. Moyses touched the rocke, and forthwith out of the rocke flowed water, Did not grace here worke belydes nature, that a

Aa iij rock

Exod. 9.
"
"
"
"
"
"
"

Ibid.
"
"
"
"
"
"

"
"
"
Exod. 14
"
"
"
Iosue 3.
"
"
"
"
Exod. 17

"
"

,, rocke ſhould ſend foorth water which na-
,, turally it had not ? The water Marath
,, was ſo bitter that the thyrſty people could
,, not drinke thereof. Moyſes caſt woode in
,, to the water, and the nature of the water
,, loſt ſtrayteway that bitterneſſe, which by
,, grace powred therupō was quickly tem-
,, pered .

,, Under Heliſeus the Prophete an axe
,, fell from the helſe out of one of the ſon-
,, nes of the Prophetes handes, and ſanke
,, vnderneth the water : he that had loſt the
,, iron of his axe beſought Heliſeus, & Heli-
,, ſeus put the woodde in to the water, and
,, the iron ſwemmed vp. And we acknow-
,, lege this alſo to haue ben brought to paſ-
,, ſe beſides the courſe of nature . for iron in
,, his kind is more heauie then the liquor of
,, water. Thus therfor doe we not perceaue
,, that grace is of greater power thē nature?
,, and yet hytherto we haue mentioned that
,, grace only, which was geuen by the bene-
,, diction of Prophetes.

S. ,, And if the bleſſing of man hath ſo much
,, preuayled ỹ it hath changed nature, what
,, ſay we to the diuine conſecration it ſelfe,
,, where the very words of our Lord & Sa-
,, uiour doe worke ? For this Sacrament
,, which thou receaueſt is made by Chriſtes
,, owne wordes. If Elias wordes were of
M   ſuch

such force that they brought fyre down frō "
heauen: shall not the wordes of Christ be "
able to change the kindes or natures of "
elementes ? Thow hast readen of the " 7.
workes of the whole worlde that he sayed "
the worde and all thinges were made, he "
commaūded, and they were created. The "
worde then of Christ which could of no- "
thing make that , which before was not , "
can it not change those thinges which are "
alredy existent, in to that thing which be- "
fore they were not ? For it is not a lesse "
thing, to geue new natures vnto thinges "
then to change natures . but what vse we "
argumentes? Let vs vse his own epsam- "
ples, and let vs confirme the truth of this "
mistery by the example of his incarna- " 8.
tion. "

when our Lorde Iesus was borne of "
Mary, was there euer befor seen any such "
course of nature? If we seeke the common "
ordre of nature, a woman is wont to con- "
ceiue by the company of a man . It ap- "
peareth therefore euidently that the vir- "
gin conceiued besydes the ordre of na- "
ture , and this bodye whiche wee doe "
make or consecrate , is that whiche came "
of the virgin. why then seekest thou here "
a naturall ordre in the bodye of Christe, "
whereas our Lorde Iesus him selfe was "
besides the ordre of nature borne of the "

9.
"
"
Matt.26
"
"
"
"
"
10.
"
"
"
"
"
"
"
"

virgin? It is truely the very true flesh of Christ which was crucified, which was buried: and therfor this is verely the Sacrament of that flesh. Our lord Jesus him self crieth, this is my body. Before the benediction of those heavenly wordes a nother kinde or nature is named, after consecration the body is signified or mentioned. He him self calleth it his blood, before consecration it is named another thing, after consecration it is called blood. And thou sayest there vnto, Amen, that is to say, it is trew. Let thy inward mynd confesse that, which thy mouth speaketh, and let thy affection thinke that whiche thy speach soundeth.

This much out of S. Ambrose who if he hath not declared his mind to haue ben plaine contary to that, whiche the Sacramentaries do teach, and altogether agreable to that which the Catholikes belieue, then fayn would I learne howe a man might vtter his minde plainly. First he

1.

proueth as you haue heard before in other how far thys Sacrament bringe the trueth passeth those figures and shadowes of the old law, by which it was foresignified. For Manna (sayeth he) was called the bread of Angels, but this is the fleshe of Christ. That came frō heauē, this is ÿ Lord hymselfe who is aboue all heauens, that

was

was corruptible , this endureth for euer.
Aske therfore of the Sacramentaries, if it
be a naked figure, how chaunce S . Am=
brose calleth it the fleshe of Christ , or lord
of heauens? and if it continue styll breade,
how it dureth for euer incorruptible ?
what nede I note vnto you how much
that confirmeth the Catholike fayth where
he bydoeth vs conceiue what a miracle
this is, by that the shadow thereof is wō=
derful , whereas that which the Sacra=
mentaries make of it is nothing so much
wonderfull as Manna, or any of the least
shadowes mentioned in the old law? But
marke a litle after how in comparing this
trueth with those shadowes he calleth it
the body of our maker. For besides that
the same maketh plainly against the Sa=
cramentaries , it proueth also that phrase
which our good Forefathers vsed in cal=
ling the blessed Sacrament theyr maker,
to haue ben of no smal antiquity but re=
ceiued together with the true faith where=
rypō it was grounded euen from the pri=
mitiue Church.

   Note also immediatly how this holy
Father putteth foorth that most common
obiection of the new bretheren , and an=
swereth to it him self. For say they not cō=
monly after this sorte? we see breade, we
taft bread , we feale bread , our senses find
                                          there

2.

3.

4.

there all the accidents of bread, how can it
then be the body of Christe? Unto whiche
sensual and carnall argumēt S.Ambrose
making answer rekoneth vp a great nōbre
of miracles out of ye old testamēt wrought
by the Prophetes: and at lenght conclu=
deth, that seing their benediction was able
to change the nature of things, much more
the wordes of Christ in the consecration of
this Sacrament, doth cōtrarie to al course
of nature & iudgemēt of the senses, change
the nature of bread into the nature of his
true body.

And note by the way before he come
to those examples that notable place,
where he saieth moste directly againste the
Sacramentaries, that this whichis in the
blessed Sacrament is not that which na=
ture formed, but that whiche benediction
consecrated. for the wordes of consecratiō
name vnto vs nothinge but the body of
Christ. And by the naturall substance of
wheat whercof it is made we learne that
it is naturally bread. if then ye benediction
being of greater power as S. Ambrose
saieth, ouercometh nature so that it is no
more that which nature formed, then it is
no more bread but the body of Christ, and
they contrariewise must nedes lye whiche
saye it is styl playnelie bread and not the
body

bodye of Christe. And likewise the Lutherans which would haue it to be bothe true bread and the true body. Note farther that if the Prophetes changed the nature of thinges as it is proued by manie examples: the wordes of Christ much more doe worke a change of nature in this diuine mysterie. And if the nature be changed, what other nature can be ment besides the substance of bread, for the outward formes wee see are not changed, and wherunto should this change be made, but into the substance of Christ his body mentioned in the wordes of consecratiõ, which do worke this miraculous change?

6.

A few lines after he compareth the workinge of Christes wordes in this blessed Sacrament to ye great worke of the creation of the worlde whiche was brought to passe by lyke meanes. and he reasoneth after this sort. It is not a lesse thing but rather a greater miracle to make somewhat of nothing then to change some one thing into an other, but God by the vertue of his worde made not somewhat onlie, but the whole worlde of nothinge, & by vertue thereof the Sonne yet continuallie shyneth, and all other creatures euen to this daye haue theyr being: how can we choose therefore but beleue, that the

7.

same

same worde of the same God should bring
y to passe which is not altogether so great
a miracle, that is, to change one nature into an other, the nature of bread into the
nature of his body? And what absurditie
is it that these wordes once spoken by him
should worke that effect euen to the end of
the world, seing those wordes by which he
created lyght and other thinges in the beginning of the world, haue euer synce had
theyr true and perfite working.

But note diligently I pray you, that
sentence whiche conteineth this whole argument and where he demaudeth whether
the worde of God which of nothing made
somewhat, can not change one thing that
is alredie made into an other. for although
the same proueth as you see moste plainly
that S. Ambrose ment a true change to
be wrought in the blessed Sacramente by
the almighty word, yet some Sacramentaries haue alleged an other like sentence
out of this doctor, hauing altogether the
same sense and in manner the same words
also, to proue that ther is no change at al,
but the nature of bread continually remayning. I will not now stay to discusse after
what manner they doe wreste the words,
for so much as the same is perfitly handeled in the answer lately made to the Apo-
logie, Let it be sufficiēt for me to haue war

ned

ned you only of this impudency which I am sure is practised, that your self beinge more conuersant emong them, if perchance herafter you shal happē to heare of y same, you may readinge together this whole discourse, be able more easely to espye theyr falshoode.

You may worthely note also that place where this holy doctor laying all other argumentes asyde proueth this great miracle which is wrought in the Sacrament by the miraculous incarnatiō which was of the blessed virgin without seed of man: geuinge you thereby that leasson whiche you haue now often heard, howe you shall answer al suche as by natural reason and by theyr outward senses goe about to discusse this veritie, for the same body is here miraculously present, which was miraculously conceiued of the blessed virgin. And that body is as wel able to remayne wholy vnder the form of bread contrarie to the course of nature, as to be conceaued aboue nature without the seed of man. Note also that he maketh no difference betwen that body which was crucified and that which is in the Sacrament, but rather argueth y because the true flesh of Christ suffered & was buried, therefore the same muste be here truely present.

Last of al beare wel away y he wriceth
one

8.

9.

10.

one name to haue ben geuen to these my=
steries before the cōsecration and an other
name after consecration. For the change
of names (which are commenly geuen ac=
cordinge to the nature of thinges) impor=
teth also the chāge of the things thēm sel=
ues. And S. Ambrose him selfe sayeth that
as Christ called these misteries after con=
secration his body and blood, so the who=
le church was wōt by the word Amen, to
witnesse that they beleiued the same to be
most true. & therefore he exhorteth euery
Christen man to beleiue that in harte vn=
faynedly which these wordes plainly doe
sound. By which few wordes the Sacra=
mentaries faythlesse doctrine is vtterly
confounded. for if ther lay hide any tropi=
call or figuratiue speach in these wordes
of Christ, Thisis my body , S. Ambrose
would neuer haue willed vs to beleiue ȳ
sence to be true which they doe plainly by
their sounde expresse & signifie, but would
him selfe rather haue expounded the ma=
ner & phrase of speach which were in them
vsed. for a metaphoriall or tropicall speach
hath commonly an other diuerse meaning
from that which the wordes literally doe
importe . as when Christ called his father
a husband man, and him selfe a rocke. for
he nether ment thereby that him self was
a material rocke, as the worde soundeth,

nor

nor that his father was a common fermer
or tiller of the ground. But here S. Am=
brose playnlie declareth, that we must take
the wordes of the blessed Sacrament euen
as they sounde in our eares, and are pro=
nounced by our mouthes. J report me
therefore to all indifferent eares, whether
those wordes This is my body, doe sounde
any other thing, then that the same whiche
was then in Christes handes, was his
body, whether any parte of them maketh
any mention of bread or figure. And seing
they doe not, let vs conclude withe S.
Ambrose and beleue hartely with y̆ whole
Catholike Church, that which these words
without any farther wresting doe signifie
most plainly. And if any other doctor be=
fore hath seemed any thing obscure,
let the plainesse and perspienity
which S. Ambrose hath vsed
in this whole discourse
perfitely recompence
the same

The Conclusion

IT remaineth now that you weigh diligently with your self, which side is more
worthy credite, that which hath the consent not only of the foure Euangelistes,
and the blessed Apostle S. Paul vttering
in so plain wordes the meaning of our sauiour, but also of these auncient Greke &
Latin doctors, agreeing in one exposition
therevpon: or els that other side and sect
which by new found gloses doth both mis-
construe the plaine wordes of holy scripture, and vtterly ouerthrow that vniform
interpretation of the auncient doctors. you
must weygh I say, and put in one balance
the auncient faith of these holy & learned
fathers whiche liued al so far within the
compasse of the first six hundred yeres, that
the yongest of them was wel nigh xii hundred yere before our dayes: & in the other
balance set this new fangled doctrine,
which is not yet half one hundred yere old.
And although wicliffe and Berengarius
be named for their Apostles, neither of the
reacheth yet to very many hundreds: and
besides that, they were both in their life
time condemned for blasphemous heretikes. And Berengarius the elder of the
two openly also recanted his heresie. So
that if antiquity deserueth any whit to be

credite

credited in this matter, which dependeth
so much vppon antiquity, you may easely
iudge which balance is the lyghter, and
which doctrine is more solishe.

But if you adde herevnto also the con=
sent of these auncient Fathers on the one
side, and the discorde which is among the
new brethern in this very matter of ý blef
sed sacramēt on the other side, this might
easely by it selfe declare their syde to be as
light, as a thing of naught. For as they
are far wyde from the true Catholike faith
and altogether disagreing from those ho=
ly Fathers, so they can not by any meanes
agree amonge them selues. This matter
is so euident that they them selues cannot
deny it, although some of them would
fayne dissemble and kepe it secret if it were
possible. For besides that many vaine me=
tinges haue bene solemnly appointed in
Germany to bring the Lutherans and
Zuinglians at one in this matter, vehe=
ment and ernest bokes are dayly set foorth
of one sect agaist the other, euidently de=
claring this discorde. And who soeuer tra=
uayleth through Germany shal find, that
the Lutheran hateth continually the Zuin
glian and Caluinist as a most deadly ene=
my. But my purpose hath not bene to de=
clare the manifold disagreing which is be=
twen them in this chief point, only I haue
Bb　　　　　endeuo=

endeuored to shew you how wel auncient
Doctors agree with that Catholike faith
which hath ben alwayes taught of the Ca
tholikes, & which they at this day all impugne, & in doing the same I haue somtimes noted vnto you specially ꝑ falshode
of that opinion which our Englishe Zuin
glians or Caluinistes teach. And therfore
I wil not at this present labor any farther
to ryppe vp their discordes & dessensions,
especially whereas they are so amply described by others. Only let it suffise you
in weyghing thys matter to vnderstand ꝑ
there is in dede such discord among them,
& considre withall how litle our Englishe
gospellers agree with that , which those
auncient Fathers before alleged do teach
you. whose auctority if they therefore impudently deny, then you ought most of all
to vse this balance , and withall you may
thinke howe litle credite they deserue,
which so arrogantly & proudly goe about
to discredit such auncient & holy wryters.

And if they doe nolesse impudently chalenge them to be on their syde, then may
you by these sewe testimonies discouer
their false dealinge in this so principall a
matter of Christen religion , and thereby
take iust occasion to discredite the whole
rable of all other their false opinions and
heresies. For although in dede they ented
nothing more then to preferre the imagi-

tations and fansies of their own braynes
before all expositions which haue bene
made synce the Apostles dayes, yet they
are loth in wordes openly to professe this
so great and manifest an arrogance, least
by so doynge, the world should quickly
espie their wickednes. And euen so the
wicked Iewes feared a long time to vtter
their malice conceiued against Christ, least
they should thereby haue fallen into the
displeasure of the people & lost their owne
credite. But as that malyce of the Iewes
after they had once gotten the multitude
on their syde did openly breake furth and
bewrayed it selfe, by putting Christ to that
most shamefull and opprobrious death: so
doubtlesse the pride of these men, had they
ye multitude somwhat more on their side,
would not long lye cloked & couered vnder that reuerece which certein of thē pretend vnto ye auncient Doctors, but would
opely shew it self by denying al antiquity
ye maketh against thē, as some alredy haue
most impudētly begonne to make a ready
patheway thereunto. And for this cause I
warne you before had not only how shamefully they abuse ye people, which would
make mē belieue ye doctors make for their
side wheras in dede they are (as you haue
heard) so clean contrari against thē: but also to prouide for such which in cōsideratiō

Bb ij of pre-

of preferring their owne heresye will vt=
terly refuse to be tried by the auncient do=
ctors, for such I say as will chalenge to
them selues more auctority now in their
life time, then that is which hath bene ge=
uen to the holy Fathers by the consent of
so many nations, many hundred yeres to=
gether, euer sence the time of their death.
then the which arrogance what can be
greater, or more impudent?

If a man which had studied the lawes a
dossen or twentie yeres, would in compa=
ring himself with a nother of equall stan=
ding, by his own verdit prefer himselfe, &
say the other knew nothing of the true
meaning of the lawes, but that only to be
true which himselfe affirmed, shuld he not
trow you seeme very arrogāt and folishe?
But what if the same lawier which he de=
spised had bene of twentie yeres more con
tinuāce? what if he had a great deale more
practise, both by reason of his yeres, & offi
ces? what if besides al this ꝑ whole realme
accounted him for a man of singular great
learning & iudgment, & none to be compa
red with him? should he seeme worthy
commēdation which in such a case would
goe about to prefer himself before such an
Auncient, & set his own opinion before ꝑ
iudgment of so many? But let vs goe yet
one degre farther. what if that man w̄ whō
the com=

the comparison is made were not aliue at
one time with the other, but dead many
yeres before? what if he liued within a
litle of those,which ether them selues were
the lawmakers,oz such as knew most per=
fitely the mind of the Lawmaker? what if
in those dayes whilest he liued he was ac=
counted foz a singular wel learned iudge,
& afterward cõtinually was of his posteri=
ty generally receaued as a true interpzeter
of the lawes, & his sentẽce in all cases most
cõmonly folowed? what shuld be thought
of ỹ lawier which in this case,in his owne
lyfe time,would himself pzeferre his own
fansie befoze such an auncient and wel ap=
pzoued iudges sentence? should ther be any
degree of impudence, oz any kinde of ar=
rogance,in which himself ought not woz=
thely to be pzeferred?

And what other thing doe these new Di
uines and late vpstart Gospellers , which
doe not only pzeferre them selues befoze
their equals & elders of this age, but also
befoze the auncient Fathers & doctozs of
the Churche, which receiued that sense of
holy Scripture,which they deliuer vs in
their wzitinges,frõ the Apostles and their
successours. which haue so many ages to=
gether bene generally receaued & allowed
foz the true interpzetours of gods wozde,
not in on oz two realmes, but thzoughout

all Christendom? what other thing I say
doe they which thus contemne these men,
but endeuour to set forth vnto the world
their excessiue pride, & as it were striue for
the best game, where presumpteous brag-
gig is rewarded? which crime as it is in al
men which professe any kind of learning
much to be detested and abhorred, so in stu-
dients of diuinity & those which professe y
knowlege of gods holy word, it is in dede
most sylthy and abhominable. For besides
a thousand other absurdities which are cō
mitted in this case, they proue them selues
therby altogether ignorāt of that, whereof they make so great bragges. dicentes
enim se esse sapientes, stulti facti sunt. For
(as S. Paul saith) whiles they call them
wise & wel learned, they become in dede
soles. Again wheras we know humility
to be the chief & only meanes to attain the
grace of the true vnderstanding & knowlege of Gods law, they must nedes be far-
thest of from it who in y same very studie
declare such a manifest and open pride.
which thing as they doe, which openly deny the auctority of the Doctors: so those
other also performe it in effect, who prete-
ding to allow them, doe teach that openly
which is contrary to their doctrine.

But let vs lay a side for a while the antiquity of those auncient fathers together
with the presumpteous impudēce of those

which contemne them. let vs not vrge the same any more, being a sufficient argumēt of it self to moue any reasonable person to forsake their wicked doctrine. But let vs considre a litle, whether if we respect these later ages only, which haue passed be=twene, synce these holy doctors liued, or this very age in which we now presently doe liue, there be any iust occasion to pre=ferre their false doctrine before ý true Ca=tholike religion. If there were no more at this day to be sayd for the Catholike faith then can be sayd for their side, if we had at this present but so many well learned and vertuous Catholikes, as they can shew ci uile Protestants: if ther were in Christen=dō but so many good Catholike Byshops as ther are amongest thē Superintēdents of all sortes, were not this alone a suffi=cient cause to moue any one of discretion to stagger and doubt, before he yelded to their innouations?

Might you not worthely reason to your self on this wise? If these haue studied scri ptures, the Catholikes also are not igno=rant of them: if some of these men liue ci uily leading a moral vertuous good life, some of the Catholikes are not therin one ace behind them: if they chalenge to them selues a special prerogatiue in vnderstan=ding holy scripture, ý Catholikes may for

    Bb iiij   their

their good conuersation, and humblenesse
of spirite, be thought to haue the assistāce
of the holy ghost as much as thei oʒ moʒe,
although they crake not thereof so much.
were not this consideratiō J say enough
to make any reasonable man looke twise
befoʒe he changed once his old religion
wherin he was Chʒistned, foʒ theyʒ new?
And yet in making this cōparison J take
those Catholikes only, which are at this
present equall with them as well in age,
learninge, and ciuil lyfe, as all other mat=
ters that belong to the commēdation of a
good religion, omitting ẏ great vantage
which might be taken of the Catholikes
graue and sage hoare heates, of their depe
knowlege in Diuinitie, and excellency in
godly lyfe, wherin they so far excell those
of the other syde, that there is in dede no
comparison to be made.

He that will moʒe at large consider
the truth hereof, nede nomoʒe but first
cal to mind those which himself knoweth
at home in his owne country where this
new religion hath so much pʒeuayled & if
he fynd the same true there (as there is no
doubt but he shall, if he be not ouer much
partial) how much moʒe is the same generally true speaking of all Chʒistendom,
where ther are so many whole countryes
Jlandes, Dominions and territoʒies,
which

which haue not yelded one iote to their
new fangled doctrine? If France & Ger=
many, where ý Protestantes haue so much
swarmed, can geue them yet two for one
able to match them in all good qualities
before mentioned, and besydes, a great
numbre far excelling them (as it may eui=
dently appeare to those, which trauell the
countries, or but reade the bookes which
are set foorth on both sydes) how much
more ought he to be persuaded herein, if he
adioyne therevnto the graue and auncient
Fathers, the learned Diuines, and holy
vertuous men, which are in the rest of
Christendome?

And he that requireth yet farther mat=
ter to discourse herevpon, let him thinke
but on the last most worthy general Coun
cel, in which there were present two hun=
dred and two graue and reuered Bishops,
besydes a great numbre of other learned
Prelates, and yet few to speake of, out of
France or Germany, for that it was ne=
cessarie for them to kepe the wolfes out
of their foldes at home. And then let him
gesse what a number of other rare learned
and vertuous men are like to be found in
al other cõtries vnder those good Bishops
where neither religious houses are plukt
down, nor collegiat churches spoiled, nor
vniuersities any whit decayed. And this

                    Bb v   much

much is sayd briefly to helpe his memorie only, who listeth to discourse farther here in.

But now let all be equall, let there be no better lyuing nor better learned men, nor more in numbre this day aliue in one syde, then in the other. Let vs suppose also such a matter to be called in controuersie the truth whereof dependeth not so much ether vppon life or learning of men this day aliue, as vpon the true meaning of some singular Legacie geuen many hundred yeres synce in a last will or Testament, and to vnderstand what was at the first beginning, among those which were present at the will making, or liued in the yeres next folowinge, the common receaued opinion thereof. If this case were put foorth in some temporall matter, as to vnderstand to whiche inheritour suche a Lordshipp or piece of ground belonged, or whether through such a fyeld any lawfull hyghe way hath bene of old tyme vsed: then I am well assured, notwithstanding both the parties which striued were of like honestie and learning, yea although the truer syde did not only not excell, but also were inferiour in those pointes, yet the Iury would take that information for most true, which were ge-

uen

nen by the eldest of the Parishe.

Our controuersie at this present is, not
of a piece of ground or Lordshipp, but of
our Sauiour Iesus Christ himselfe, who
is Lord of the whole earth. And that whe=
ther by his last will and Testament we
really and rightly, receaue and possesse,
his precious body and blood, vnder the
formes of bread and wine in the blessed
Sacrament of the altar, or no.

Also whether this faith hath bene of
old tyme alwayes receaued, for the com=
mon hyghe waye for Christian men to
walke in, and to bring them safely through
this vale of myserie vnto the heauenly
Paradise.

Now shall we not suffre that kinde
of proofe in this so weighty a matter to
take place, which in matters of lesse im=
portance should preuayle? Nay I should
saye rather, shall we admitte in this
controuersie, on which dependeth our
euerlastinge saluation or damnation, the
rash sentence of a few yong lyghtbraines,
which in a matter of temporall goodes
euery man (especially seing on the o=
ther syde graue testimonies of wise and
eldery men) would vtterly contemne and
sette at naught?   For what thinge
els doe they, who forsaking that fayth,
                                                which

which the eldery men of this age witnesse to haue bene generally receaued & taught long before our dayes, doe embrace these new mens new fangled opinions?

There are very few or none at all I suppose of yeres of discretion, but can testifie if they will, that of their eldery parents & kynsfolke they learned a contrarie faith to that which these men now teache concerning the blessed Sacrament. And if you enquire of the most aged men which are now aliue not in one Parish but through out all the Parishes of Christendome, you shall fynd them (I warrant you) in hart Catholikes, or such at the least wise as can testifie, y̆ nether their fathers nor graundfathers were any Sacramentaries. So that if we graunted them to be equal both in vertue and learning, yet of this vātage we are most assured, that both the aged mē of this tyme, and the whole age last before, or rather many whole ages one before the other, shall wholy cōdemne them. which reason I see not why it should not in this matter be much regarded, seing in other matters where the case is like, the same only ouercometh.

But they will reply perchaunce & say, as they are wont commonly, that old men doe easely dote, and that our late forefathers were all generally through their superstition

perstition & Idolatry in great blindnesse, and errour. which thing as it is more easy for them to affirme then to proue, so it is in dede most false, and plainly against the promise of God made vnto his welbeloued spouse the Church. For whereas he promised to assist the same with his holy spirite vnto the end of the world, and to teach it all truth, what assistance of the holy Ghost, or what teaching of truthe had this bene, if a false religion should generally haue bene taught & receued throughout all Christen dominions? And if there were any truth at all remayning, should that haue bene such as was kept in some one or two mens brestes only, and they also such kind of men as generally were taken of the Church, for false lying heretikes? God did neuer halfe so much forsake the Iewes froward Synagog, which neither was at any tyme halfe so great in multitude of people, nor had any such great promise made vnto it. For the Iewes had frō tyme to tyme either some true Prophete, or some other good man, which openly warned them of their Idolatry and other vices. Neither is it to be thought, but a numbre of them also thereby repented and forsoke their Idolatry. And often tymes God raysed vp good Kinges such as Dauid, Ezechias, and

and Josias were, which wholy gaue eare
vnto the true Prophetes and were diligent in extirping false religion and in setting foorth the synceere worshipping of
God. Now what good Prince can the
Protestantes name, which in our forefathers dayes embraced their religion, or
what numbre of people which thought
well of their doctrine?

God neuer suffered that litle flocke of
those stubborn Iewes to commit at any
tyme that horrible synne of Idolatrie, but
he speadely chastened them with some
great and euident plage, vntill such tyme
as they had acknowleged their fault, and
returned vnto him. So much detested he
alwayes that synne in those specially which
had professed to serue him. And shall we
thinke that he would haue permitted this
congregation of the Gentils, vnto which
he hath shewed so many prerogatiues of
loue, not only to commit Idolatry openly, but also to professe it generally so many hundred yeres together? Shall we be
persuaded that the holy hyll of Sion, that
is to say, the holy Catholike Church gathered both of Iewes and Gentils, the
gates whereof (as Dauid sayeth) God
loueth more then all the Tabernacles of
Iacob, should haue bene in such an horrible

*That our
Catholike
forefa-
thers did
not comit
Idolatry.*

Psal. 86.

rible blindnesse so long together, as the
Sacramentaries blasphemeously reporte,
that it should haue worshipped that for
God, which were in dede and in substance
no better then bare wheaten bread & common wine?

By this meanes our forefathers should
not only haue far passed the Iewes in
wickednesse, but (which is most detestable) should by their Christianitie haue fallen into a more grosse and vile kind of
Idolatrie, then was committed by their
auncesters the Heathen and Pagan infidels.

For we reade that they in their greatest blyndnesse worshipped yet diuerse
kind of liuing beastes, and some also the
Moone and Sonne, or some of the other
starres, all which are far more worthy
creatures, and haue much more likenesse
with God then a peace of bread, which is
not of it selfe properly a naturally thing,
but is made artificially, and that of corne,
a creature although very necessarie for
the sustenance of man, yet in dignitie
much inferiour to euery lyuing beast, be
it the verie least worme that crepeth on
the ground.

Also the wiser sort of Pagãs, as ý Grecians & Romans vnder whose iurisdictiõ
                                        our

our Jle of Britany was, when it first receaued the faith of Christ) vsed not altogether so grosse an Jdolatrie as that of beastes was, but chose vnto them for Gods certain men which had bene in tymes past valiaunt princes and rulers vpon y̑ earth, as Saturne, Juppiter, Hercules, Romulus, with other such like. Yea and the wyser sorte amongste them also, such as Socrates, Plato, Aristotle, and Cicero were, did not acknowlege these for true Goddes nether, but founde out by theyr philosophy and naturall discourse, that there was one moste symple and pure substance far surmounting the grossnes of mans nature, which was the true God, the supreme motor & gouernour of al the world. And shal we thinke that Christe who came specially to destroy the false Goddes of the Gentils, and to geue lyghte to them whiche sate in darkenes, would suffer his people at any tyme to become generally more ignorant in worshipping of God, not only then the hethen Philosophers & Pagan Romans, but also to excede therin the most barbarous and rude people that euer was?

Shal we imagin y̑ our good forefathers which were al regenerat in baptisme, and receaued thereby the vnspeakeable gyftes and graces of the holy Ghost, and were
after‐

afterward confirmed and strengthened in
them by the Sacrament of confirmation,
of which many were not only wel learned
and all the dayes of theyr lyfe conuersant
in reading, and preching Gods word: but
led also a merueilous vertuous lyfe allwayes in the feare of God, and loue of
theyr neighbour: can we, I say, imagine
that these men all this notwithstandinge
continued all theyr lyfe longe in a more
horrible and shameful Idolatry, then euer
the blynd Egyptians committed in worshipping theyr Idoll Apis, or any other
heathen Pagans, which adored Ceres and
Bacchus? For these also are properly the
names of those which were thought fyrste
to haue inuented the sowing of corne and
the planting of the vine, so that by these
names they honored those persons, and
not the creatures of bread and wine. Neither doe I read that euer any barbarous
nation was so fonde or folyshe. And yet
all Christen men of these later ages, among
whome we are assured the most ignorant
and symplest soule knew more of the true
worshippige of God, then the beste learned Heathen Philosopher that euer was,
did by these slaunderous Sacramentaries
iudgemēt manie hundred yeres together,
committe this grosse and detestable Idolatrie.

              Cc   Cham

Cham that wicked childe was together with his offspring cursed of God, for that finding his father dronke and his priuities discouered, he laughed and scorned thereat, neither woulde goe about with his other good brethern to hyde and couer them. But what shall we say of these cursed and wicked children of our dayes, which do not only scorne their forefathers both spirituall and temporall, neither only not endeuour to hyde their turpitude if any happen to appeare, but secke all meanes possible to amplify and set foorth their faultes to the world in the most spitefull maner that can be deuised? And for lacke of matter sufficient for their malice, they faile not to forge millions of fayned fables to bring vpon them greater shame and infamie. yea and whereas they find many of them in dede to haue bene very sobre and vertuous to their liues end, so that there is no doubt but thousandes are blessed Sainctes in heauen, they preache and teache in effect no other thing but that they were generally all more then sow dronke, in the most detestable and grosse Idolatry that euer was: And therefore must nedes be now consequently drowned lower then the Mahometical Turkes and faithlesse Pagans in the deepest pit

of

of euerlasting damnation.

Truly if Cham was cursed for laugh=
ing at his Father, being in dede dronke
with the wine of the grape which he had
planted, they are a thousand tymes more
cursed, who vntruly and wrongsully con=
demne their fathers and graundfathers
of that spirituall dronkuesse of Idolatrie,
which before the face of God is a thousand
fold more haynous, then that other which
Noe committed.

But herein the iust iudgement of God
doth meruelously appeare, who suffe=
reth them falsly to accuse their forefathers
of such a grosse and dronken vice, to the
end it should more manifestly appeare vn=
to the world, how they them selues are
altogether cupshotten and ouerladen with
the poysoned draughtes of heresie, and
false doctrine, which they haue learned of
those wicked Apostates and drousy Tosse=
pottes of Germanye. For were they
them selues sobre and in their right wit=
tes, they would neuer haue layed that
to their forefathers charge, the contra=
rie whereof is so plainly proued by Scri=
pture it selfe.

How many places haue we there in
whiche playne mention is made of the

pure and syncere worship, which should be continually geuen vnto God among the Gentils after that the voice of the Gospell were once by the Apostles caried abrode into al nations? Malachie the Prophete writing hereof in the person of God sayeth: From the East vnto the west my name is great amongst the Gentils, and in all places there is sacrificed and offered vnto my name a pure oblation, for because my name is great amongst the Gentils sayeth the Lord God of Hostes. Now what pure oblation could I pray you either outwardly or inwardly be made vnto God, so long as our forefathers euery where committed such Idolatry, as these men doe imagine?

Moreouer whereas that pure oblation which Malachie speaketh of, is (according to the interpretation, not only of S. Damascen and S. Chrysostome, but of S. Ireneus also who liued immediatly after the Apostles) ment of the very blessed Sacrament of the altar, which is the only chief sacrifice of the Gentils: how could that haue bene so much commended by God himselfe, speaking in his Prophete, if so many hundred yeres together, such abhominable Idolatry should therein, in that sacrifice it selfe, haue bene committed? But will you yeare one or two testimonies

Malac 10
„
„
„
„
„

Irin.li.4.
cap.32.

vice more of holy Scripture, which may
serue in stede of many, and which alone
may quite choke them?

Looke in the Prophete Zacharie, ther you
shal find the god promised by his Prophete,
so to destroy al Idolatrie after the coming
of Christ into the world, that amongst his
people that grosse vice should neuer raig-
ne any more. His words are these: And it
shall come to passe in that day, sayeth the
Lord God of Ostes, I will destroy the
names of Idols from of the earth, and they
shalbe no more remembred. He promiseth
so perfitely to rote out all Idolatry, that
neither name nor memorie shall remaine
of any Idoll to be worshipped any more
among his people. Esaie sayeth also, that
in that day God alone shall be extolled &
Idola penitus conterentur, and all the I-
dois shall throughly be destroyed. Wherefore if Gods promise be true, they must
nedes be confounded and proued false
lyers, which so impudently accuse our forefathers of that blindnesse.

Zach. 13.

Esaiæ 2.

This much I haue sayed by way of a
digression in the defence of those good
Christen folke our parentes and frindes
heretofore departed, to the end it should
appeare more manifest, that although I
graunted the Protestantes to be equall
in vertue and learning with the Catho-

Cc iij   likes

likes now lyuing, and that there were nothing els to confound them (whereas in dede of a great many this is the leaſt) yet this alone were ſufficient, ỹ we are aſſured and they cannot denie, all our forefathers and great grandfathers generally throughout all Chriſtendom lyued and dyed in this Catholike fayth which we nowe defend.

This I ſay were ſufficient, ſeing we are warranted both by good reaſon, & alſo by holy ſcripture , that they could not generally fall in to that groſſe idolatry & blindnes, which theſe new men haue imagined, eſpecialy whereas the ſame ſcripture willeth vs alſo more thē in one or two places to geue no ſmall credite vnto thoſe thinges which our Parents ſhould teach vs. Moyſes in that godly ſong which he made in remēbrance of gods beneſites beſtowed vppon the children of Iſraell hath theſe wordes: Interroga patrem tuum & annunciabit tibi, maiores tuos & dicent tibi, Aſke thy father and he ſhall declare vnto thee, aſke thy elders and they ſhall tell thee. Dauid likewiſe being about to rekon vp the wonderfull workes of God beginneth hys ſong in this manner: Deus auribus noſtris audiuimus, patres noſtri annunciauerunt nobis.

Deut.32.

Pſal. 43.

bis. O God we haue heard with our eares
our fathers haue told vs. Also the wyse
man Salomon commaundeth vs not to Prou.2²
& 23.
passe the boundes which our forefathers
haue appointed , but to hearken vnto
those which haue begotten vs.

And why doe not we then gene eare to
that faith , whiche our temporall forefathers so diligently obserued ? why doe
we passe those lymites of the Catholike
Church, which our spiritual and ghostly
Forefathers taught vs?

If we will not credite those of the last
age next before vs , at the least why doe
we not yeld to our great graundfathers
auncestours ? why doe not we Englishmen content our selues with that faith
whiche they taught , who first brought
vs vnto the faith ? were they them selues
ignorant, that they knew not how to in-
struct vs perfitely ? Or were they so en-
uious & malicious, that they would not ?
To accuse thē of ignoráce it were to great
presumption, seing the disciple is not a-
boue his master, and seing all that knowlege which we haue of Christ, came by thē.
On the other syde to lay malice or enuy
to their charge it were to great a vilany.

for seing they did not enuy vs that singular benifite of baptisme, which is the only
entry to saluation, who can thinke that
they would kepe from vs any truth, that
might afterward strengthen and confirme
vs in the hope thereof: or who can presume
any parentes to be so vnnatural, that after
their children were with their great paine
and trauell brought forth into the worlde,
they would geue them poyson in stede of
wholsom meate to nourish them withall?
Or if men may be so malicious, yet who
can thinke that God who wrought our regeneration by those liuely instrumentes,
would suffre the effect of his holy Sacramentes to be so longe tyme voyde and
frustrat?

But if on the other side we mistrust not
but the Sacrament of baptisme receaued
at their handes was the right way to heauen, why should we mistrust that doctrine
whiche they taught our greate grandsyrs
concerning the blessed Sacrament of the
altar? If we credite the scriptures whiche
they brought vs together with our Christendome, howe can we refuse that true
sense of them which they taught those men
from whom we are from hand to hand instructed? Truely there is no nay, but it is
as muche absurde to denye one parcell
as to

as to denie altogither, and with as good
reason may they denie all, as one part,
seing all dependeth vpon one auctority.
And therefore it is not a litle to be teared,
least p, as many haue easely forsaken this
one trueth of Christ his reall presence in
the blessed Sacrament & therewith many
moe: so onlesse spedy repentaunce be called
for they forsake vtterly their whole Christendome, and become as they were before
rude Paynimis, and plain infidels. For
that S. Gregorie the Pope who was occasion of our Christendom taught this Catholike faith touching the blessed Sacrament, or that those holy monkes S. Augustin & S. Melitus sent by him to con-
uert vs Englishmen preached the same, it
is so manifest by all chronicles and old
monuments besides the tradition it selfe,
that I nede not spend many wordes in
the profe thereof. And if all other profes
failed, the very stonies of Churches, chap-
pels, and aultars erected in the honor of
this trueth, were sufficient to proue the
same.   Neither doe I thinke the contrary but the Sacramentaries them selues doe also confesse it. For otherwise
we should donbtles haue heard longe or
this, the name of that place where in stede
of aultars, Comunion tables had bene set
vp, or in stede of the reall presence of Chri-
                    Cc v   sies

ftes body, their figuratiue eating had bene
preached. But they witnesse most plainly
their consent herein by that they admit no
auctority of auncient wryters which liued
then or synce that time, that is to say, with
in the compasse of these nyne hundred
yeres. For thereby they confesse that all
such haue writen to plainly against them.

And therfore also they often times raile
and scoffe both at S. Augustine, and S.
Melitus, and at S. Gregory, calling him
Gregory the dreamer. Which doings of
theirs as they are in dede most absurd and
wicked, seing we haue as good cause to
estrme and credite these men being the first
founders of our faieth, and the trne Apostles of the Saxons in England, as the
Corinthians had to credite S. Paul, the
Indians to credite S. Bartholmew, or
p Romans to credite S. Peter: so J doubt
not but if you pondre diligently, what
great auctority in dede we geue them, how
incredible thinges we beleue vppon their
worde, and by their first instruction, you
wil easely condescend vnto that faith, which
they taught in this point also. Do we not
beleue through their first preaching that
God almighty, the chief gouernour and
creator of all thinges, came downe from
heauen, toke on him the nature of his
crea=

creature and seruant, and for the loue of
him being then his deadly enemy suffered
so many cruel torments, and last of al that
most shamefull death of the crosse? Do we
not beleue that he rose the third day and
triumphed ouer death, and that we like=
wise shal rise at the later day in the same
flesh which we now cary about, be it be=
fore that time neuer so much rotted and
corrupted? If then our fathers being Pa=
gans did credite them in these matters
naturally to mans reason so incredible, &
if we haue receued and beleued the same
together with all that is conteined in the
holy Bible vpõ their worde, you ought to
thinke their auctority also to be vnto you
a sufficient warrant for the truth of the Ca
tholike faith in the blessed Sacrament, and
consequently of all other matters which
are this day in controuersie.

But for so much as the aduersaries of
the Catholike Church, puffed vp altoge=
ther with singular arrogance and pride, to
bring those first teachers of our faith into
discredite, haue pretended a greater anti=
quitie and reformation of religion accor=
ding to Christes owne institution and
the vse of the primitiue Church, as though
they were better able to vnderstande
now what the primitiue Church taught,
then those which were neuer by eight
                              or nine

or nine hundred yeres, for this cause I say, although the common reasons now last mentioned might haue bene sufficiēt to stay you & euery other reasonable person in the Catholike faith: yet to satisfye you more fully & to confound them more euidetly I haue gathered those places out of the auncient Fathers and Doctors of the primitiue Church, which are here before translated. I haue for those first six hundred yeres, which they in vain crake of, geuen you six auncient Bishopes liuing all with in that compasse, so that by the helpe of these testimonies you may most truely stoppe their mouthes which crake of the primitiue Church, and in vaine houle and barke against this vndoubted veritie.

As for that stubborn and stiffnecked sort of them, which as I sayd before will not sticke to denye the auctority of these also, because they make so plainly against thē, yea and prefer Zuinglius, Peter Martyr, Caluin, Beza and them selues before. S. Chrysostome, S. Cyrill, S. Cyprian, S. Hilarie, S. Ambrose, S. Augustin: with such desperat persons there is small hope: that any kind of persuasion wil doe good. Yet that you may as it were in a glasse see their deformed visage, and thereby take occasion, if any of your frindes or mine be in that case, to make thē behold their own

deformi-

deformitie: I wil to make an end set breifly before your eyes that notable example of Roboam sonne and successour vnto Salomon in the Kingdom of Israell.

This Roboam, as you may read more at large in the Byble, refused to folow that good counsell which his Fathers graue & elderie counsell gaue him, and preferred the light opinion of certain rashe headed yonkers. By occasion whereof he lost not only the fauor of God and the greatest part of his Kingdom, but which was a great deale more, caused thousandes of soules to be lost and perishe, which so ne after departing frō the vniforme seruing of God in Hierusalē, erected aultars vnto idols and false Godes according to their own fancies, in the schismatical Hylles of Dan and Bethel. They forsoke also those Priestes appointed vnto them by God out of the tribe of Leui, and chose other meeter in dede for such sacrifices as the text noteth de extremis populi, of the basest and vilest sort among the people, by coniecture not much vnlike the Coblers and Tinkers, Mortermakers & Tilers, which in these our miserable dayes occupie the romes of graue and learned prelates. But you shall heare these wordes write in scripture concerning Roboam, whereby you may see how he was cause of all that mysery. they

are

are these: Dereliquit consilium senū quod dederunt ei,& adhibuit adolescentes qui nutriti fuerant cum eo , & assistebant illi. He forsoke the counsell which the olde men gaue him, and toke vnto him yong laddes which were brought vp with him and wayted on him. In which few wordes their perfite image is as it were in a glasse most liuely represented, who refuse the auctority of those auncient Doctors of the Church, and in stede thereof admitte the hereticall opinions newly inuented by a few yong renegate fryers and lecherous Apostates?

And as this example of Roboam doth in dede truly represent their deformity, so God geue them grace to espie and amend the same , and graunt other the grace to take hede they be not likewise entrapped, especially wheras we see to the hartsore of many good men, those inconueniences mentioned there in the scripture, to haue alredy ensewed thereof . For who seeth not the Kyngdom of Christ most pitefully diuided and mangled ? who sigheth not to behold those which were somtime parcels of his deare spouse the Church to be now most miserably cut of through sectes and schismes ? who hath not compassion on the numbre of soules which are daylie by this occasion tombled into the deep
dongeon

dongeon of euerlasting darknes? Ponder well therefore I pray you, and confer diligently with our time this terrible example of holy scripture written chiefly for our instruction. take occasion thereby to folow & reuerence the more that counsell which the auncient Fathers before alleaged doe geue you: and by so doing you shall folow the counsell & commandment of God himselfe, who by the mouth of his holy Prophet Hieremie saith: Stand vpō the wayes, loke about & aske of the auncient fathers which is the right way, and walke therin, & you shall find refreshing for your soule. Aske (as S. Cyril expoundeth the same place) of those holy Fathers which haue troden the right path of saluation before you, and you shall finde both quietnesse of conscience in this world, and peace euerlasting in the world to come, which he of his infinite mercy graunt vs, who w his most pretious body & blood hath redemed vs, and with the same in the blessed Sacrament of the aultar continually feedeth vs, to whom with the Father and the holy Ghost be al honor and glory for euer and euer.
Amen.

Hiere.6.
Cyrill.
cotr a hę
ret.l.b.
cap.4.

Volumen hoc *Roberti* *Pointz* de
facrofancta Euchariftia perlectu
& approbatum eft a viris *Angli-*
ci idiomatis & Theologiæ peri-
tißimis quibus meritò creden-
dum effe iudico.

Cunerus Petri, Paftor fancti
P. i I uanij. 7. Auguft.
Anno 15 5.